AF352480

THE HISTORY OF AL-ṬABARĪ

AN ANNOTATED TRANSLATION

VOLUME XXVII

The ʿAbbāsid Revolution

A.D. 743–750/A.H. 126–132

Bibliotheca Persica
Edited by Ehsan Yar-Shater

The History of al-Ṭabarī
(Ta'rīkh al-rusul wa'l-mulūk)

VOLUME XXVII

THE
ʿAbbāsid Revolution

translated and annotated
by

John Alden Williams
University of Texas at Austin

State University of New York Press

The preparation of this volume was made possible by a grant from the Translation Program of the National Endowment for the Humanities, an independent federal agency; and by the Persian Heritage Foundation.

Published by
State University of New York Press, Albany
 1985 State University of New York

For information, address State University of New York
Press, State University Plaza, Albany, N.Y., 12246
Library of Congress Cataloging in Publication Data

Library of Congress Cataloging in Publication Data

Ṭabarī, 744–754.
    The Abbasid revolution.

    (The History of al-Ṭabarī Tarīkh al-rusul
wa'l-mulūk ; v. 27) (SUNY series in Near Eastern studies)
    1. Islamic Empire—History—661–750. 2. Abbasids—
Early works to 1800. 3. World history—Early works to
1800. I. Williams, John Alden. II. Title. III. Series:
Ṭabarī, 838?–923. Tārīkh al-rusul wa-al-mulūk.
English ; v. 27. IV. Series: SUNY series in Near
Eastern studies.
DS38.6.T32   1984   909'.1   83-24 249
ISBN 0-87395-884-5

10 9 8 7 6 5 4 3 2 1

Acknowledgement

In 1971 the General Editor proposed to the UNESCO to include a translation of al-Ṭabarī's *History* in its Collection of Representative Works. UNESCO agreed, but the Commission in charge of Arabic works favored other priorities. Deeming the project worthy, the Iranian Institute of Translation and Publication, which collaborated with UNESCO, agreed to undertake the task. After the upheavals of 1979, assistance was sought from the National Endowment for the Humanities. The invaluable encouragement and support of the Endowment is here gratefully acknowledged.

The General Editor wishes to thank sincerely also the participating scholars, who have made the realization of this project possible; the Board of Editors for their selfless assistance; Professor Franz Rosenthal for his many helpful suggestions in the formulation and application of the editorial policy; Professor Jacob Lassner for his painstaking and meticulous editing; and Dr. Susan Mango of the National Endowment for the Humanities for her genuine interest in the project and her advocacy of it.

Preface

THE HISTORY OF PROPHETS AND KINGS (*Ta'rīkh al-rusul wa'l-mulūk*) by Abū Jaᶜfar Muḥammad b. Jarīr al-Ṭabarī (839–923), here rendered as the *History of al-Ṭabarī*, is by common consent the most important universal history produced in the world of Islam. It has been translated here in its entirety for the first time for the benefit of non-Arabists, with historical and philological notes for those interested in the particulars of the text.

Ṭabarī's monumental work explores the history of the ancient nations, with special emphasis on biblical peoples and prophets, the legendary and factual history of ancient Iran, and, in great detail, the rise of Islam, the life of the Prophet Muḥammad, and the history of the Islamic world down to the year 915. The first volume of this translation will contain a biography of al-Ṭabarī and a discussion of the method, scope, and value of his work. It will also provide information on some of the technical considerations that have guided the work of the translators.

The *History* has been divided here into 38 volumes, each of which covers about two hundred pages of the original Arabic text in the Leiden edition. An attempt has been made to draw the dividing lines between the individual volumes in such a way that each is to some degree independent and can be read as such. The page numbers of the original in the Leiden edition appear on the margins of the translated volumes.

Each volume has an index of proper names. A general index volume will follow the publication of the translation volumes.

Ehsan Yar-Shater

Contents

The Caliphate of Abū al-ʿAbbās al-Saffāḥ

Translator's Foreword

In this volume I have followed the transliteration system adopted by the Series, in deference to the judgement of the editor. My personal preference would always be to eliminate the Greek suffix *id* on Arabic and Persian names and nouns to obtain an adjectival form, e.g. ᶜAbbāsid, ᶜAlid, Umayyad, and to use the Islamic *nisba* form used in the Middle East ending in *-ī*, which has gained currency in modern English usage, e.g. Israel*i*, Pahlav*i*, Saud*i*. The terminal *h* for a *tā marbūṭa(h)* might also in my view be left to the general desuetude into which it is falling, e.g. in the new *Enclopaedia of Islam*.

I must express my deep gratitude to the Center for Middle Eastern Studies of Harvard University which kindly sustained me with a research fellowship for one year during which parts of this volume and of others were completed; to the Harvard Center for the Study of World Religions, which offered me and my family its hospitality during the year, and to the American University in Cairo which allowed me a year of leave. My colleagues Ahmed Sharkas at Harvard and Adel Sulaiman Gamal at American University in Cairo and University of Arizona helped me often with the poetry passages, and I would record my thanks to them here.

Professor George Makdisi of the University of Pennsylvania read the greater part of the translation against the originals and offered invaluable suggestions in the midst of trying circumstances: a most generous act. Professor Jacob Lassner made many thoughtful additions to the footnotes, and where this occurred I have indicated it in the notes. To Professor Ehsan Yar-Shater who has seen to the publication of this volume and others of al-Ṭabarī, very special thanks are due.

John Alden Williams
Center for Middle Eastern Studies
The University of Texas at Austin

The Caliphate of Marwān b. Muḥammad

In this year the oath of allegiance was given in Damascus to Marwān b. Muḥammad as Caliph.[1]

Why The Oath of Allegiance Was Given to Marwan

ʿAbd al-Wahhāb b. Ibrāhīm reported the following from Abū Hashīm Mukhallad b. Muḥammad, the mawlā of ʿUthmān b. ʿAffān: When people announced that Marwān's cavalry had entered Damascus, Ibrāhīm b. al-Walīd fled and went into hiding. At this, Sulaymān (b. Hishām) seized what was in the treasury, divided it among his troops, and left the city. Those mawlās of al-Walīd b. Yazīd who were in the city rushed to the house of ʿAbd al-ʿAzīz b. al-Ḥajjāj and slew him. Then they ransacked the grave of Yazīd b. al-Walīd and hung his body on the Jābiyah Gate. Marwān entered Damascus, and

---

Footnotes followed by (J.L.) have been added by Jacob Lassner. Others are those of the translator.

1. See Ṭabarī, II/3, 1879; Ibn Khayyāṭ, II, 392; Azdī, 62ff; *FHA*, 156; Yaʿqūbī, *Taʾrīkh*, II, 404ff; Masʿūdī, *Murūj*, VI, 46; Ibn Qutaybah, *Maʿārif*, 366.

stopped at ʿĀliyah.[2] The two young sons of al-Walīd b. Yazīd who had been slain were brought to him, as well as the body of Yūsuf b. ʿUmar, and he ordered that they be given burial.[3] Abū Muḥammad al-Sufyānī was carried to him in shackles, and he saluted Marwān as [1891] Caliph. Up until that day, Marwān had only been hailed with the title of amīr, so he asked al-Sufyānī, "What's this?" Al-Sufyānī replied, "Both [the sons of al-Walīd] made the Caliphate over to you as their successor."

He then recited some verses composed by al-Ḥakam in prison.

Our source adds that they had both reached legal maturity; al-Ḥakam had begotten offspring, and the other had reached puberty two years before.[4]

The verses of al-Ḥakam were:

Who shall tell Marwān about me,
    and my noble uncle, yearning long there,

That I have been oppressed and my people
    have become parties to the slaying of al-Walīd?

Shall their Kalb (also: dog) take my blood and my substance
    while I obtain neither gristle nor fat?

And Marwān is in the land of the Banū Nizār
    like a lion of the thicket, a neckbreaker in his lair.

Does not the slaying of that youth of Quraysh afflict you,
    and their shattering the staff [of unity] of the Muslims?

Now convey my regards to Quraysh.
    and to Qays in the Jazīrah, all of them:

---

2. The text is ʿĀliyah; perhaps it should be read al-ʿĀliyah. Yaʿqūbī, *Taʾrīkh*, II, 403 reads *Dayr al-ʿĀliyah*. The term *al-ʿāliyah* generally means the heights of an area as distinct from the low lying areas. See Yāqūt, *Muʿjam*, III, 592.

3. Yūsuf had been imprisoned throughout the reign of al-Walīd. His death and that of al-Walīd was ordered by ʿAbd al-ʿAzīz. The two boys are elsewhere identified as ʿUthmān and al-Ḥakam. They are also called the "two lambs" (*ḥaml*). See n.1 above.

4. That is, it was legal for them to transfer their authority. A short variant of these verses is found in *FHA*, 156–57.

The deficient Qadarī[5] has lorded it over us
   and incited war among the sons of our father.

Had the riders of Sulaym taken part in the battle,
   and those of Kaʿb, I would not be a prisoner.

Had the lions of the Banū Tamīm taken part,
   we'd not have sold the inheritance we had from our fathers.

Did you break your oath to me because of my mother?
   you have sworn allegiance before to a concubine's son.

Would that my maternal uncles were other than Kalb,
   and had been born to some other people!

Yet if I and my heir-presumptive should perish,
   then Marwān shall be Commander of the Faithful.

[1892]

Then Abū Muḥammad said, "Stretch out your hand and I'll swear allegiance to you." Those of the Syrian army *(ahl al-shām)* who were with Marwān heard him, and the first to come forward was Muʿāwiyah b. Yazīd b. al-Ḥusayn b. Numayr with the chief people of Ḥims. They swore allegiance to Marwān, whereupon he commanded them to choose governors for their military districts. The men of Damascus chose Zāmil b. ʿAmr al-Jibrānī; the men of Ḥims chose ʿAbdallāh b. Shajarah al-Kindī; the people of the Jordan chose al-Walīd b. Muʿāwiyah b. Marwān; and those of Palestine chose Thābit b. Nuʿaym al-Judhāmī, whom Marwān had extricated from Hishām's prison, and who then had betrayed him in Armenia.[6] Marwān took sure promises and binding oaths from them when they

---

5. Yazīd b. Walīd had been a Qadarī, or believer in free will. He was called "the Deficient," because he reduced his soldiers' pay. See Ṭabarī, II/3, 1874.

6. As chief of the local Yamanī faction, Thābit acted out of partisan motives against Marwān whose support was mostly from the Qays. Thābit took the title al-Qaḥṭānī to indicate descent from the alleged progenitor of the southern tribes and to thus draw wide support. See Ṭabarī, II/3, 1871ff; Ibn Khayyāṭ, II, 393; Azdī, 66; Masʿūdī, *Tanbīh*, 314.

gave him the handclasp of allegiance; then he withdrew to his residence in Ḥarrān.[7]

Abū Jaʿfar reported that when order had been restored in Syria (al-Shām) on behalf of Marwān b. Muḥammad and he had gone off to his residence in Ḥarrān, Ibrāhīm b. al-Walīd and Sulaymān b. Hishām asked for a guarantee of security *(amān)*, and Marwān granted it.[8] Sulaymān, who was then at Tadmur (Palmyra), came to Marwān with his brothers, the members of his family and his mawlās, the Dhakwāniyyah,[9] who were there, and they swore allegiance to Marwān.

In this year, too, the people of Ḥimṣ as well as some of the other people of Syria rebelled against Marwān, and he fought with them.

Revolt of the People of Ḥimṣ[10]

According to Aḥmad—ʿAbd al-Wahhāb b. Ibrāhīm—Abū Hāshim Mukhallad b. Muḥammad b. Ṣāliḥ: When Marwān left for his residence in Ḥarrān after settling with the Syrian army, he had not been there more than three months before they openly opposed him and rebelled against him. The one who incited them to that was Thābit b. Nuʿaym, who sent them messengers and wrote them letters. Information about them reached Marwān, and he marched against them himself. The army of Ḥimṣ sent word to the Kalb who were at [1893] Tadmur, whereupon al-Aṣbagh b. Dhuʾālah al-Kalbī set off toward them, accompanied by three of his sons, full grown men, Ḥamzah, Dhuʾālah and Furāfiṣah. Also accompanying him were Muʿāwiyah al-Saksakī, one of the Syrian cavalry, and ʿIṣmah b. al-Muqshaʿirr, Hishām b. Maṣād, Ṭufayl b. Ḥārithah and about a thousand horsemen of their tribe. They entered the city of Ḥimṣ on the night of the

---

7. Ḥarrān thus became the unofficial capital of the new Caliph. Not surprisingly Marwān wished to avoid taking up residence among the followers of his enemies, preferring to remain instead in the area where he had long resided. For Ḥarrān see Le-Strange, *Lands*, 103.

8. See Ibn Khayyāṭ, II, 393; Azdī, 64; *FHA*, 157; Ibn ʿAbd Rabbihi, IV, 468.

9. A Syrian regiment named after its commander Muslim b. Dhakwān. These were apparently Sulaymān's guard. While Ṭabarī's terming them mawlās does not necessarily mean they were non-Arabs, it suggests that some of them may not have been Arabs. Such elite regiments supplied the backbone of Marwān's support. See Wellhausen, *Arab Kingdom*, 372, 375. For a challenging and highly speculative view of the late Umayyad military, see P. Crone, *Slaves on Horses*, esp. 42–57.

10. See Ibn Khayyāṭ, II, 393ff; Azdī, 66; *FHA*, 158ff.

'Id al-Fiṭr[11] in 127 (June 25, 745). Marwān was at Ḥamāh, no more than thirty miles[12] from Ḥimṣ when the news of them reached him on the morning of the 'Id al-Fiṭr, so he moved quickly. With him at the time were Ibrāhīm b. al-Walīd, the deposed Caliph, and Sulaymān b. Hishām. They had sent him messages and asked him for a guarantee of security, and (having received it) they traveled with him as part of his army. Treating them generously, he positioned them both near him, so they sat at his table for dinner and supper and rode with him in his train. He reached Ḥimṣ two days after the 'Id al-Fiṭr, and the Kalb in the city had blocked the gates from inside. He was prepared, as his guard (rābiṭah) was with him. Surrounding the city with his horsemen, he stationed himself opposite one of the gates and looked out over a group of defenders along the wall. His herald then called out, "What call had you to break faith?" They answered, "We still obey you; we have not broken faith with you!" He then told them, "If what you say about yourselves is true, then open the gate!" At this, they opened it. 'Amr b. al-Waḍḍāḥ burst in at the head of the Waḍḍāḥiyyah,[13] who numbered about three thousand men, as they fought the Kalb inside the city. When Marwān's cavalry became too much for them, they ran for one of the gates, called Bāb Tadmur. They went out by it, but Marwān's guard was stationed there and fought them; most of them were thus killed. Al-Aṣbagh b. Dhu'ālah and al-Saksakī got away, but Dhu'ālah and Furāfiṣah, the two sons of al-Aṣbagh, and more than thirty of their men were captured. They were brought to Marwān, who had them killed on the spot. He ordered that all their slain, some five or six hundred, be collected and crucified around the city, and he tore down about a bowshot's length of the city wall. [1984]

The inhabitants of the Ghūṭah (the oasis of Damascus), attacked the city, besieged their governor, Zāmil b. 'Amr, and chose Yazīd b. Khālid al-Qasrī to rule over them. The city and its inhabitants and an officer, named Abū Habbār al-Qurashī, with about four hundred men held fast with Zāmil. Marwān sent Abū al-Ward b. al-Kawthar b. Zufar b. al-Ḥārith, whose name was Majza'ah, from Ḥimṣ to aid the defenders, as well as 'Amr b. al-Waḍḍāḥ and ten thousand men.

---

11. 'Id al-Fitr is the Feast of Fast-breaking at the end of Ramaḍān, see *EI* s.v. 'īd.

12. One Arabic mīl is 2 km., one third of a *farsakh*. See E.I2, s.v.

13. The Waḍḍāḥiyyah were a military contingent similar to the Dhakwāniyyah. See n.8 above.

When they came near the city they attacked the besiegers. Abū al-Habbār and his horsemen came out from the city, and they routed the rebels and seized their camp. Then they burned al-Mizzah, one of the villages of the Yamanīs. Yazīd b. Khālid and Abū ʿIlāqah sought refuge with a man of the Lakhm tribe from al-Mizzah. Their whereabouts was reported to Zāmil, who sent for them, but they were both killed before they were brought before him. He then sent their heads to Marwān at Ḥimṣ.

Thābit b. Nuʿaym of the army of Palestine rebelled, advancing as far as Tiberias,[14] and besieged its people. Their governor was Walīd b. Muʿāwiyah b. Marwān, son of the brother of the Caliph ʿAbd al-Malik b. Marwān. They fought the rebel for several days, whereupon Marwān wrote to Abū al-Ward ordering him to go there and assist them. Abū al-Ward set off from Damascus some days later. When word reached the inhabitants that he was near, they came out of the city against Thābit and his men and seized their camp. Thābit fled to Palestine and gathered his kinsmen and military forces (jund). Abū al-Ward now moved against him and put him to flight a second time, and those who were with Thābit deserted him. Three of his grown sons were captured: Nuʿaym, Bakr, and ʿImrān. Abū al-Ward sent them to Marwān; they were brought to him at Dayr Ayyūb,[15] wounded, and he gave orders for their wounds to be treated.

Thābit b. Nuʿaym went into hiding, and al-Rumāḥis b. ʿAbd al-ʿAzīz al-Kinānī was made governor of Palestine. Escaping with Thābit was one of his sons, Rifāʿah, who was the worst of them all. (Later) he joined Manṣūr b. Jumhūr,[16] who honored him with gifts, gave him a position and made him his lieutenant along with a brother of his called Manẓūr b. Jumhūr. But Rifāʿah assaulted Manẓūr and murdered him. This came to Manṣūr's ears as he was setting out for Multān—his brother had been at Manṣūrah,[17] so Manṣūr

[1895]

---

14. Tiberias (Ṭabariyyah) was the headquarters of the military district of the Jordan (al-Urdunn). See *EI* s.v. Ṭabariyya.

15. A village situated in the Ḥawrān district near Damascus. See Yāqūt, *Muʿjam*, II, 645.

16. Manṣūr b. Jumhūr was a leader of the Kalb who had helped plan the death of al-Walīd b. Yazīd. He was subsequently made governor of Iraq and later, of Sind. See Ṭabarī, II, 1778, 1800, 1809, 1836; also Wellhausen, *Arab Kingdom*, 367, 368.

17. Yāqūt, *Muʿjam*, IV, 629 lists a Multān which he indicates is also recorded as Mūltān. It was a great city in Hind on the way to Manṣūrah (the capital of Sind). For Manṣūrah, see LeStrange, *Lands*, 331.

turned back and seized Rifāʿah. He then built a hollow column of burnt brick, placed Rifāʿah inside it, fastened him to it, and bricked him in.[18] Marwān wrote al-Rumāḥis to look for Thābit and display kindness to him. At last a man from Thābit's tribe told where he was, and he was taken, along with a number of others. After two months, he was brought in. Marwān ordered that Thābit and his sons, who were already in Marwān's hands, be brought forward. Then their hands and feet were cut off, and they were transported to Damascus. Abū Hāshim stated, "I saw them cut in pieces and fixed on the gate of the city mosque." This was done because word had reached Marwān that people were spreading alarming rumors about Thābit, saying that he had gone to Egypt, gained control there, and slain Marwān's governor.

Marwān now came from Dayr Ayyūb to arrange the oath of allegiance to his sons ʿUbaydallāh and ʿAbdallāh. He married them to two daughters of (the Caliph) Hishām b. ʿAbd al-Malik, Umm Hishām and ʿĀʾishah. For this occasion he gathered together all the people of his family; Muḥammad, Saʿīd and Bakkār, the sons of (the Caliph) ʿAbd al-Malik, and the children of (the Caliphs) al-Walīd, Sulaymān, Yazīd and Hishām, and others of the Quraysh and the chiefs of the Arabs.

He mobilized the army of Syria, strengthened it, and placed one of the Syrian officers over each corps. He then ordered them to join Yazīd b. ʿUmar b. Hubayrah, whom he had sent ahead before his Syrian campaign with twenty thousand men of Qinnasrīn and the Jazīrah. He had ordered Ibn Hubayrah to camp at Dūrayn[19] until he should come, thus establishing this force as his vanguard. Marwān [1896] left Dayr Ayyūb for Damascus when all of Syria except for Tadmur had been pacified. He ordered that Thābit b. Nuʿaym, his sons, and the group he had mutilated be brought forward. They were put to death and then crucified on the gates of Damascus. Abū Hāshim reports, "I saw them at the time they were slain and gibbeted." He

---

18. This elaborate execution may be indirectly explained by a variant in Yaʿqūbī, *Taʾrīkh*, II, 407. The victim is identified here as one Ibn ʿArār, governor of Sind and a relative. When the treacherous Ibn ʿArār was apprehended, Manṣūr put him to death without shedding his blood, because he was a kinsman. On the legal ramifications of such executions see Lassner, *ʿAbbāsid Rule*, 39–57, esp. 43–46. (J.L.)

19. There is no entry for this place in Yāqūt's geographical dictionary. Dūr and Dūrān were common place names in Iraq.

adds, "Marwān spared one man among them, called ʿAmr b. al-Ḥārith al-Kalbī; it is claimed he had knowledge of the wealth which Thābit had deposited with certain kinsmen." Then Marwān moved on with his men to camp at Qasṭal,[20] in the territory of Ḥimṣ adjacent to that of Tadmur, the distance between them being three days' march. Word reached him there that the enemy (i.e., the Kalb) had spoiled all the wells lying between him and Tadmur, filling them in with stones, so he prepared waterskins, canteens, fodder, and camels to transport the provisions for him and his men. Al-Abrash b. al-Walīd, Sulaymān b. Hishām and other Umayyads interceded with him and asked that they (the Kalb) be excused, and that they make representations to them. He agreed to this, and al-Abrash sent them his brother ʿAmr b. al-Walīd. Al-Abrash wrote them a letter urging caution and informing them that he feared they would be the death of him and all their kinsmen. They drove ʿAmr away, however, and did not comply. Al-Abrash now asked Marwān to let him go to them himself, and to give him a few days. This, Marwān did. Al-Abrash went to them, spoke to them, and put fear into them. He told them that they were stupid and that they could not withstand Marwān and his troops. Most of them agreed with this, while those who did not trust him fled into the desert lands of the Kalb. These were al-Saksakī, ʿIṣmah b. al-Muqshaʿirr, Ṭufayl b. al-Ḥārithah, and Muʿāwiyah b. Abī Sufyān b. Yazīd b. Muʿāwiyah, who was the son-in-law of al-Abrash. Al-Abrash wrote to Marwān informing him of this, and Marwān wrote back to him, "Tear down the walls of their city and come back to me with those who have given you their allegiance." He therefore went back to Marwān with their chief men, al-Aṣbagh b. Dhuʾālah and his son Ḥamzah, and a number of others. Marwān

[1897] then set out with them on the desert road for Sūriyyah[21] and Dayr al-Lathiq[22] until he came to Ruṣāfah (residence of the Caliph Hishām). With him were Sulaymān b. Hishām, his paternal uncle Saʿīd b. ʿAbd al-Malik and all his brothers, as well as Ibrāhīm the deposed Caliph and a number of the sons of the Caliphs Walīd, Sulaymān and Yazīd. They stayed there for a day; and then Marwān left for

---

20. A place between Ḥimṣ and Damascus. See Yāqūt, *Muʿjam*, IV, 95.

21. A place in Syria between Khunāṣirah and Salamiyyah. See Yāqūt, *Muʿjam*, III, 87.

22. Vocalization conjectural. This place is not listed by Yāqūt.

Raqqah. Sulaymān b. Hishām asked for permission and begged Marwān to allow him to stay on for some days, so that his mawlās might
recover their strength and his beasts be rested. Sulaymān would
then follow after him. Marwān gave him permission and went on
his way, halting at a camp on the bank of the Euphrates where he
used to stay, near Wāsiṭ.[23] He remained there for three days and
went on to Qarqīsiyyah (Circesium), where Ibn Hubayrah was waiting to precede him to Iraq to fight al-Ḍaḥḥāk b. Qays al-Shaybānī al-
Ḥarūrī.[24] At this time about ten thousand men of those whom Marwān had mobilized for the campaign in Iraq while he was at Dayr
Ayyūb came up with their officers and stopped at Ruṣāfah. Here
they called on Sulaymān to renounce his allegiance to Marwān and
fight him.

This year al-Ḍaḥḥāk b. Qays al-Shaybānī entered Kūfah.

The Revolt of al-Ḍaḥḥāk the Khārijite (Muḥakkim)[25]

Sources differ in their accounts of this affair. As for Aḥmad b. Zuhayr—ʿAbd al-Wahhāb b. Ibrāhīm—Abū Hāshim Mukhallad b. Muḥammad: The occasion for the revolt of al-Ḍaḥḥāk was that when
al-Walīd was slain, a Ḥarūrī called Saʿīd b. Bahdal al-Shaybānī rebelled in the Jazīrah at the head of two hundred men of the region.
One of them was al-Ḍaḥḥāk, who took advantage of al-Walīd's death
and Marwān's preoccupation with Syria to rebel in the territory of
Kafartūtha.[26] At the same time Bisṭām al-Bayhasī, who differed
with Saʿīd in his views, set out with a like number of the Rabīʿah,
and each of them marched against the other. When the two forces
were near each other, Saʿīd b. Bahdal sent al-Khaybarī, one of his of-

[1898]

---

23. Not to be confused with the famous city of Wāsiṭ founded by al-Ḥajjāj b. Yūsuf.
This city was situated near Qarqīsiyāh. See Yāqūt, *Muʿjam*, II, 882 ff.

24. Ḥarūrāʾ was the district near Kūfah where the Khārijites rebelled against ʿAlī in
Rabīʿ I, 37 (August 17-September 15, 758). It subsequently gave its name to the sect
known as the Ḥarūriyyah. See *EI²* s.v. Ḥarūrāʾ.

25. Literally one who submits only to God's judgment; that is, the Khārijites who
opposed the arbitration at Ṣiffīn by crying out *la ḥukm illā li-llāh*. For al-Ḍaḥḥāk's
entry, see Ibn Khayyāṭ, II, 395ff; Azdī, 67ff; *FHA*, 157; Wellhausen, *Arab Kingdom*,
389–92, and *The Religious Political Opposition Parties*, 164ff; *EI²* s.v. ad-Daḥḥak b.
Ḳays al-Shaybānī.

26. The Kafartūthā mentioned here is a large village in the Jazīrah some five
*farsakh*s (30 km) from Dārā.

ficers, the one who later routed Marwān, with about a hundred and
fifty riders to attack Bistām by night. He came to Bistām's camp un-
detected, and ordered each of his men to have with him a white
cloth to wrap around his head so they might recognize each other.
Then they gave the cry of "Allāhu Akbar!"[27] in Bistām's camp and
smote them hard for their neglect (to keep watch). On this, al-Khaybarī recited:

> Though he was Bistām, surely I am al-Khaybarī;
> I strike with the sword and set guards in my camp.

They slew Bistām and all who were with him except for fourteen
men who escaped to Marwān. They stayed with him, and he gave
them positions in his personal guard (rābitah), putting one of them,
a man called Muqātil who had the patronymic (kunyā) of Abū al-
Na'thal, in charge of the others.

Sa'īd b. Bahdal then moved in the direction of Iraq, because word
had reached him of the disorders there and of the differences within
the Syrian army leading to clashes between the supporters of 'Abdallāh b. 'Umar (b. 'Abd al-'Azīz) and al-Nadr b. Sa'īd al-Harashī. The
Yaman tribesmen among the Syrians were with 'Abdallāh b. 'Umar
at Hīrah, while the Mudar tribesmen were with Ibn al-Harashī at
Kūfah, and they fought each other morning and evening in the area
between them.[28]

Sa'īd b. Bahdal died of pestilence he contracted en route to Iraq,
and al-Dahhāk b. Qays was appointed his successor. Sa'īd had a wife
named Hawmā', and in connection with this, al-Khaybarī recited
the verse:

> God moisten, O Hawmā', the grave of Ibn Bahdal;
> When the night riders saddle up, he'll no longer depart.

[1899]
Around a thousand men joined al-Dahhāk, and they turned toward Kūfah. He passed through the territory of Mosul, and around
three thousand men from there and from the army of the Jazīrah followed him. Al-Nadr b. Sa'īd al-Harashī and the Mudarīs were in Kūfah at this time, and 'Abdallāh b. 'Umar and the Yamanīs were in

---

27. The text is *bakkarū*; it should be read *kabbarū*, following the Cairo edition.
28. The distance between the old Christian town of Hīrah and the Muslim city of
Kūfah was three *farsakh*s (18 km).

Ḥīrah. (They were) engaged in a tribal feud in the territory between,
but when al-Ḍaḥḥāk approached, Ibn ʿUmar and al-Ḥarashī made
peace and joined forces to fight him. They entrenched themselves at
Kūfah, and between them at that time they had about thirty thousand men of Syria, a strong force well armed and provisioned. With
them was an officer from the forces of Qinnasrīn called ʿAbbād b. al-
Ghuzayyil, commanding a thousand horsemen whom Marwān had
sent to reinforce Ibn al-Ḥarashī. The enemy challenged them to give
combat, and they fought. ʿĀṣim b. ʿUmar b. ʿAbd al-ʿAzīz and Jaʿfar
b. ʿAbbās al-Kindī were both slain that day, and al-Ḍaḥḥāk's forces
put them to a most ignominious flight. ʿAbdallāh b. ʿUmar escaped
to Wāsiṭ with his men, and Ibn al-Ḥarashī, i.e., al-Naḍr, and the Mu-
ḍarīs set out along with Ismāʿīl b. ʿAbdallāh al-Qasrī for Marwān. Al-
Ḍaḥḥāk and the men of the Jazīrah thus took possession of Kūfah
and its territories, and they collected the taxes of the Sawād. Al-
Ḍaḥḥāk put one of his followers, a man called Milḥān, in charge of
Kūfah with two hundred horsemen, and set off with most of his men
after ʿAbdallāh b. ʿUmar at Wāsiṭ. There, he laid siege to the city.
ʿAbdallāh had with him an officer of Qinnasrīn called ʿAṭiyyah al-
Thaʿlabī, one of the hardiest of men. When it seemed likely that al-
Ḍaḥḥāk would besiege the city, ʿAṭiyyah left with seventy or eighty
of his own men intending to reach Marwān. They left by way of Qādisiyyah, and Milḥān received word of their movements; so he
moved out quickly, seeking him. ʿAṭiyyah met him at the bridge of
Saylaḥūn,²⁹ where Milḥān had hastened with about thirty horsemen. Milḥān engaged ʿAṭiyyah, and the latter killed him and some   [1900]
of his men. The rest of them fled until they came into Kūfah, and ʿAṭiyyah went on with his men until he reached Marwān.

Another account, from Abū ʿUbaydah Maʿmar b. al-Muthannā—Abū Saʿīd: When Saʿīd b. Bahdal al-Murrī died and the
Khārijites gave their allegiance to al-Ḍaḥḥāk as their Imām, he
stayed at Shahrazūr.³⁰ The Ṣufriyyah³¹ came to him from every direction, until he headed some four thousand of them. No such num-

---

29. Al-Saylaḥūn or Saylaḥīn was a village situated between Kūfah and Qādisiyyah.
See Yāqūt, *Muʿjam*, III, 219 and index, 125.

30. A large district in Jibāl between Irbīl and Hamadhān. This places al-Ḍaḥḥāk surprisingly far from the events he was to participate in. See Yāqūt, *Muʿjam*, III, 320.

31. The Ṣufriyyah were a less intransigent subgroup of the Khārijites. A brief de-
scription of them can be found in Watt, *Islamic Thought*, 24–27.

ber had ever joined any Khārijite leader before him. When Yazīd b. al-Walīd perished, his functionary in Iraq was ʿAbdallāh b. ʿUmar. Marwān then came down from Armenia and ultimately camped in the Jazīrah. He appointed al-Naḍr b. Saʿīd, one of the officers of Ibn ʿUmar, as his governor for Iraq. Al-Naḍr set out for Kūfah, and Ibn ʿUmar settled in Ḥīrah. The Muḍar tribesmen rallied to al-Naḍr and the Yaman to Ibn ʿUmar, who fought the former for four months. Then Marwān reinforced al-Naḍr with Ibn al-Ghuzayyil, but al-Daḥḥāk advanced on Kūfah. This was in 127 (744–5). Ibn ʿUmar sent a message to al-Naḍr saying, "This man means [harm] to none but you and me; so come, let us unite against him." And they made a pact agreeing to this.

Ibn ʿUmar came forward and camped at Tall al-Fatḥ, while al-Daḥḥāk advanced to cross the Euphrates, so Ibn ʿUmar sent Ḥamzah b. al-Aṣbagh b. Dhuʾālah al-Kalbī to prevent him from crossing. Then ʿUbaydallāh b. ʿAbbās al-Kindī said, "Let him cross over; it is easier for us than looking for him." Hence Ibn ʿUmar sent a message to Ḥamzah telling him to desist from this. Ibn ʿUmar then camped at Kūfah. He would pray at the governor's mosque with his followers, while al-Naḍr b. Saʿīd would pray with his own followers in the outskirts of Kūfah. He neither associated with Ibn ʿUmar nor prayed with him; however, they had both stopped fighting each other and had agreed to fight al-Daḥḥāk. When Ḥamzah returned, al-Daḥḥāk advanced. He crossed the Euphrates and camped at Nukhaylah[32]

[1901] on the fourth of Rajab, 127 (April 9, 745). The Syrian troops of Ibn ʿUmar and al-Naḍr rushed upon them before they were settled in their camp, and killed fourteen horsemen and thirteen women. Al-Daḥḥāk then dismounted, bivouacked, and set his followers in order, and they rested. Beginning early the next morning, a Thursday, the two forces fought a fierce battle. Ibn ʿUmar and his followers were put to flight, and the Khārijites slew his brother ʿĀṣim. The man who killed him was al-Birdhawn b. Marzūq al-Shaybānī. The descendants of al-Ashʿath b. Qays buried him in their residence.[33] The Khārijites also slew Jaʿfar b. al-ʿAbbās al-Kindī, the brother of

---

32. A place situated near Kūfah. See Yāqūt, *Muʿjam*, IV, 771.

33. Burial within a residence was a common practice in early Islam. There was, of course, the example of the Prophet, who was buried under the floor of his wife ʿĀʾishah's quarters.

'Ubaydallāh. Ja'far was in command of the security force *(shurṭah)*
of 'Abdallāh b. 'Umar, and the one who slew him was 'Abd al-Malik
b. 'Alqamah b. 'Abd al-Qays. Just as this man was overtaking him,
Ja'far called to a paternal cousin of his named Shāshilah. The latter
wheeled toward him, but one of the Ṣufriyyah struck him, splitting
his face in two.

Abū Sa'īd reported: I saw him after that; as if he had two faces.
'Abd al-Malik bent down and slit Ja'far's throat. Umm al-Birdhawn
al-Ṣufriyyah[34] made up these verses:

> We slew both 'Āṣim and Ja'far, also
> The Ḍabbī rider, when they came out,
> And we came to the hollowed-out trench.

The followers of Ibn 'Umar took flight and the Khārijites came after us, stopping at our defensive trench until nightfall. Then they
went away. We got up early Friday morning, and by God we hadn't
come out at all before they put us to flight; we retreated behind our
trench. On Saturday we got up and our people were all slipping out
and running away to Wāsiṭ. They'd seen an enemy whose like they
had never seen before, of the fiercest courage, like a lion over its
cubs. Ibn 'Umar went to look at his followers, and lo, most of them
had run away under cover of night. The majority of them reached   [1902]
Wāsiṭ. Some of those who got there were al-Naḍr b. Sa'īd, Ismā'īl b.
'Abdallāh, Manṣūr b. Jumhūr, Aṣbagh b. Dhu'ālah with his two sons
Ḥamzah and Dhu'ālah, al-Walīd b. Ḥassān al-Ghassānī and all of the
chiefs *(wujūh)*. Only Ibn 'Umar remained, leading such of his followers as stayed; he stood his ground and did not quit.

It is said that when 'Abdallāh b. 'Umar was made governor of Iraq,
he appointed 'Ubaydallāh b. 'Abbās al-Kindī governor of Kūfah with
'Umar b. al-Ghaḍbān b. al-Qaba'tharī in charge of security. Neither
one of them stepped down until Yazīd b. al-Walīd died; then Ibrāhīm
b. al-Walīd came and reappointed Ibn 'Umar as governor in Iraq. Ibn
'Umar made his brother 'Āṣim governor of Kūfah, and reappointed
Ibn al-Ghaḍbān to take charge of security. They continued in this
capacity until 'Abdallāh b. Mu'āwiyah rebelled,[35] whereupon

---

34. Khārijite women often rode with their men in battle. This is evidence that some
of them also improvised mocking verses about enemies in the old Arab manner.

35. For this rebellion, see text above.

'Umar b. al-Ghaḍbān came under suspicion. When the affair of 'Abdallāh b. Mu'āwiyah was ended (in Kūfah), 'Abdallāh b. 'Umar appointed 'Umar b. 'Abd al-Ḥamīd b. 'Abd al-Raḥmān b. Zayd b. al-Khaṭṭāb governor of Kūfah, with al-Ḥakam b. 'Utaybah al-Asadī, from the army of Syria, over security. Then he removed 'Umar b. 'Abd al-Ḥamīd from his position at Kūfah, appointing 'Umar b. al-Ghaḍbān governor there with al-Ḥakam b. 'Utaybah al-Asadī over security. Then he removed 'Umar b. al-Ghaḍbān as governor of Kūfah[36] and gave this post to al-Walīd b. Ḥassān al-Ghassānī. Ibn 'Umar then appointed Ismā'īl b. 'Abdallāh al-Qasrī governor, with Abān b. al-Walīd in charge of security. He then relieved Ismā'īl and appointed 'Abd al-Ṣamad b. Abān b. al-Nu'mān b. Bashīr al-Anṣārī. Removing him, he appointed his brother 'Āsim b. 'Umar governor.

Al-Ḍaḥḥāk b. Qays al-Shaybānī advanced. It is also said that al-Ḍaḥḥāk only advanced when Ismā'īl b. 'Abdallāh al-Qasrī [1903] was residing in the governor's palace at Kūfah. 'Abdallāh b. 'Umar was situated at Ḥīrah, and Ibn al-Ḥarashī was at the Convent of Hind.[37] Then al-Ḍaḥḥāk prevailed over Kūfah, and made Milḥan b. Ma'rūf al-Shaybānī governor there, with Ṣufr, a Ḥarūrī Khārijite of the Banū Ḥanẓalah, in charge of security. Then Ibn al-Ḥarashī came out, seeking to make his own way to Syria. Milḥan opposed him and Ibn al-Ḥarashī slew him. After this, al-Ḍaḥḥāk made Ḥassān governor of Kūfah, with Ḥassān's son al-Ḥārith in charge of security. Lamenting his brother 'Āsim when the Khārijites killed him, 'Abdallāh b. 'Umar said:

> The ill vicissitudes of time cast at the object of their aim,
>   leaving to the morrow no arrow in the hand for bow to throw;
>
> They cast at my most precious target and killed 'Āsim,
>   a brother; to me a fortress, a shelter, and a refuge.
>
> If grief and flowing tears have dissolved
>   the fresh blood of my vitals pooled,

---

36. Following the suggestion of the editor in the apparatus to the Leiden edition. The text reads, "from [his position in charge of] security."

37. There were two convents of that name at Ḥīrah. One was built by Hind bt. al-Nu'mān b. Mundhir (Dayr Hind al-Ṣughrā), the other by Hind the mother of 'Amr b. Hind (Dayr Hind al-Kubrā). Both were from the pre-Islamic period. See Yāqūt, *Mu'jam*, II, 707–708.

I've swallowed them, sipping them slowly for ʿĀṣim.
    much greater are those he's supped and swallowed.

And would the Dooms had left me ʿĀṣim,
    so we might live together, or taken us together!

It is mentioned that ʿAbdallāh b. ʿUmar used to say, "I have heard that ʿAyn b. ʿAyn b. ʿAyn slew Mīm b. Mīm b. Mīm. He had hoped to kill him, but ʿAbdallāh b. ʿAlī b. ʿAbdallāh b. ʿAbbās b. ʿAbd al-Muṭṭalib killed him (Marwān b. Muḥammad b. Marwān)!"[38] [1904]

It is also mentioned that when the followers of ʿUmar fled and got away to Wāsiṭ, they asked him, "What are you staying for, when these people have run away?" He told them, "I'll linger and see!" They stayed a day or two, and saw no one but deserters whose hearts were filled with dread of the Khārijites. At last he ordered the journey to Wāsiṭ. Khālid b. al-Ghuzayyil gathered his followers together and joined Marwān, staying in the Jazīrah. ʿUbaydallāh b. ʿAbbās al-Kindī saw what had befallen the people, and did not feel that he was safe, so he went over to al-Ḍaḥḥāk, swore allegiance to him and served in his army. Abū ʿAṭāʾ al-Sindī[39] coined these verses, shaming him for following al-Ḍaḥḥāk, who had slain his brother:

Tell ʿUbaydallāh, "If it were Jaʿfar who
    had lived, he'd not submit once you were slain.

He'd not have followed the heretics when revenge was due
    while in his hand was a sharp and shining blade!

A rabble who killed your brother and called your
    father an infidel; what do you say to that?"

When ʿUbaydallāh b. ʿAbbās heard this verse of Abū ʿAṭāʾ, he said, "Why, I say, 'God make you bite your mother's clitoris!'" Abū ʿAṭāʾ's verses continue:

May your kinship be disowned by any relative
    or one seeking revenge: low lies the lowly.

---

38. The literary device using the first initials of a name to predict a future event is characteristic of the apocalyptical traditions. For other examples of these traditions see Lassner, ʿAbbasid Rule, 42–43; also Thaʿālibī, Laṭāʾif, 87–88 (J.L.)

39. A pro-Umayyad poet from Kūfah. See EI[2] s.v. Abū ʿAṭaʾ al-Sindī.

> You let the brother of Shaybān plunder his weapons
> while a fleet-wheeling horse on a long rein rescued you!

[1905]   Ibn ʿUmar occupied the residence of al-Ḥajjāj b. Yūsuf at Wāsiṭ, it is said, with the Yaman, while al-Naḍr b. Saʿīd and his brother Sulaymān and Ḥanẓalah b. Nubātah with his sons Muḥammad and Nubātah settled with the Muḍar on the right side of the road as you come up from Baṣrah. They abandoned Kūfah and Ḥīrah to al-Ḍaḥḥāk and the Khārijites, and everything there fell into their hands. The war between ʿAbdallāh b. ʿUmar and al-Naḍr b. Saʿīd al-Ḥarashī reverted to its situation before the advent of al-Ḍaḥḥāk, al-Naḍr demanding that Ibn ʿUmar deliver the government of Iraq to him according to Marwān's writ and Ibn ʿUmar refusing; the Yaman (siding) with Ibn ʿUmar and the Nizār with al-Naḍr. This was because the forces *(jund)* of the Yaman were on the side of Yazīd the Deficient[40] in their feud with al-Walīd, after he delivered Khālid al-Qasrī over to Yūsuf b. ʿUmar al-Thaqafī who put him to death. The Qays, however, were with Marwān, since he had called for vengeance for al-Walīd. The Qays were the maternal relatives of al-Walīd, by way of Thaqīf, since his mother was Zaynab bt. Muḥammad b. Yūsuf, the niece of al-Ḥajjāj. Thus, war resumed between Ibn ʿUmar and al-Naḍr.

Al-Ḍaḥḥāk entered Kūfah and stayed there, and he appointed as governor of the city Milḥān al-Shaybānī in Shaʿbān 127 (May 745). At the head of the Khārijites, al-Ḍaḥḥāk moved swiftly against Wāsiṭ in pursuit of Ibn ʿUmar and al-Naḍr, and he camped at the Hippodrome Gate (Bāb al-Miḍmār). When they saw that, Ibn ʿUmar and al-Naḍr abstained from fighting each other and united against al-Ḍaḥḥāk, as they had at Kūfah. Al-Naḍr and his officers would cross the bridge and fight al-Ḍaḥḥāk and his followers alongside Ibn ʿUmar; then they would return to their own places, and not stay with Ibn ʿUmar. They continued in this fashion during the months
[1906]   of Shaʿbān, Ramaḍān and Shawwāl (May–July 745). One day, they were engaged in combat when the battle grew fierce. At the gate called Bāb al-Quraj, Manṣūr b. Jumhūr charged at one of al-Ḍaḥḥāk's officers, a man of great rank with the Khārijites called ʿIkrimah b. Shaybān, and struck him, cutting him in two and killing him. Al-

---

40. See n. 5 above.

Ḍaḥḥāk sent one of his officers called Shawwāl—he was from the Banū Shaybān—to the Zāb Gate, saying, "Burn it down over them; the siege has gone on too long for us." Shawwāl set off in the company of al-Khaybarī, also one of the Banū Shaybān, at the head of their horsemen. ʿAbd al-Malik b. ʿAlqamah met them and asked, "Where are you going?" Shawwāl told him, "We're going to the Zāb Gate. The Commander of the Faithful (i.e., al-Ḍaḥḥāk) has ordered me to do this and that." ʿAbd al-Malik then said, "I'm with you," and went back with them, though he was bare-headed and had no breastplate on him. He, too, was an officer of al-Ḍaḥḥāk and a most redoubtable man. They went to the Zāb Gate and set fire to it, and ʿAbdallāh b. ʿUmar sent out Manṣūr b. Jumhūr against them with six hundred cavalry of the Kalb. The latter engaged them in fierce combat. ʿAbd al-Malik b. ʿAlqamah attacked them, although he had no armor, and killed a number of them. Manṣūr b. Jumhūr saw this, and ʿAbd al-Malik's prowess enraged him. He therefore charged him and struck him between his shoulder and neck, cutting him to the haunch, and he fell dying. A hardy Khārijite woman then came forward and seizing the bridle of Manṣūr's horse cried, "You sinner! Answer to the Commander of the Faithful!" But he cut off her hand —or, it is also said, he cut the rein of his horse while it was in her hand—and got away. Al-Khaybarī came into the city after Manṣūr, and a paternal cousin of Manṣūr from the Kalb came at him, but al-Khaybarī struck and killed him.

(Ḥabīb b. Khudrah, the mawlā of the Banū Hilāl)[41] claimed that ʿAbd al-Malik b. ʿAlqamah was a descendant of the kings of Persia, and composed these verses lamenting him:

The woman speaks while tears flow from her eye: [1907]
    "may peace be on the soul of Ibn ʿAlqamah!"

Has death overtaken you in mid-career?
    each man in his due course finds death.

And so there is no trembling of the hands, nor slowing down of age;
    no slackening in the battle, nor weakening with time.

---

41. This phrase is missing from the Leiden text and is supplied from the Cairo edition.

Being killed for the Khārijites is no disgrace;
but they are slain, and they are noble.

The dregs of mankind have no path to follow;
'tis they who make me mourn, O Ibn ʿAlqamah, the dregs.

Manṣūr then said to Ibn ʿUmar, "I've never seen anyone like these people," meaning the Khārijites. "Why are you fighting them and keeping them too busy to deal with Marwān? Give them your approval, and put them between yourself and Marwān. If you do that, they'll let us alone and go off to [fight] him. Their intensity and courage will be directed against him, and you can remain at rest here in your own place. If they defeat him, you will have gotten what you wanted, and you'll be on good terms with them. If he should defeat them and you want to oppose him and fight him, you'll do battle with him fully rested; his dispute with them will go on a long time, and they'll give him ample trouble." But Ibn ʿUmar said, "Don't rush; let's wait and see!" "What shall we wait for?" Manṣūr asked. "You can't get out with them, and you can't go on. If we went out against them, we could not stand up to them. What can we expect will happen to them? Meanwhile, Marwān is untroubled, because we have absorbed the cutting edge of their power and diverted them from him! As for me, I'm going out and joining them!" He then went out, and, standing opposite their lines, he cried, "I am ready to listen! I want to submit as a Muslim and hear the Word of God!" The informant adds, "This is their trial [mihnah]." Then Manṣūr went over to them and gave them his oath of allegiance, saying, "I have become a Muslim." With that, they invited him to the mid-morning meal, and he ate. Then he asked them, "Who was the rider who seized my bridle that day by the Zāb?" meaning the day he slew Ibn ʿAlqamah. They called, "O Umm al-ʿAnbar!" Lo, the most beautiful woman came out to them. She asked him, "Are you Manṣūr?" "Yes," he answered. "May God shame your sword wherever you mention it," she told him. "By God, it did nothing, and gave nothing!" She meant by this, why could he not have killed her when she seized his bridle so she would have entered Paradise (as a martyr). Until that moment, Manṣūr had not known that she was a woman. He said, "O Commander of the Faithful, marry her to me!" Al-Ḍaḥḥāk replied, "She has a husband." She was, in fact, the wife of

[1908]

'Ubaydah b. Sawwār al-Taghlibī.[42] Finally, 'Abdallāh b. 'Umar sent out to them at the end of Shawwāl (late April 745) and gave al-Ḍaḥḥāk the oath of allegiance.

In this year, 127 (744–745), Sulaymān b. Hishām b. 'Abd al-Malik b. Marwān threw off his allegiance to Marwān b. Muḥammad, and waged open war.[43]

The Revolt of Sulaymān b. Hishām

According to Aḥmad b. Zuhayr—'Abd al-Wahhāb b. Ibrāhīm—Abū Hāshim Mukhallad b. Muḥammad b. Ṣāliḥ: When Marwān set out from Ruṣāfah to Raqqah to send Ibn Hubayrah to Iraq to fight al-Ḍaḥḥāk b. Qays al-Shaybānī, Sulaymān b. Hishām requested his permission to stay behind a few days to rest his forces and set his affairs in order. Marwān consented and went his way. About ten thousand men came forward, of those whom Marwān had levied at Dayr Ayyūb to campaign in Iraq. They journeyed with their officers to Ruṣāfah, where they called on Sulaymān to throw off his allegiance to Marwān and fight him. They told him, "You are considered more acceptable than he is by the army of Syria, and more worthy of the Caliphate." On this, Satan caused Sulaymān to err, and he agreed. He went out to them with his brothers, his sons, and his mawlās. He formed his army, and then he marched with all his forces to Qin-nasrīn. He wrote letters to the troops of Syria, and they slipped away to join him from every direction and from the district forces *(jund)*. Then Marwān drew near, having turned back after he had gone above Qarqīsiyyā.[44]

He wrote to Ibn Hubayrah ordering him to secure himself with his troops at Dūrayn until he moved his camp to Wāsiṭ. The mawlās of Sulaymān and the children of Hishām who had been at Hanī[45] gathered together with their families and entered the fortress of al-

[1909]

---

42. Al-Taghlibī was one of the leading Khārijites and a member of the electoral council *(shūrā)* that chose al-Ḍaḥḥāk.

43. See Azdī, 51; *FHA*, 158ff; Ya'qūbī, *Ta'rīkh*, II, 405ff.

44. Qarqīsiyyah (ancient Circesium) was situated on the left bank of the Euphrates 200 miles below al-Raqqah. See LeStrange, *Lands*, 105.

45. the Hanī was one of two canals (the other being the Mārī) dug by the Caliph, Hishām b. 'Abd al-Malik. They gave their names to adjacent estates. See Yāqūt, *Mu'jam*, IV, 994.

Kāmil, fortifying themselves within and barring the doors against Marwān. He sent to them asking, "What have you done? Have you thrown off obedience and broken your oath of allegiance to me after you gave me solemn pledge and covenants?" They replied to his messengers, "We are with Sulaymān, against all who oppose him." He then told them, "I earnestly warn you and caution you that if you oppose any one of those following me in my army, or let any harm come to him from you, you will bring my punishment upon you. There will be no safety for you from me." They sent word, "We shall desist." And Marwān passed on. Then they took to coming out of their fortress, attacking stragglers and scattered groups of the army who were following Marwān, and stripping them of their horses and weapons. Word of this came to him, and he burned with rage against them. Around seventy thousand men of the Syrian army had gathered around Sulaymān, including the Dhakwāniyyah and other groups, and camped at a village of the Banū Zufar, called Khusāf,[46] in the territory of Qinnasrīn. When Marwān drew near there, Sulaymān sent out al-Saksakī at the head of about seven thousand men, and Marwān sent ʿIsā b. Muslim with about the same number. The two forces met in the area between the two camps and fought a fierce battle. Al-Saksakī and ʿIsā, each one a heroic cavalryman, clashed in battle. They jousted until their lances were broken, then they drew their swords. Al-Saksakī struck the forepart of ʿIsā's horse so its harness fell down to its chest, and the horse went out of

[1910] control. Al-Saksakī cut him off, struck him with his mace, and felled him. He then dismounted and took him prisoner. At this, one of the cavalry of Antioch called Silsāq,[47] an officer of the Slavs (Ṣaqālibah)[48] appeared and captured al-Saksakī. Marwān's vanguard was put to flight, and word of this reached him en route. He kept on, concentrating on his preparations, and did not dismount until he reached Sulaymān. Marwān had set his troops in order and was now ready to fight. Sulaymān did not expect him and was taken by surprise. He and those with him fled. Marwān's horsemen pursued them, killing some and capturing others, until he reached and

---

46. Yāqūt, *Muʿjam*, II, 441 lists a Khusāf but makes no mention of this particular village.

47. Silsāq: the initial 'i' is conjectural.

48. The Ṣaqālibah were captives of Slavic origin who were brought to the Islamic lands as slaves. The initial "*i*" in Silsāq is conjectural.

overran their camp. Then Marwān took up his position, and commanded his two sons to take theirs, while Kawthar, the chief of security, was in another place. He then ordered his army to take no
prisoners except those who were slaves *(mamlūk)*. The count of the
slain on Sulaymān's side that day exceeded thirty thousand. Ibrāhīm
the oldest son of Sulaymān was slain, and a maternal uncle of
Hishām b. ʿAbd al-Malik called Khālid b. Hishām al-Makhzūmī was
brought in. A big and very fleshy man, he was brought up to Marwān
with his tongue lolling out. "You profligate!" cried Marwān.
"Weren't the wines and slave girls of Madīnah[49] enough to keep
you from running out with this excrement to fight against me?" He
said, "Commander of the Faithful, he made me do it! I beg you, for
God's sake, and that of kinship!" Marwān answered, "So you tell
lies, too! How would he have forced you, when you came out with
your singing-girls and wineskins and guitars *(barabīṭ)* with you in
his camp!" Marwān then killed him. Many of the prisoners from the
district forces claimed that they were slaves. He therefore refrained
from slaying them and commanded that they be sold with the other
slaves, along with the booty taken from their camp.

Sulaymān fled on until he reached Ḥimṣ, where he was joined by
those of his supporters who had escaped. He made camp there and
rebuilt that part of the city walls which Marwān had ordered torn
down. On the day that Sulaymān was routed, Marwān sent ahead officers and guards *(rabiṭah)* with a detachment of cavalry. He ordered
them to reach the fortress of al-Kāmil before any news (of the battle)   [1911]
arrived, and in his rage against those within (he ordered this detachment) to surround it until he came there. The advance force arrived
and set up camp, and Marwān advanced and halted at his camp at
Wāsiṭ. He sent a message to the defenders to deliver themselves to
his judgment, but they replied, "No, not until you guarantee all of
us safety." He took his time with them, and had mangonels set up
against them. When the stones began to fall on them, they sub-
mitted to his judgment. He made an example of them, mutilating
them, but the people of Raqqah transported them, gave them shelter
and treated their wounds. Some of them perished, but most of them
survived. Their number altogether was around three hundred.

---

49. Madīnah was the resort of the idle rich in the Umayyad period and noted for its
pleasures; see Masʿūdī, *Murūj*, IV, 254–44, or Hitti, *History of the Arabs*, 236–37.

Then Marwān set out after Sulaymān and those who had gathered around him at Ḥimṣ. As he drew near, they had a meeting, and some of them said to the others, "How long shall we be forced to run from Marwān? Come, let us make a covenant to seek death, and not disperse once we have seen him until all of us are dead!" Around nine hundred of their cavalry who were prepared to die agreed to this. Sulaymān put Muʿāwiyah al-Saksakī in charge of half his forces, setting Thubayt al-Bahrānī over the other half. They set out against Marwān, having agreed to attack him by night, if they could take him unawares. News of them and their plan reached Marwān, however, and he took precautions. He marched slowly, digging trenches, and staying in defensive battle formation. They were eager to attack him by night but could not, so they prepared for him by setting an ambush among some olive groves above the route he would take, in a village named Tall Mannas of Jabal al-Summāq.[50] They came out against him while he was marching in battle formation, and turned their weapons on those who were with him, so he withdrew and called up his cavalry. Elements of his vanguard, the two wings and the rearguard gathered about him, and they fought [1912] the enemy from midmorning until after the afternoon prayer. Al-Saksakī[51] encountered one of the riders of the Banū Sulaym, and they clashed. The Sulamī pulled him off his horse, and dismounted to deal with him. He was assisted by a man of the Banū Tamīm, and together they brought him prisoner to where Marwān had stationed himself. He said, "Praise to God who has empowered us over you; you've had too much from us!" Al-Saksakī cried, "Spare me, for I am the best rider among the Arabs!" But Marwān told him, "You lie, for the man who brought you in is a better rider than you are." He gave the order, and he was bound. The number of those bound like him and put to death was six thousand. Thubayt and those who had been put to flight escaped.

When they came to Sulaymān, he put his brother Saʿīd b.

---

50. Yāqūt, *Muʿjam*, IV, 871 lists Tall Mannas as a village in the district of Ḥimṣ and as a fortress near Maʿarrat al-Nuʿmān. The latter was situated between Ḥimṣ and Ḥalab (Aleppo) and was famous for its olive groves. See Yāqūt, *Muʿjam*, IV, 575. The Jabal al-Summāq was a large mountain region with many settlements. It was considered part of the western districts of Ḥalab. Yāqūt, *Muʿjam*, II, 21.

51. At least two men of the Banū Saksak are identified in the accounts of the times: Muʿāwiyah and Abū ʿIlāqah. The text rarely distinguishes between them. The identity of the individual here cannot be ascertained.

Hishām in charge of the city of Ḥimṣ. Recognizing that there was nothing he could do there, Sulaymān went to Tadmur and stayed there. Marwān encamped against Ḥimṣ and besieged the defenders for ten months. He erected more than eighty mangonels and bombarded them with stones night and day. Throughout this time they made daily sallies and fought him. At times they raided the outskirts of his camp by night, attacking positions where they hoped they would find a breach or a gap in his defenses. When one setback after another had befallen them, they were forced to act humbly. They asked him to guarantee them all safety on condition they deliver to him Saʿīd b. Hishām and his two sons ʿUthmān and Marwān, as well as a man named al-Saksakī,[52] who used to raid Marwān's camp, and an Abyssinian who used to insult and slander him. Marwān consented to these terms. The story of the Abyssinian was that he would climb up on the city wall and fasten to his own penis that of a donkey. Then he would shout, "O Banū Sulaym, you sons of this and that, here is your banner!"[53] and he would revile Marwān. When Marwān got control of him, he handed him over to the Banū Sulaym, who cut off his male organs and his nose and made an example of him. Marwān ordered the man called al-Saksakī killed , and Saʿīd and his two sons tightly secured. Then he began to move against al-Ḍaḥḥāk.

[1913]

A source other than Abū Hāshim Mukhallad b. Muḥammad gives a different account of what happened to Sulaymān b. Hishām after he was routed at the Battle of Khusāf: When Marwān routed Sulaymān b. Hishām b. ʿAbd al-Malik on the day of Khusāf, he fled to ʿAbdallāh b. ʿUmar and went with him to al-Ḍaḥḥāk. He gave al-Ḍaḥḥāk his oath of allegiance and informed him of Marwān's transgressions and injustice. Inciting them against him, Sulaymān said, "I'll march with you, with my mawlās and all who follow me." He accompanied al-Ḍaḥḥāk when he moved against Marwān.

Shubayl b. ʿAzrah al-Ḍubbaʿī says of their pledging allegiance to al-Ḍaḥḥāk:

> See ye not that God made His religion prevail,
> so Quraysh prayed behind Bakr b. Wāʾil?

---

52. See n. 51 above.

53. This was an insult to Marwān who was called Marwān "al-Ḥimār," that is, "the ass." The expression "al-Ḥimār" was not intended to denigrate the Caliph's intelligence. On the contrary, it denoted strength and endurance.

Ibn ʿUmar and his companions were of one accord in opposing al-Naḍr b. Saʿīd. Thus he he knew that there was nothing he could do with them, so he departed at once to seek Marwān in Syria.

According to Abū ʿUbaydah—Bayhas: By Dhū al-Qaʿdah 127 (early August 745), Syria was pacified under Marwān and he had removed all those opposing him. Hence he summoned Yazīd b. ʿUmar b. Hubayrah and sent him as governor to Iraq, adding the troops of the Jazīrah to his command. He advanced until he camped at the Canal of Saʿīd b. ʿAbd al-Malik,[54] and Ibn ʿUmar sent a message to al-Ḍaḥḥāk informing him of this. Bayhas continues: Al-Ḍaḥḥāk assigned Maysān[55] to us, saying, "That will suffice you until we see what transpires." Ibn ʿUmar appointed his mawlā al-Ḥakam b. Nuʿmān in charge of it.

[1914] As for Abū Mikhnaf—Hishām:[56] ʿAbdallāh b. ʿUmar made peace with al-Ḍaḥḥāk with the understanding that al-Ḍaḥḥāk should retain all of Kūfah and its surrounding lands, while Ibn ʿUmar should retain all that he still held of Kaskar, Maysān, Dastmaysān, the districts of the Tigris, Ahwāz and Fārs. Al-Ḍaḥḥāk moved on to encounter Marwān at Kafartūthā in the Jazīrah territory.

Abū ʿUbaydah reported: Al-Ḍaḥḥāk made preparations to go against Marwān, and al-Naḍr passed making for Syria. He camped at Qādisiyyah, and word of it came to Milḥān al-Shaybānī, al-Ḍaḥḥāk's governor of Kūfah. Milḥān came out against al-Naḍr and fought him, although he had with him only a few of the Khārijites. Al-Naḍr gave battle, and Milḥān persisted until al-Naḍr slew him. In a lament for him and ʿAbd al-Malik b. ʿAlqamah, Ibn Khudrah said:

> How many are like Milḥān, Khārijite trusted brother,
>   and Ibn ʿAlqamah, a Khārijite who found martyrdom?
>
> A sincere man to whom I devoted my affection,
>   who sold my house at highest bargain of any abode;[57]

---

54. The canal (*nahr*) named after Saʿīd b. ʿAbd al-Malik was situated outside of Raqqah. The reference here is probably to a second Nahr Saʿīd which was in the area of Baṣrah. See n. 54 below and Yāqūt, *Muʿjam*, IV, 840.

55. Maysān was a district between Baṣrah and Wāsiṭ. See Yāqūt, *Muʿjam*, IV, 840.

56. Hishām b. ʿAmmār al-Dimashqī d. 244–46/858–60. See *Taʾrīkh Dimashq*, I, pp. 581, 586, 587.

57. I.e., exchanged this world for paradise.

Brothers in truth whom I hoped for and forsook;
  I complain to God of my desertion and abandonment.

Word reached al-Ḍaḥḥāk of the slaying of Milḥān, so he appointed
al-Muthannā b. ʿImrān of the Banū ʿAʾidah as his governor in Kūfah.
Then al-Ḍaḥḥāk marched in Dhū al-Qaʿdah 127 (May 745), and took
Mosul. Ibn Hubayrah now moved from the Canal of Saʿīd and
camped at Ghazzah by ʿAyn al-Tamr.[58] Word of this reached al-   [1915]
Muthannā b. ʿImrān al-ʿĀʾidhī, al-Ḍaḥḥāk's governor in Kūfah, so he
marched against Ibn Hubayrah with the Khārijite troops at his disposal. With him was Manṣūr b. Jumhūr, who had gone over to him
when he pledged allegiance to al-Ḍaḥḥāk, in opposition to Marwān.
The two forces met at Ghazzah and fought a violent battle for several days. Al-Muthannā was slain, as were ʿUzayr and ʿAmr, two of
al-Ḍaḥḥāk's chieftains, while Manṣūr fled and the Khārijites were
routed. Muslim, the chamberlain of Yazīd, said concerning this:

War let al-Muthannā see his death, that day of Ghazzah,
  and flung ʿUzayr dead among those boulders,

She brought to ʿAmr doom, while already
  about Manṣūr were drawn the ropes of the snare.

Ghaylān b. Ḥurayth says in his panegyric of Ibn Hubayrah:

You vanquished on the Day of al-ʿAyn those whom you met,
  like the victory of a David over a Goliath.

When those slain on the Day of al-ʿAyn were slain and Manṣūr b.
Jumhūr had fled, he went straight on until he entered Kūfah and
gathered together a group of the Yaman faction and the Ṣufriyyah,
including those who had dispersed the day Milḥān was slain and
those who had held back from following al-Ḍaḥḥāk. Manṣūr gathered all these together and marched with them to camp at
Rawḥāʾ,[59] while Ibn Hubayrah advanced with his troops until he
encountered them. He fought them for several days and then put

---

58. ʿAyn al-Tamr is situated between al-Anbār and Kūfah. It commanded the military approaches from the western desert to Iraq and especially Kūfah. See *EI²* s.v.
ʿAyn al-Tamr. The Ghazzah mentioned here cannot be identified.
59. Yāqūt, *Muʿjam*, II, 820 lists al-Rawḥāʾ as a village in the vicinity of Baghdad
along the ʿĪsā Canal.

them to flight. Al-Birdhāwn b. Marzūq al-Shaybānī was slain, and Manṣūr fled. Concerning this, Ghaylān b. Ḥurayth said:

> The day of Rawḥāʾ al-ʿUdhayb when they dispatched
> Ibn Marzūq, a deadly swift poison.

[1916]   Ibn Hubayrah advanced until he was settled in Kūfah and drove the Khārijites from the city. Word of what had happened to his followers reached al-Ḍaḥḥāk, who sent for ʿUbaydah b. Sawwār al-Taghlibī and sent him against Ibn Hubayrah's forces. Ibn Hubayrah moved from Kūfah, intending to get to Wāsiṭ while ʿAbdallāh b. ʿUmar was there. He appointed ʿAbd al-Raḥmān b. Bashīr al-ʿIjlī as governor of Kūfah. On the next day ʿUbaydallāh b. Sawwār came up with his cavalry and stationed himself at the Ṣarāt Canal,[60] where he was joined by Manṣūr b. Jumhūr. Word of this reached Ibn Hubayrah and he marched against them. The two forces encountered each other at the Ṣarāt in the year 127 (745).

According to what is mentioned,[61] in this year (the ʿAbbāsid *naqībs*) Sulaymān b. Kathīr, Lāhiz b. Qurayẓ, and Qaḥṭabah b. Shabīb went to Mecca, where they met with Ibrāhīm b. Muḥammad the Imām (of the ʿAbbāsid Shīʿah). They informed him that they had with them twenty thousand dīnārs and two hundred thousand dirhams, as well as much musk and other goods. He ordered them to turn it over to Ibn ʿUrwah the mawlā of Muḥammad b. ʿAlī. This

---

60. It is not clear from context whether the reference to the Ṣarāt is to the canal that emptied into the Tigris at Baghdad (at this time a village) or to the Shaṭṭ al-Nīl which Ibn Serapion called the "Great Ṣarāt" that linked the Euphrates and Tigris north of the ruins of Babylon. See LeStrange, *Lands*, 72.

61. General surveys of the ʿAbbasid Revolution can be found in G. Van Vloten, *De Opkomst der Abbasiden in Khunasan* (Leiden, 1882), *Recherches sur la domination arabe, le chiitisme et les croyances messianiques sous le Khalifat des Omayyades* (Amsterdam, 1890); Wellhausen, *Arab Kingdom*, 357–566; R. Frye, "The ʿAbbāsid Conspiracy and Modern Revolutionary Theory," *Indo-Iranica*, 5/3 (1952–53): 9–14; C. Cahen, "Pointes de vue sur la revolution ʿAbbāside," *Revue Historique*, 230 (1963): 295–338; F. Omar, *The ʿAbbāsid Caliphate 132–70/750–80* (Baghdad, 1969), 57–136; *Al-ʿAbbāsiyyūn al-awāʾil: 132–70/750–86* (Beirut, 1970), v.1; M. Shaban, *The ʿAbbāsid Revolution* (Cambridge, 1970); H. Kennedy, *The Early Abbasid Caliphate* (New York, 1981), 35–45. See also the dissertations of M. Sharon, "ʿAlīyat ha-ʿAbbāsīm la-Shilṭōn," Hebrew University, Jerusalem, 1970 (soon to be published in Hebrew and in an expanded two-volume work in English); and D. Dennet, "Marwān b. Muḥammad; the passing of the Umayyad Caliphate," Harvard University, 1939. (J.L.)

year they had brought Abū Muslim with them, and Ibn Kathīr told Ibrāhīm b. Muḥammad, "This is your mawlā."

Also this year, Bukayr b. Māhān wrote to Ibrāhīm b. Muḥammad informing him that he was at death's door, and that he had chosen (Abū Salamah) Ḥafṣ b. Sulaymān as his successor and the latter was willing.[62] Ibrāhīm wrote to Abū Salamah instructing him to take command of his followers, and wrote to his people in Khurāsān informing them that he had entrusted Abū Salamah with their affairs. Abū Salamah then went to Khurāsān. The Khurāsānīs approved of him and accepted his leadership, and turned over to him what had been gathered on their behalf as contributions of their Shī'ah, and the fifth part of their wealth. [1917]

'Abd al-Azīz b. 'Umar b. 'Abd al-Azīz led the Pilgrimage this year. He was Marwān's governor for Madīnah, Mecca and Ṭā'if. Aḥmad b. Thābit al-Rāzī reported this from someone—Isḥāq b. 'Isā—Abū Ma'shar; al-Wāqidī and others have said the same.

The governor of Iraq in this year was al-Naḍr b. al-Ḥarashī. We have already mentioned what transpired between him and 'Abdallāh b. 'Umar and al-Ḍaḥḥāk al-Ḥarūrī. In Khurāsān Naṣr b. Sayyār was governor, but there were also those who contended with him for power there, such as Juday' al-Kirmānī (leader of the Yamanīs) and al-Ḥārith b. Surayj (al-Murji'ī).[63]

---

62. Bukayr was the non-Arab leader of the revolutionary apparatus of the 'Abbāsid Shī'ah in Kufah. Abū Salamah, his son-in-law, had taken his place on a mission to Khurāsān the previous year. See *Akhbār al-Dawlah*, 247–49; Balādhurī, *Ansāb*, III, 118 seemingly refers to this event and places it in the lifetime of Muḥammad b. 'Alī (d. 125 or 125 .AH.).

63. Al-Ḥārith is identified elsewhere as a Murji'ī, or member of a sect which left judgment of others to God.

The Events of the Year

128

(October 3, 745 – September 21, 746)

Among the events of this year was the slaying of al-Ḥārith b. Surayj in Khurāsān.[64]

The Slaying of al-Ḥārith b. Surayj

We have already mentioned the letter of Yazīd b. al-Walīd b. al-Walīd to al-Ḥārith with a pardon for him, and how al-Ḥārith then left the land of the Turks for Khurāsān and went to Naṣr b. Sayyār. We also mentioned how Naṣr treated him,[65] and how adherents collected around al-Ḥārith in answer to his call.

According to ʿAli b. Muḥammad (al-Madāʾinī)—his shaykhs: When Ibn Hubayrah took control of Iraq, he wrote to Naṣr b. Sayyār of his appointment, and Naṣr gave his allegiance to Marwān. Then al-Ḥārith said, "It was only Yazīd b. al-Walīd who gave me his promise of safety, and Marwān will not confirm a pardon made by Yazīd —I do not trust him."

Naṣr called for the oath of allegiance to Marwān, but Abū al-Salīl reviled Marwān. When he called on al-Ḥārith to give the oath, Salm

---

64. See Ibn Khayyāt, II, 405.
65. See Ṭabarī, II/3, 1887ff, *sub anno* 126.

b. Aḥwaz al-Tamīmī came to him, as well as Khālid b. Huraym,
Qaṭan b. Muḥammad, ʿAbbād b. al-Abrad b. Qurrah and Ḥammād b.   [1918]
ʿĀmir. They spoke with him, saying, "Why should Naṣr render his
authority and his governorship into the hands of your people? Didn't
he bring you out of the land of the Turks, away from the rule of the
Khāqān? He delivered you so that your enemies would not take
heart against you. But you opposed him; you forsook the rule of your
own tribe [ʿashīrah] and emboldened their enemy against them. We
would remind you of God, lest you scatter our unity [jamāʿah]!" Al-
Ḥārith replied, "Truly, I see the governorship in the hands of al-
Kirmānī, but the rule in the hands of Naṣr." Thus he would not
agree with them as they desired. He went out to a walled garden be-
longing to Ḥamzah b. Abī Ṣāliḥ al-Sulamī, opposite the palace of the
Bukhārākhudā,[66] and camped there. He sent a message to Naṣr say-
ing, "Submit the [question of] rule to consultation [shūrā]."[67] But
Naṣr refused. Then al-Ḥārith came out and went to the dwellings of
Yaʿqūb b. Dāwud. He ordered Jahm b. Ṣafwān the mawlā of the Banū
Rāsib[68] to read a document describing al-Ḥārith's program (sīrah) to
the people. At that, they went away exclaiming "Allāhu Akbar!" Al-
Ḥārith sent a messenger to Naṣr saying, "Discharge Salm b. Aḥwaz
from your security force and employ Bishr b. Bisṭām al-Burjumī."
There occurred some words between him and Mughallis b. Ziyād,
whereupon the Qays and the Tamīm split into separate factions.[69]
At this, Naṣr discharged Salm, but employed Ibrāhīm b. ʿAbd al-
Raḥmān. The two groups then chose some men to nominate for
them men mindful of the Book of God. Naṣr chose Muqātil b. Sulaymān and Muqātil b. Ḥayyān, while al-Ḥārith selected al-Mughīrah
b. Shuʿbah al-Jahḍamī and Muʿādh b. Jabalah. Naṣr instructed his
secretary to record whatever precedents (sunan) were acceptable to

---

66. Bukhārākhudā was the title of the native prince of Bukhārā.

67. That is, the ruler would have been chosen by an electoral council (shūrā). The
decision would thus have been taken out of the hands of Naṣr b. Sayyār and given to a
wider community.

68. Jahm b. Ṣafwān was the secretary and advisor of al-Ḥārith as well as the intel-
lectual protagonist of his revolt. His views were obscure, but a sect identified as his
followers was later condemned by Aḥmad b. Ḥanbal as propagating belief in the
created Qurʾān. They also held to an extreme view of predestination. See *EI*[2] s.v.
Djahmiyya. The Banū Rāsib were a sub-group of the Azd, a major group of the Yaman
in Khurāsān. See *EI*[2] s.v. Azd.

69. Text: *faqarrat*; read *fatafarraqat Qays wa Tamīm* following the Cairo ed.

them[70] and the governors they chose, so that he might appoint them to the two frontier zones, that is, the frontier of Samarqand and that of Ṭukhāristān.[71] He also instructed him to write to those who governed there what they saw fit in the way of programs and precedents. At this, Salm b. Aḥwaz asked Naṣr for permission to assassinate al-Ḥārith, but he refused, and appointed in his stead Ibrāhīm b. ʿAbd al-Raḥmān al-Ṣāʾigh, who used to send his son Isḥāq to Marw with turquoises.

Al-Ḥārith had proclaimed that he was "He of the Black Banners."[72] Naṣr sent to him saying, "If you are the one you claim, you will tear down the walls of Damascus and bring the rule of the Banū Umayyah to an end. So take five hundred men from me and two hundred camels, and load up with whatever wealth and weapons you will, and go! By my life, if you are the one you mention, then I am indeed in your hands; but if you are not that one, then you have destroyed your tribe." Al-Ḥārith replied, "I have learned that this [claim] is true, but none of my followers have given me an oath of allegiance on that basis." Naṣr answered, "Then it is clear that they are not of your opinion, and have nothing like your clairvoyance, and that they are sinners and ruffians. I exhort you in God's name for the twenty thousand of the Rabīʿah and the Yaman that shall perish in the conflict between you!" Naṣr also proposed to make al-Ḥārith governor of Transoxiana, and to give him three hundred thousand (pieces of silver), but he did not accept. Then Naṣr told him, "If you wish then begin with al-Kirmānī, and if you kill him, then I will obey you. Or if you wish, stay out of our quarrel, and if I am victorious over him, then do as you see fit. Or if you wish, then

---

70. Perhaps the precedents of the Prophet and his companions. Al-Ḥārith's movement had called for governing by the book of God and the precedent (*sunnah*) of the Prophet, and Naṣr was trying to conciliate al-Ḥārith and the pietists, who demanded justice for the convert element.

71. These areas had a large Turkish population and many Iranians who had converted to Islam. Ibn Surayj had a large following there.

72. That is, he who leads the revolt against the Umayyad regime and ushers in the messianic age. The movement of Ibn Surayj had many parallels to that of the ʿAbbāsids who were similarly imbued with messianic fervor and saw themselves as restoring the *sunnah* of the Prophet. See Sharon, *ʿAlīyat*, 139ff. On the black flags see Omar, "al-Alwān," *Bulletin of the College of Arts* (Baghdad University, XIV (1571): 828ff.

go with your followers,[73] and once you pass Rayy then I shall do as
you say!"

Naṣr and al-Ḥārith came face to face, and agreed that Muqātil b.
Ḥayyān[74] and Jahm b. Ṣafwān should arbitrate their differences.
Their judgment was that Naṣr should abdicate, and the government
be decided by consultation *(shūrā)*, but Naṣr did not accept it. Jahm
kept telling stories in his tent in al-Ḥārith's camp, while al-Ḥārith
kept opposing Naṣr. Then Naṣr issued orders to his people of the
Banū Salamah and others. He sent Salm into the city to the house of
Ibn Sawwār, and gave him command of the guard *(rābiṭah)*. He gave   [1920]
Hudbah b. ʿĀmir al-Shaʿrāwī some cavalry, and sent him into the
city as well. Naṣr appointed ʿAbd al-Salām b. Yazīd b. Ḥayyān al-
Sulamī governor of the city, and transferred the weapons and the
government registries to the Quhandiz.[75] He suspected that a group
of his followers had corresponded with al-Ḥārith. He thus had those
whom he suspected, and who had not been put to the test, sit to his
left, and he had those whom he had empowered and entrusted sit at
his right. He then spoke, and mentioned the Banū Marwān and
those who had rebelled against them, and how God had given him
victories. Then he said, "I praise God, but I blame those on my left
hand. I took over Khurāsān when you, O Yūnus b. ʿAbd Rabbihi,
were one of those who wanted to flee from the burden of providing
for Marw. You and the people of your family were of those who
wanted Asad b. ʿAbdallāh[76] to put his seal on their necks, and make
foot-soldiers of them.[77] Yet I befriended you when I became your
governor and treated you well. I commanded you to take away what
you had received when I wanted to travel to al-Walīd. Some of you

---

73. Text: *aṣḥābī* "my followers;" read *aṣḥābuka* "your followers" as in the Cairo
ed.

74. Muqātil b. Ḥayyān was the son of the Iranian convert and mediator Ḥayyān al-
Nabaṭī. For the latter see Ṭabarī, index, 158, and Wellhausen, *Arab Kingdom*, pp. 473,
496, 536.

75. The Quhandiz was the inner citadel at Marw, the size of a small city. It was surrounded by a larger walled urban area beyond which were the suburban districts that
stretched along the canals of the oasis. See LeStrange, *Lands*, 358.

76. That is Asad b. ʿAbdallāh al-Qasrī, the former governor of Khurāsān who favored the Yamani faction and brought Judayʿ al-Kirmānī in as his lieutenant.

77. Arabs rode to battle. To be made infantry was regarded as degrading. Foot-
soldiers were usually non-Arabs.

took a million [pieces of silver], more or less. And then you con-
spired with al-Ḥārith against me. Why didn't you look at these free
men who stuck with me, recipients of bounty, suffering no distress?" Here he indicated those who were on his right hand. At this,
those on his left apologized to him, and he accepted their plea.

A number of people came to Naṣr from the districts of Khurāsān
when word reached them of the internal strife he was encountering.
Among them were 'Āṣim b. 'Umayr al-Suraymī, Abū al-Dhayyāl al-
Nājī, 'Amr al-Fādusbān[78] al-Sughdī al-Bukhārī and Ḥassān b. Khālid
al-Asadī from Ṭukhāristan with their cavalry. They also included
'Āqil b. Ma'qil al-Laythī, Muslim b. 'Abd al-Raḥmān b. Muslim and
Sa'īd al-Ṣaghīr with more horsemen.

Al-Ḥārith b. Surayj wrote out his program and it was read in the
[1921]   great public street of Marw and in the mosques, and many people responded to it.

A man read it out at Naṣr's door in Majān,[79] whereupon Naṣr's
slaves beat him. At this, al-Ḥārith broke his compact with Naṣr.
Hubayrah b. Sharāḥīl and Yazīd Abū Khālid came and informed
Naṣr, and he summoned al-Ḥasan b. Sa'd, the mawlā of Quraysh, ordering him to proclaim, "Al-Ḥārith b. Surayj is the enemy of God.
He has broken faith and declared war, so call upon God for aid; there
is no might nor power save in God!" That same night he sent 'Āṣim
b. 'Umayr to al-Ḥārith, and asked al-Khālid b. 'Abd al-Raḥmān,
"What shall we employ as our battle cry tomorrow?" Muqātil b.
Sulaymān said, "When God sent a prophet and he fought the enemy,
his battle cry was '*Ḥā-Mīm*, they shall not be victorious!'" Thus
their battle cry was "*Ḥā-Mīm*, they shall not be victorious!" The
emblem on their lances was wool.[80]

Salm b. Aḥwaz, 'Āṣim b. 'Umayr, Qaṭan, 'Āqil b. Ma'qil, Muslim
b. 'Abd al-Raḥmān, Sa'īd al-Ṣaghīr, 'Āmir b. Mālik, and a number of
others were on the edge of the Ṭukhāriyyah quarter, while Yaḥyā b.
Ḥudayn and the Rabī'ah were in (the quarter of) the Bukhārīs. A
man from the city of Marw guided al-Ḥārith to a hole in the wall,
and al-Ḥārith went there, breached the wall and entered the city in

---

78. Text: *al-Qāwusān*; Cairo ed. *al-Fādusbān*.

79. A large western suburb of Marw where the Government Palace (Dār al-Imārah)
stood in 'Abbāsid times. See LeStrange, *Lands*, 399.

80. The wearing of wool was a sign of asceticism in early Islam. It appears that
Naṣr's forces were countering pietism with pietism.

the area near the Bālīn Gate[81] with fifty men. They cried out *"Yā Manṣūr!* [O divinely aided],"[82] al-Ḥārith's battle cry. They then came to Bāb Nīq, where Jahm b. Masʿūd al-Nājī fought them. A man charged at Jahm, but he speared him in the mouth, killing him. Then they went out through Bāb Nīq until they came to the pavilion *(qubbah)* of Salm b. Aḥwaz, where ʿIṣmah b. ʿAbdallāh al-Asadī, Khaḍir b. Khālid and al-Abrad b. Dāwud of the family of al-Abrad b. Qurrah fought them. At the Bālīn Gate was Ḥāzim b. Ḥātim, and they slew all who were guarding it and began to plunder the dwellings of Ibn Aḥwaz and of Qudayd b. Maniʿ, Al-Ḥārith forbade them to take anything except mounts and weapons from these houses or from the house of Ibrāhīm and ʿĪsā, the two sons of ʿAbdallāh al-Sulamī. This occurred on Sunday night at the end of Jumādā II (March 14, 746).   [1922]

A messenger from Salm came to inform Naṣr that al-Ḥārith was nearby, and he sent back the message, "Delay him until morning." Then Muḥammad b. Qaṭan b. ʿImrān al-Asadī also sent word to him that most of his followers had rebelled, and Naṣr replied, "Don't you be the one to begin the fighting." What provoked the conflict was that a slave of al-Naḍr b. Muḥammad the Jurist, a man called ʿAṭiyyah, went over to Salm's followers. At this, the followers of al-Ḥārith said, "Give him back to us." This they refused, and so they started fighting. A slave of ʿĀṣim was struck in the eye and died, and ʿĀṣim fought them along with ʿAqīl b. Maʿqil and put them to flight. They ran off to al-Ḥārith, who was saying the prayer of daybreak in the mosque of Abū Bakrah, the mawlā of the Banū Tamīm. As soon as he finished the prayer he went up to them, and they went back to the edge of the Ṭukharian quarter. Then two men approached him and ʿĀṣim called out to them, "Hamstring his horse!" At this, al-Ḥārith struck one of them with his mace killing him, and retreated to the street of the Sughdīs. There he saw Aʿyan, the mawlā of Ḥayyān, and forbade him to fight, but he fought (nonetheless) and was killed. Al-Ḥārith turned into the street of the Banū ʿIṣmah, and Ḥammād b. ʿĀmir al-Ḥimmānī and Muḥammad b. Zurʿah followed

---

81. The Bālīn Gate was the northwest gate of the inner city. See LeStrange, *Lands,* 399.

82. For messianic titles in late Umayyad and early ʿAbbāsid times see Lewis, "Regnal Titles" in the *Dr. Zakir Hussain Presentation Volume* (New Delhi, 1968).

him. He broke both their spears, and then charged Marzūq, the mawlā of Salm. As he drew near him, however, al-Ḥārith's horse bolted with him into a shop. He drove his mount into the rear wall, and it was killed.

When Salm awoke in the morning, he rode to Bāb Nīq and ordered the people to dig a trench. They dug it, and he instructed a herald to proclaim, "Whoever brings in [an enemy] head shall have three hundred [silver pieces]." The sun had hardly risen before al-Ḥārith was routed—he had fought them all night long. When we awoke in the morning Naṣr's followers took the Razīq Canal.[83] They overtook 'Abdallāh b. Mujjā'ah b. Sa'd, and slew him. Salm went as far as al-Ḥārith's camp and then turned back to Naṣr, who forbade him to advance, but he said, "I'm not stopping until I get into the city and fight that *dabbūsī* [club-wielder]!"[84] Muḥammad b. Qatan and 'Ubaydallāh b. Bassām went with him to the Dar Sankan Gate,[85] which is in the Quhandiz, and found it shut. However, 'Abdallāh b. Mazyad al-Asadī climbed the wall with three men and opened the gate. Ibn Aḥwaz entered, and set Abū al-Muṭahhar Ḥarb b. Sulaymān to guard the gate. That day Salm slew a secretary of al-Ḥārith b. Surayj whose name was Yazīd b. Dāwud. He gave the order to 'Abd Rabbihi b. Sīsan, who killed him. Salm went on to Bāb Nīq and opened it and killed a man from the Butchers' Quarter who had showed al-Ḥārith the hole (in the wall).

Al-Mundhir al-Raqqāshī, the paternal cousin of Yaḥyā b. Ḥudayn said, mentioning the fortitude of al-Qāsim al-Shaybānī:

None of you fought the enemy but our comrade,
With a band who fought steadfastly, unafraid;

They fought at the gate of the fortress and weakened not
Till God's help came to them and they conquered.

---

83. The Razīq was one of the four main canals which issued from the basin created by damming the Murghāb River. The canals watered the Marw Oasis and then ran into a marsh and were lost in the desert. See LeStrange, *Lands*, 398–99.

84. *Dabbūsī* was a disparaging term. Clubs, which were a favored weapon of the Iranian converts to Islam, may have acquired a symbolic meaning, e.g. schismatics.

85. That is the gate leading to Dar Sankān, a village adjacent to Marw. According to Yāqūt the village was also called Sinjān or Sanjān. See *Mu'jam*, III, 160.

Thus Qāsim following God's command guarded it,
While you confined yourself to withdrawal from that place.

It is said that when the matter of al-Kirmānī and al-Ḥārith grew rough, Naṣr sent a message to al-Kirmānī, who came to him under a truce. Present with them were Muḥammad b. Thābit the Qāḍī, Miqdām b. Nuʿaym the brother of ʿAbd al-Raḥmān b. Nuʿaym al-Ghāmidī, and Salm b. Aḥwaz. Naṣr called on them to unite, and said to al-Kirmānī, "You will be the happiest of men in that." Then some words occurred between Salm and Miqdām, and Salm spoke rudely to him. Miqdām's brother then took his part, and al-Sughdī b. ʿAbd al-Raḥmān al-Ḥazmī became angry with them both. Salm said, "I'd like to cut your nose off with a sword." And al-Sughdī told him, "Were you to touch your sword, your hand would not come back to you." At this, al-Kirmānī feared that this was a plot on Naṣr's part, so he rose and clung to Naṣr. He would not sit down, but went back to the door of the *maqṣūrah*.[86] His followers met him with his horse, and he mounted there in the mosque. Naṣr said, "He intended treachery to me." Al-Ḥārith then sent Naṣr the message, "We do not accept you as a leader of prayer." Naṣr replied, "How should you know [of such things]? You dissipated your life in the land of idolatry and raided the Muslims with idolators! Do you think that I would humble myself to you more than I have already done?"

That day Jahm b. Ṣafwān, the leader of the Jahmiyyah[87] was taken prisoner and he told Salm, "I have a promise[88] from your son Ḥārith!" He replied, "He should not have given it, and even if he did, I would not give you protection. Even if you filled this wrapper with stars, and Jesus the son of Mary pronounced you guiltless to me, you would not be delivered! By God, if you were in my belly, I would cut my belly open to kill you! And by God, no one will rise against us with the Yamanīs to an extent greater than you have done!" He then ordered ʿAbd Rabbihi b. Sīsan to kill him, and the people said, "Abū Muḥriz is slain;" for Jahm's patronymic was Abū Muḥriz.

[1924]

---

86. It appears that this meeting was arranged in the *maqṣūrah* of the mosque, the governor's prayer enclosure, so as to afford the participants maximum privacy and protection.

87. See n. 68 above.

88. The text is *walī*; it should be read *walth*, following the Cairo edition.

[1925] Hubayrah b. Sharāḥīl and ʿAbdallāh b. Mujjāʿah were taken prisoner that day, and he (Salm) said, "May God not spare him who spares you, though you are both of Tamīm." It is also said that Hubayrah was killed when the cavalry overtook him at the house of Qudayd b. Manīʿ.

When Naṣr routed al-Ḥārith, the latter sent his son Ḥātim to al-Kirmānī. At this, Muḥammad b. al-Muthannā[89] told al-Kirmānī, "They are both your enemies. Let them fight each other." But al-Kirmānī sent al-Sughdī b. ʿAbd al-Raḥmān al-Ḥazmī back with him, and al-Sughdī entered the city near the Maykhān Gate.[90] Then al-Ḥārith came, and entered the tent of al-Kirmānī. With al-Kirmānī were Dāwud b. Shuʿayb al-Ḥuddānī and Muḥammad b. al-Muthannā. The time for prayer came, and al-Kirmānī prayed with them.[91] Then al-Ḥārith mounted, and Jamāʿah b. Muḥammad b. ʿAzīz Abū Khalaf went with him. The next day al-Kirmānī went to the gate of Maydān Yazīd, and fought Naṣr's followers. Saʿd b. Salm al-Marāghī was slain, and the banner of ʿUthmān b. al-Kirmānī was captured.

The first to bring the news of al-Ḥārith's rout to al-Kirmānī—he was encamped at Bāb Māsarjasān, one *farsakh* (6 km) from the city —were al-Naḍr b. Ghallāq al-Sughdī and ʿAbd al-Wāḥid b. al-Munakhkhal. Then came Sawādah b. Surayj[92] (Ḥātim b. al-Ḥārith, and Khālil b. Ghazwān al-ʿAdawī, bringing him the oath of al-Ḥārith b. Surayj).[93] The first to give the oath of allegiance to al-Kirmānī was Yaḥyā b. Nuʿaym b. Hubayrah al-Shaybānī. Then al-Kirmānī sent
[1926] Sawrah b. Muḥammad al-Kindī to al-Ḥārith (at Asmānīr),[94] as well

---

89. According to Dīnawarī, 352, this man was a chief of the Rabīʿah in Marw who joined al-Kirmānī, while Ṭabarī's accounts seem always to associate him with the Azd. Dīnawarī's extended account (352–62) of the tribal war contains details not found in Ṭabarī, but there is no mention of Ibn Surayj. The account is confined to al-Kirmānī's quarrel with Naṣr b. Sayyār.

90. Both editions read *maykhān*, "tavern;" *mijān* is also possible.

91. This was the forging of a coalition against the Qays. It was, however, an inherently unstable alliance, for while al-Ḥārith had a following of converts and tribesmen of the Yaman, he and his core following were from the Tamīm. Some of the Tamīm, such as Salm b. Aḥwāz, supported Naṣr b. Sayyār. The Tamīm were the natural allies of the Qays.

92. The brother of al-Ḥārith b. Surayj.

93. This phrase is missing from the text and is supplied from the Cairo edition.

94. The text records that a word is missing. The reading is supplied by the Cairo edition. There is no entry for Asmānīr in Yāqūt.

as al-Sughdī b. ʿAbd al-Raḥmān Abū Ṭuʿmah, and Saʿb or Suʿayb, and Ṣabbāḥ. They entered the city from Bāb Maykhān until they came to Bāb Rakak. Then al-Kirmānī advanced to the gate of Ḥarb b. ʿĀmir and sent his followers against Naṣr on Wednesday. They exchanged volleys, but abstained from further combat, and there was no fighting on Thursday. Then they encountered each other on Friday, and the Azd fled back to al-Kirmānī. He took their standard in his hand and fought with it. Al-Khaḍir b. Tamīm charged (Naṣr's men) wearing a coat of mail, and they shot arrows at him. Then Ḥubaysh, a mawlā of Naṣr, dashed at him, and wounded him in the throat. Al-Khaḍir tore the spearhead from his throat with his left hand and his horse set off with him. He charged Ḥubaysh, speared him and threw him off his horse, and al-Kirmānī's foot-soldiers finished him off with clubs.

Naṣr's followers fled, and al-Kirmānī's men captured eighty of their horses. Tamīm b. Naṣr was thrown, and two mounts of his were taken; al-Sughdī b. ʿAbd al-Raḥmān took one of them, and al-Khaḍir took the other. Al-Khaḍir encountered Salm b. Aḥwaz, took a mace from his nephew and clubbed Salm, and wrested him off his horse. Two men of Tamīm charged Salm, but he got away, and threw himself from the bridge. He had sustained some ten blows on his iron helmet, and he collapsed. Muḥammad b. al-Ḥaddād carried him to Naṣr's camp, and the forces withdrew. A few nights later, Naṣr came out of Marw, and ʿIṣmah b. ʿAbdallāh al-Asadī was slain. He was defending Naṣr's men, and Ṣāliḥ b. al-Qaʿqāʿ al-Azdī overtook him. ʿIṣmah called, "Come on, Mazūnī!"[95] And Ṣāliḥ replied, "Hold tight, eunuch!" For ʿIṣmah was childless. ʿIṣmah turned his horse and it reared, whereupon he fell. Then Ṣāliḥ speared him and killed him. Ibn al-Daylīmarī,[96] a *rajaz* poet, fought and was slain at ʿIṣmah's side. ʿUbaydallāh b. Ḥawtamah al-Sulamī was slain; Marwān al-Bahrānī hurled an iron bar at him, and he was killed. They brought his head to al-Kirmānī, and he recoiled, for ʿUbaydallāh had been a friend of his. A Yamanī man seized the reins of Muslim b. ʿAbd al-Raḥmān b. Muslim's horse, but he recognized him, so he let him go. They fought each other for three days and on

[1927]

---

95. This was an insult reserved for the Azd (Mazūn was once a Persian name for ʿUmān). The Azd regarded it as an ethnic sneer. See *Lisān al-ʿArab*, XVII, 294 and n. 103.

96. Vocalization conjectural.

the last day the Muḍar put the Yaman to flight. Then al-Khalīl b. Ghazwān called, "O men of Rabiʿah and Yaman, al-Ḥārith has entered the bazaar; Ibn al-Aqṭaʿ [Naṣr] is slain; Muḍar's strength has been broken!" The first who fled was Ibrāhīm b. Bassām al-Laythī. Tamīm, Naṣr's son, dismounted to fight on foot, and ʿAbd al-Raḥmān b. Jāmiʿ al-Kindī took his horse. Hayyāj al-Kalbī was slain, and Laqīṭ b. Akhḍar was killed by a slave of Hāniʾ al-Bazzār.

It is said that when Friday came, they prepared for battle and tore down (part of) the walls in order to give themselves more space. Al-Naṣr sent Muḥammad b. Qaṭan to al-Kirmānī with the message, "You are not like this club-wielder; fear God, and do not enter civil war *[fitnah]*." Tamīm b. Naṣr sent his armed retinue (Shākiriyyah),[97] who were within the house of Janūb bt. al-Qaʿqāʿ, but the followers of al-Kirmānī shot at them from the roofs and were wary of them. Then ʿAqīl b. Maʿqil said to Muḥammad b. al-Muthannā, "Why are we killing ourselves for Naṣr and al-Kirmānī? Come, let us return to our own country in Ṭukhāristān!" However, Muḥammad replied, "Naṣr did not keep faith with us, and we shall not stop fighting him."

The partisans of al-Ḥārith and al-Kirmānī used to shoot at Naṣr and his followers with a ballista. Naṣr's awning was struck while he was under it, but he did not move from it. Then he sent Salm b. Aḥwaz against them, and he engaged them in battle. At first, the victory went to Naṣr, but when al-Kirmānī saw that, he took his banner from Muḥammad b. Muḥammad b. ʿUmayrah and fought with it until he broke it. Muḥammad b. al-Muthannā then set out with al-Zāgh and Ḥiṭṭān for Kārābakul,[98] so that they emerged on the Razīq Canal where Tamīm b. Naṣr held the bridge. When he came up to Tamīm, Muḥammad told him, "Stand aside, boy!" Muḥammad was carrying a yellow banner while al-Zāgh accompanied him. They unhorsed Aʿyan the mawlā and chief clerk of Naṣr and slew him, along with a number of his Shākiriyyah. Al-Khaḍir b. Tamīm attacked Salm b. Aḥwaz and speared him, but he deflected the blow. Then al-Khaḍir struck him on the chest with an iron bar,

[1928]

---

97. Shākiriyyah are frequently mentioned in Arabic sources of the early period. Their precise composition and function however remains unknown.

98. Reading conjectural. Al-Zāgh and Ḥiṭṭān seem to be non-Arab names, and Kārābakul a place.

and again on his shoulder. He struck him a third time on his head, and Salm fell down. Naṣr defended his followers with eight hundred men, and kept the enemy from entering the market.

When the Yaman had put the Muḍar to flight, al-Ḥārith sent Naṣr the message, "The Yaman blame me for your getting away, and I am refraining from fighting. Now set the staunchest of your followers in front of al-Kirmānī." At this, Naṣr sent Yazīd al-Nahawī or Khālid[99] to him to ascertain from him that he would keep his word to refrain from fighting. It is said that al-Ḥārith only desisted from fighting Naṣr so that ʿImrān b. al-Faḍl al-Azdī and the people of his house, and ʿAbd al-Jabbār al-ʿAdawī and Khālid b. ʿUbaydallāh b. Ḥabīb al-ʿAdawī and most of his followers might be avenged on al-Kirmānī for what he did to the people of Tabūshkān.[100] That was when Asad had sent al-Kirmānī against them, and they came out to submit themselves to Asad's judgment. However, he slit open the bellies of fifty men and threw them into the Oxus, and cut off the hands and feet of three hundred of them. He crucified three men and sold their households to the highest bidder. They were thus taking revenge on al-Ḥārith for helping al-Kirmānī and fighting Naṣr.

When matters changed between him and al-Ḥārith, Naṣr said to his followers, "Muḍar will not unite in support of me as long as al-Ḥārith is with al-Kirmānī. They cannot agree on anything; the best idea is to leave them both, since they are quarreling." He then went out to Julfar[101] where he found ʿAbd al-Jabbār al-Aḥwal al-ʿAdawī and ʿUmar b. Abī al-Haytham al-Sughdī, and asked them, "Are you pleased to stand with al-Kirmānī?" ʿAbd al-Jabbār told him, "May you never lack for affliction so long as you occupy this place!" When Naṣr came back to Marw, he ordered that ʿAbd al-Jabbār be given four hundred lashes.

[1929]

Naṣr now went to Kharaq[102] and stayed there for four days. With him were Muslim b. ʿAbd al-Raḥmān b. Muslim, Salm b. Aḥwaz and Sinān al-Aʿrābī. Naṣr told his wives, "Al-Ḥārith will take my place,

---

99. The text has "and Khālid," but the Cairo edition says it should read "or Khālid."

100. Tabūshkān was a fortress in upper Tukhāristān where in 117 (January 31, 735—January 20, 736), Asad b. ʿAbdallāh al-Qasrī had al-Kirmānī massacre the relatives of al-Ḥārith b. Surayj. See Ṭabarī, II/3, 1589 *sub anno* 118.

101. Julfar (also Julfār) was one of the villages of Marw. See Yāqūt, *Muʿjam*, II, 104.

102. Yāqūt lists Kharaq as a village in the Marw oasis. See *Muʿjam*, II, 445.

and will protect you." When he drew near to Naysābūr the people sent messengers asking, "What has brought you? Has some tribal quarrel flared up which God had extinguished?" Naṣr's governor at Naysābūr was Ḍirār b. 'Īsā al-'Āmirī, and Naṣr sent him Sinān al-A'rābī, Muslim b. 'Abd al-Raḥmān and Salm b. Aḥwaz, who spoke to the Naysābūrīs. Then they came out, and met Naṣr with a princely retinue, slave-girls, and gifts. At this, Salm told him, "God make me your ransom! This tribe is of Qays, and Qays was only remonstrating." Naṣr replied:

> I am the son of Khindif; its tribe increases me
> In good deeds, and my paternal uncle is Qays 'Aylān!

When Naṣr departed from Marw, Yūnus b. 'Abd Rabbihi, Muḥammad b. Qaṭan and Khālid b. 'Abd al-Raḥmān accompanied him, with others who were their peers.

The source says that 'Abbād b. 'Umar al-Azdī, 'Abd al-Ḥakīm b. Sa'īd al-'Awdhī and Abū Ja'far 'Īsā b. Jurz came to Naṣr at Abrashahr[103] from Mecca, and Naṣr told 'Abd al-Ḥakīm al-'Awdhī, "Do you not see what the foolish men of your folk have done?" He replied, "Say rather the foolish men of your own folk. Their rule was prolonged in your governorship, and you rendered the government to your own people, excluding Rabī'ah and Yaman, so that they became insolent. There are forbearing people and foolish ones in both the Rabī'ah and Yaman, and the foolish ones prevailed over the wise." 'Abbād said, "Do you receive the Amīr with such words?" But Naṣr told him, "Let him alone; he's spoken the truth." Then Abū Ja'far 'Īsā b. Jurz—a man who came from a village on the river of Marw—said, "O Amīr, you have merit [ḥasab] in these matters and in your governorship, for truly a momentous matter is at hand. A man of obscure origins will rise and display black colors, and call men to a revolution [dawlah][104] which is to come. He will take the authority, and you shall see it and be shaken." However, Naṣr said, "I do not think that will be, because of the lack of agreement among the people, their rancor and their mutual enmity. I sent an emissary

[1930]

---

103. In early Islamic time Naysābūr (Nishāpūr) was known as Abrashahr. See Le-Strange, *Lands*, 383.

104. For the term *dawlah*, see *EI²* s.v. Dawla. The man of unknown origins is a reference to Abū Muslim al-Khurasānī, and the aim of the account is to score a propaganda point for the 'Abbāsids.

to al-Ḥārith when he was in the land of the Turks and offered him a
governorship and money, yet he refused and stirred up mischief, and
rose up against me." Then Abū Jaʿfar ʿĪsā said, "Al-Ḥārith is already
slain and crucified, and al-Kirmānī is not far from that fate." Naṣr
bestowed gifts on ʿĪsā for this. Salm b. Aḥwaz used to say, "I never
saw a folk more generous in response or more giving of their blood
than the Qays."

When Naṣr departed from Marw, al-Kirmānī gained the upper
hand there, and told al-Ḥārith, "I want only the Book of God."
(Later) Qaḥṭabah said, "If he'd been telling the truth, I would have
reinforced him with a thousand horsemen."[105]

Muqātil b. Ḥayyān asked, "Is it in the Book of God to tear down
houses and seize wealth?" And al-Kirmānī confined him in a tent in
the camp. Then Muʿammar b. Muqātil b. Ḥayyān, or Muʿammar b.
Ḥayyān, spoke to al-Kirmānī, and he let Muqātil go. Later al-Kirmānī went to the mosque, and al-Ḥārith stood by. Al-Kirmānī addressed the people and gave all of them a guarantee of safety, except
Muḥammad b. al-Zubayr and one other man. Dāwud b. Abī Dāwud [1931]
b. Yaʿqūb then asked him for surety for Muḥammad b. al-Zubayr.
The secretary came in and gave Muḥammad a guarantee. Al-Ḥārith
went to the Gate of Dūrān and Sarakhs,[106] while al-Kirmānī
camped in Muṣallā Asad. He sent for al-Ḥārith, who came before
him and denied that he had destroyed people's homes and taken
their possessions. Al-Kirmānī pondered but did nothing, and he remained for several days. Then Bishr b. Jurmūz al-Ḍabbī rebelled at
Kharqān,[107] summoning men to the Qurʾān and the *sunnah*. He
told al-Ḥārith, "I only fought beside you seeking justice, but since
you have been with al-Kirmānī I have realized that you only fight so
that it will be said 'al-Ḥārith has won.' These people are [only] fighting out of tribalism, so I'm not fighting on your side." He then with-

---

105. The reference here is to Qaḥṭabah b. Shabīb, the great ʿAbbāsid general who
did much to defeat the Umayyads (see *EI*² s.v. Ḳaḥṭaba b. Shabīb). This interjected
tradition supports the "message" that the ʿAbbāsids alone were able and willing to
support the Book of God, and so fulfill the apocalyptic traditions.

106. That is, the main gate of Marw, Bāb al-Madīnah, to the southwest. See Le-
Strange, *Lands*, 399.

107. Yāqūt, *Muʿjam*, II, 424–25 lists several places under Kharaqān, Kharqān and
Kharraqān, but none seems to be the place mentioned here. He also mentions a Kharqān Canal in the vicinity of Marw (I, 66), which is mentioned later in Ṭabarī's narra-
tive. There is also the possibility that Kharaq was intended. See n. 102 above.

drew *(iʿtazal)*[108] at the head of fifty-five hundred men—some say with only four thousand—and said, "We are the just detachment; we summon [people] to the truth, and we fight none but those who fight us." Al-Ḥārith came to the Mosque of ʿIyāḍ, and sent to al-Kirmānī calling upon him to let the government be decided by consultation, but al-Kirmānī refused. Al-Ḥārith sent his son Muḥammad, and he moved his household[109] from the house of Tamīm b. Naṣr. At this, Naṣr wrote to his own tribe and the Muḍar, "Stay with al-Ḥārith as good advisers." So they came to him, and al-Ḥārith told them, "You are the root and branch of the Arabs, but you are about to be routed, so come out to me with your households." They replied, "We never agree on anything without encountering it."

One of the administrative assistants in al-Kirmānī's camp was Muqātil b. Sulaymān. A man of the Bukhārīs came to him and said, "Give me the payment for the mangonels I set up." He told him, "Establish the proof that you set them up for the sake of the Muslims." At this, Shaybah b. Shaykh al-Azdī testified for him. A draft on the treasury was then written for the man at Muqātil's behest.

[1932]   The followers of al-Ḥārith wrote to al-Kirmānī, "We advise you to fear God and to obey Him, to follow the path of imāms of guidance and to forbid of your blood what God has forbidden. If God joins us together, it will be for al-Ḥārith's earnest desire for a relationship with God and his sincere advice to His servants. We have exposed ourselves to war, our blood to spilling, and our property to destruction. All that is little to us, beside the reward we hope for from God. We are all brothers in religion, and helpers against the enemy. So fear God and return to the truth, for truly we desire not the spilling of blood unless it be lawful."

They remained for several days, and then al-Ḥārith b. Surayj came and bored a hole in the wall, near Nawbān at the house of Hishām b. Abī Haytham. At this, cautious people parted company with al-

---

108. Bishr b. Jurmūz had fought with the Murjiʾites of Jahm b. Ṣafwān earlier. Some of the early Muʿtazilah were accused of following the teachings of Jahm later on. The Muʿtazilah, whose political program was "an upright Imām," took their name from a ḥadīth which orders withdrawal from factions when the Imāmate is in doubt. The expression *iʿtazala*, "he withdrew," is at least suggestive of possible connections between the followers of Jahm b. Ṣafwān and the Muʿtazilah.

109. The text is *naqalahu*, "he moved him;" it should be read *ḥawala thaqalahu*, "he moved his household," as in the Cairo edition.

Ḥārith, saying, "You have acted treacherously." Al-Qāsim al-Shaybānī and Rabīʿ al-Taymī remained in one group, while al-Kirmānī came into the city from the Sarakhs Gate. Al-Ḥārith opposed them. Al-Munakhkhal b. ʿAmr al-Azdī passed by, whereupon al-Samaydaʿ, one of the Banū al-ʿAdawiyyah, slew him, crying out, "Now for the avengers of Laqīṭ!" Thereupon the two sides fought one another. Al-Kirmānī put Dāwud b. Shuʿayb and his brothers Khālid, Mazyad and Muhallab on his right wing, and Sawrah b. Muḥammad b. ʿAzīz al-Kindī on his left, leading the Kindah and the Rabīʿah. The fighting grew fierce and al-Ḥārith's followers were put to flight and slain in the area between the breach in the wall and al-Ḥārith's camp. Al-Ḥārith, who was on a mule, got off it and mounted a horse. He struck it, and it sped off as his followers fled. He stayed with some of his followers, and was slain at a tree. His brother Sawādah, Bishr b. Jurmūz and Qaṭan b. al-Mughīrah b. ʿAjrad were also killed. Then al-Kirmānī stopped the fight. A hundred men were slain along with al-Ḥārith, and so were a hundred of al-Kirmānī's followers. Al-Ḥārith's headless body was crucified at the city of Marw. Hid death came thirty days after Naṣr's departure [1933] from Marw, the last Sunday of Rajab (April 25, 746).

It was said that al-Ḥārith was killed in this manner under an olive or sorb tree in the year 128 (745–746). Al-Kirmānī found sheets of gold belonging to al-Ḥārith, which he seized. He put al-Ḥārith's concubine *(umm walad)* in confinement; then he let her go—she had once belonged to Ḥājib b. ʿAmr b. Salamah b. Sakan b. Jawn b. Dabīb. He also seized the property of those who departed with Naṣr, and he took his choice of the furnishings of ʿĀṣim b. ʿUmayr. Ibrāhīm[110] asked him, "By what right do you acquire his property?" At this, Ṣāliḥ of the family of al-Waḍḍāḥ said, "Pour out his blood for me!" But Muqātil b. Sulaymān stepped between them and brought him to his house.

According to ʿAlī (al-Madāʾinī)—Zuhayr b. al-Hunayd: Al-Kirmānī went out to Bishr b. Jurmūz and camped outside the city of Marw. Bishr had four thousand men, and al-Ḥārith camped with al-Kirmānī. Al-Kirmānī stayed thus for some days, at a distance of two *farsakh*s (12 km) from Bishr's camp. Then he advanced until he was close to it, intending to do battle with Bishr. He told al-Ḥārith,

---

110. Perhaps Ibrāhīm b. ʿAbdallāh al-Sulamī, mentioned above.

"Move up." But al-Ḥārith regretted having followed al-Kirmānī and said, "Don't be in a hurry to fight them; I'll get them back for you." He left the camp with ten horsemen and rode until they came to Bishr's camp in the village of Darzījān and stayed with them, saying, "I was not one to fight against you with the Yamanīs!" Then the Muḍar began to steal away from the camp of al-Kirmānī to al-Ḥārith until none of the Muḍar remained with al-Kirmānī except two men: Salamah b. Abī ʿAbdallāh the mawlā of the Banū Sulaym, who said, "By God, I shall never follow al-Ḥārith, for I know that he is a deceiver;" and Muhallab b. Iyās, who said, "I will not follow him, for I have never seen him except leading cavalry which has been repulsed."

[1934]

Then al-Kirmānī engaged them repeatedly. They would fight each other, and then go back behind their trenches. One time the advantage would be with one side, and another time with the other. On one such day they met in battle when Marthad b. ʿAbdallāh al-Mujāshiʿī had been drinking. He went out drunk on a horse belonging to al-Ḥārith. He was hit with a lance and thrown from his mount. Some horsemen of the Banū Tamīm protected him until he was safe, but the horse ran away. When he came back, al-Ḥārith blamed him, and said, "You almost killed yourself." He told al-Ḥārith, "You only say that because of your horse; may his wife be divorced if I don't bring you a livelier [horse than yours from their camp!" The next day they fought again, and Marthad said,][111] "Who has the liveliest horse in their camp?" They told him, "ʿAbdallāh b. Daysam al-ʿAnazī," and pointed to where he stood. Marthad fought until he reached him, and then struck him. Ibn Daysam threw himself from his horse, and Marthad hooked the reins of the horse on his lance and led it until he came to al-Ḥārith. Then he said, "Take this in place of your horse." Mukhallad b. al-Ḥasan encountered Marthad later, and said in jest, "How fine the horse of Ibn Daysam is under you!" At this, he dismounted and said, "Take it!" He replied, "You want to disgrace me! You took it from us in war, and shall I take it in peace?"

They remained thus for some days. Then al-Ḥārith moved off by night and came to the walls of Marw and bored an opening and entered within the walls. Then al-Kirmānī entered, and al-Ḥārith

---

111. The text lacks the bracketed words, which are supplied by the Cairo edition.

moved off. At this the Muḍar told al-Ḥārith, "We left the trenches when the day was ours, and you've run away more than once, so dismount and fight on foot!" He told them, "I'm more good to you as a horseman than as a foot-soldier." However, they said, "We will not be satisfied unless you dismount." He thus dismounted to fight between the wall of Marw and the city. Al-Ḥārith was killed along with his brother and Bishr b. Jurmūz and a number of cavalry from the Tamīm, while the rest were put to flight. Al-Ḥārith was crucified, and Marw was given over to the Yaman, who tore down the houses of the Muḍar.

[1935]

When al-Ḥārith was slain, Naṣr b. Sayyār composed these verses:

> Now, bringer of humiliation upon his folk,
>   may removal and distance be yours in death!

> Your evil fortune made all Muḍar to fall,
>   and diminished the reputation of your people.

> Azd and its partisans were not wont [before you]
>   to hope to overcome ʿAmr or Mālik

> Nor the Banū Saʿd, when they bridled
>   each swift horse deadly black in color!

It is also said that Naṣr addressed these verses to ʿUthmān b. Ṣadaqah al-Māzinī. Umm Kathīr al-Ḍabbiyyah said:

> May God not bless any female, but torment her
>   to the end of time, if she marries a Muḍarī!

> Convey to the men of Tamīm the word of a woman distressed,
>   whom you lodged in the house of humiliation and poverty!

> If you return not to the battle after your wheeling,
>   until you make the men of Azd retreat in a victory,

> I am ashamed for you that you give your obedience
>   to this Mazūnī who mulcts you by oppression.

ʿAbbād b. al-Ḥārith said:

Now, O Naṣr, the hidden is revealed,
　　though hope and expectation were protracted.

The Mazūn have exercised in the Land of Marw
　　the office of the governor, decreeing as they will.

Their ruling is held lawful in every judgment
　　against Muḍar, though the ruling is unjust

While Ḥimyar[112] sit in their assemblies,
　　and blood is pouring from their [Muḍar's] necks.

If Muḍar is content with that and is abased,
　　then may their abjection and distress be long!

And if they turned from that 'twere well; if not,
　　then let destruction fall upon their armies!

[1936]

He also recited:

Well then, O you man whom
　　emotions have split asunder,

Wake up! and leave aside the thing
　　you sought, and we also sought for.

For there have occurred in our presence
　　matters of strange condition.

I beheld the Azd become mighty
　　in Marw, while the Arabs were humiliated,[113]

And brass became current when that
　　happened, while gold became a trifle.

---

112. The Banū Ḥimyar were a kingly Yamanī tribe. Here apparently all Yaman tribes are meant.

113. The Azd were taunted with being fisherfolk of 'Umān, and no true Arabs. See *EI*² s.v. Azd.

Abū Bakr b. Ibrāhīm, addressing ʿAlī and ʿUthmān the sons of
al-Kirmānī:

> I travel intending with my poem of praise
>   two brothers whose qualities excel those of all men,
>
> Outracing noble stallions, never lacking forage,
>   while the guest, the stranger, never lacks their cheer.
>
> Ascendant and yet racing for the height,
>   their tribe lives under their protection.
>
> I mean that ʿAlī and his chief helper
>   ʿUthmān; never was humiliated one who followed them,
>
> Still racing that they may overtake their father,
>   like stallions from afar who near the goal.
>
> And if they did attain it, 'tis partly due to noble sire,
>   that they race up the slope to catch up to a father.
>
> And if he should outrun them, many times
>   he ran surpassing them and others too.
>
> Indeed I shall praise them for what my eyes
>   have seen, though I've not numbered all their qualities.
>
> They are two pious men, to whom all are directed;
>   both bearers of their tribe's burden, perfect men;
>
> They removed from the haughtiness of kingly state
>   a Naṣr, who found humiliation in opposing them;
>
> They drove Ibn Aqtaʿ [Naṣr] away after slaying his defenders;
>   divided are his spoils among their horsemen.
>
> Also al-Ḥārith b. Surayj, when they aimed at him
>   so that their swords took turns in striking his head.

They took the best part of their father in his prime
                    so that their folk are mighty, and those who follow them.

In this year Ibrāhīm b. Muḥammad (the ʿAbbāsid) sent Abū Muslim to Khurāsān, and wrote his followers there, "I have given him
my command, so listen to him and accept his words, for I have given
him command over Khurāsān and whatever he may gain control
over beyond it."[114] Abū Muslim came to them, but they did not accept his words. Those who were opposed went and met in Mecca in
the presence of Ibrāhīm. Abū Muslim informed Ibrāhīm that they
had not acted in accord with his letter and command, and Ibrāhīm
said, "I have offered this authority to more than one, and they have
refused it." This was because, before he sent Abū Muslim, he had offered it to Sulaymān b. Kathīr al-Khuzāʿī, who said, "I shall never
take on two functions." Then he offered it to Ibrāhīm b. Salamah,
and he refused. He now informed them that he had decided on Abū
Muslim, and commanded them to hear and to obey. Then he said to
Abū Muslim, "ʿAbd al-Raḥmān,[115] you are one of us, people of the
House, so learn my instructions well. Look to this tribe of Yaman;
honor them and settle among them, for truly God will not complete
this matter without them. Look to this tribe of Rabīʿah, and be suspicious of all they do. Look to this tribe of Muḍar; they are indeed
the enemy close to the House, so slay anyone of whom you are in
doubt, or in whose actions there is ambiguity, or anyone of whom
you come to feel any suspicion. If you can not leave one Arab tongue
in Khurāsān,[116] then do it; any boy who has attained five hand-
spans height, whom you suspect, slay! But do not quarrel with the
shaykh, that is, Sulaymān b. Kathīr, and do not disobey him. If any
matter gives you difficulty then go to him rather than to me."

---

114. For Abū Muslim's mission to Khurāsān see *Akhbār al-Dawlah*, 267ff; *FHA*,
164ff; Kūfī, *Futūḥ*, VIII, 155ff; Ibn ʿAbd Rabbihi, IV, 478ff; Balādhurī, *Ansāb*, III,
120ff; Azdī, 65; Dīnawarī, 360.

115. One of several proper names attributed to him. The most detailed treatment of
his origins is found in the *Akhbar al-Dawlah*, 253ff.

116. Given the instruction to court one group of Arabs and known ʿAbbāsid practice, this is a very problematic statement. (On it, see Sharon, *Alīyat*, 156-J.L.) The
need to rely on the Yaman and Rabīʿah vis-a-vis the Muḍar is found in various traditions. See for example Kūfī, *Futūḥ*, VIII, 154; Ibn ʿAbd Rabbihi, IV, 477.

According to Hishām b. Muḥammad who reported it from Abū   [1938]
Mikhnaf, in this year al-Ḍaḥḥāk b. Qays al-Khārijī was killed.

The Death of al-Ḍaḥḥāk b. Qays the Khārijite

When al-Ḍaḥḥāk was besieging ʿAbdallāh b. ʿUmar b. ʿAbd al-ʿAzīz
at Wāsiṭ and Manṣūr b. Jumhūr gave him the oath of allegiance,
ʿAbdallāh b. ʿUmar saw that he could not withstand al-Ḍaḥḥāk. He
therefore sent him a message, "Your stand against me is worth nothing. Here is Marwān, so march against him. If you do battle with
him I shall be with you." He became reconciled with him, as we
have mentioned in the conflicting accounts of this event. Hishām
reported from Abū Mikhnaf that al-Ḍaḥḥāk set out from Ibn ʿUmar
to engage Marwān at Kafartūtha in the territory of the Jazīrah, and
was slain the day the armies met.

According to Abū Hāshim Mukhallad b. Muḥammad b. Ṣāliḥ—
Aḥmad b. Zuhayr—ʿAbd al-Wahhāb b. Ibrāhīm: ʿAṭiyyah al-
Thaʿlabī[117] slew Milḥān, al-Ḍaḥḥāk's follower and governor for
Kūfah, at the Bridge of Saylaḥūn. News of Milḥān's slaying reached
al-Ḍaḥḥāk while he was besieging ʿAbdallāh b. ʿUmar at Wāsiṭ, and
al-Ḍaḥḥāk sent as replacement one of his followers called Muṭāʿin.
ʿAbdallāh b. ʿUmar and al-Ḍaḥḥāk made peace on the condition that
Ibn ʿUmar enter into obedience to al-Ḍaḥḥāk. Ibn ʿUmar did this,
and prayed behind him. Al-Ḍaḥḥāk went off to Kūfah, and Ibn
ʿUmar stayed with his followers at Wāsiṭ. Al-Ḍaḥḥāk entered Kūfah,
and the inhabitants of Mosul wrote to him inviting him to come
there, whereupon they would give him control of their city. After
twenty months he marched with all his troops to Mosul. Ruling
there at that time was Marwān's governor, a man of the Banū Shaybān of the Jazīrah called al-Qaṭirān b. Akmah. The people of Mosul   [1939]
opened the city for al-Ḍaḥḥāk, and al-Qaṭirān fought them with a
small number of his tribe and the people of his house to the last
man. Al-Ḍaḥḥāk thus took possession of Mosul and its districts.

Word of this reached Marwān while he was besieging Ḥimṣ and

---

117. The text is al-Taghlibī; it should be read al-Thaʿlabī as in the Cairo edition.
This is supported by *FHA*, 164, and is more probable, since many of the Taghlib were
fighting for the Khārijites.

preoccupied in fighting its inhabitants. He wrote to his son ʿAbdallāh, who was his viceregent for the Jazīrah, ordering him to march with those of his guard *(rawābit)* whom he had with him to the city of Naṣībīn[118] in order to prevent al-Ḍaḥḥāk from cutting the Jazīrah in half. ʿAbdallāh set out for Naṣībīn with all of his guard, about seven or eight thousand men, leaving as his deputy at Ḥarrān an officer with one thousand men or thereabouts. Al-Ḍaḥḥāk, too, marched from Mosul toward ʿAbdallāh at Naṣībīn. ʿAbdallāh fought him but could do nothing against the great number of troops who were with al-Ḍaḥḥāk. These were, according to the accounts which have reached us, one hundred and twenty thousand. He paid monthly stipends of one hundred and twenty dirhams to a cavalryman, one hundred to a footsoldier, and eighty to a mule driver.

Al-Ḍaḥḥāk stayed at Naṣībīn besieging it, and he sent two of his officers, named ʿAbd al-Malik b. Bishr al-Taghlibī and Badr al-Dhakwānī the mawlā of Sulaymān b. Hishām, with four or five thousand men and they came to Raqqah. Marwān's cavalry there, about five hundred horsemen, fought them. As soon as word reached Marwān of their presence at Raqqah, he sent cavalry from his guard. As they neared the city, al-Ḍaḥḥāk's followers began leaving to go back to him. Marwān's cavalry pursued them, and more than thirty of the men in their rearguard were unhorsed. Marwān had them cut in pieces when he came to Raqqah. He went on, intent on battle against al-Ḍaḥḥāk and his forces, until they encountered each other at a place called Ghazz[119] in the territory of Kafartūtha. They

[1940] fought a battle that same day. When it was evening, al-Ḍaḥḥāk and almost six thousand of his most steadfast followers dismounted to fight on foot, though the people of his camp for the most part did not know what had become of him. Marwān's cavalry surrounded them and pressed them hard until they killed them around nightfall. The remainder of al-Ḍaḥḥāk's followers went back to their camp, and neither Marwān nor al-Ḍaḥḥāk's followers knew that he was among the slain until they missed him in the middle of the night. Some of those who had seen him when he dismounted to fight on foot came and told them of it and that he was killed. They wept for him and be-

---

118. One of the most important towns in upper Mesopotamia on the reaches of the Hirmās, a tributary of the Tigris. See LeStrange, *Lands*, 94, 95.

119. The vocalization is conjectural. This place is not listed by Yāqūt.

wailed his death. ʿAbd al-Malik b. Bishr al-Taghlibī, the officer he had sent against Raqqah, went out to Marwān's camp, and entering Marwān's presence informed him that al-Ḍaḥḥāk had been killed. Marwān sent men from his guard with him carrying firebrands and candles to the site of the battle. They turned over the slain until they found al-Ḍaḥḥāk and carried him to Marwān. There were more than twenty cuts on his face. The people of Marwān's camp shouted "God is Great!" Then those in al-Ḍaḥḥāk's camp realized that they had learned of his death. Marwān sent his head that night to the cities of the Jazīrah, where it was paraded about.

Some say that al-Khaybarī and al-Ḍaḥḥāk were only killed in the year 129 (746–47).

According to Hishām who heard it from Abū Mikhnaf, in this year al-Khaybarī the Khārijite was slain.[120]

The Slaying of al-Khaybarī and Shaybān's Succession

According to Aḥmad b. Zuhayr—ʿAbd al-Wahhāb b. Ibrāhīm—Abū Hāshim Mukhallad b. Muḥammad b. Ṣāliḥ: When al-Ḍaḥḥāk was slain, the people in his camp arose at daybreak and gave their oath of allegiance to al-Khaybarī. They remained there that day and went to him the morning of the next day. They lined up before him and he put their ranks in order. Sulaymān b. Hishām was there that day with his mawlās and the people of his house; he had come to al-Ḍaḥḥāk at Naṣībīn with more than three thousand of the people of his house and his mawlās. Sulaymān also married the sister of Shaybān al-Ḥarūrī, the man to whom they gave the oath of allegiance after the slaying of al-Khaybarī. Al-Khaybarī attacked Marwān with about four hundred Khārijite riders, and routed Marwān's men, and him in the midst of them. Marwān fled his encampment, and al-Khaybarī entered it with his followers. They shouted their battle cry, "O Khaybarī, Khaybarī!" They also killed all those whom they overtook, until they came to Marwān's tent. They cut its ropes, and al-Khaybarī sat upon Marwān's own carpet. Marwān's right wing, commanded by his son ʿAbdallāh, had held its ground, and his left wing commanded by Isḥaq b. Muslim al-ʿUqaylī was still firm. When the people of Marwān's camp saw how few were accompa-

[1941]

---

120. See Ibn Khayyāṭ, I, 400ff; Azdī, 71ff; *FHA*, 159ff.

nying al-Khaybarī, some slaves from the camp assaulted him with tentpoles and slew him and all of his companions at Marwān's tent and in the area around it. The news reached Marwān when he had fled five or six miles *(mīl)* from the camp. At this he returned to his camp, ordered his cavalry back from their places and stations, and spent that night in his camp. The people of al-Khaybarī's army went back and elected Shaybān as their ruler and gave him the oath of allegiance. After this, Marwān fought them only with cavalry squadrons *(karādīs)*,[121] and he gave up using battle lines from that day forward. On the day al-Khaybarī was slain Marwān had sent Muḥammad b. Saʿīd, one of his trusted men and secretaries, to al-Khaybarī (with a message). However, word reached Marwān that this man had incited the enemy and encouraged them at that time. He was brought to Marwān as a prisoner, and Marwān cut off one of his hands and a foot and then cut out his tongue.

Yazīd b. ʿUmar b. Hubayrah is Sent to Iraq

In this year Marwān sent Yazīd b. ʿUmar Hubayrah to Iraq to fight the Khārijites who were still there.

[1942]   ʿAbd al-ʿAzīz b. ʿUmar b. ʿAbd al-ʿAzīz led the Pilgrimage at Mecca in this year; that is what Abū Maʿshar (al-Sindī) said, according to Aḥmad b. Thābit—from one who mentioned it—Isḥāq b. ʿIsā—Abū Maʿshar. Al-Wāqidī and others say the same.

Al-Wāqidī reported: Marwān conquered Ḥimṣ and tore down its walls, and took Nuʿaym b. Thābit al-Judhāmī captive and slew him in Shawwāl 128 (June 26–July 24, 746). We have mentioned those who differ with him on this earlier.

The governor of Madīnah, Mecca and Ṭāʾif, according to what is mentioned for this year, was ʿAbd al-ʿAzīz b. ʿUmar b. ʿAbd al-ʿAzīz. In Iraq were the governors of al-Ḍaḥḥāk and ʿAbdallāh b. ʿUmar. In charge of the judiciary of Baṣrah was Thumāmah b. ʿAbdallāh. Naṣr b. Sayyār was (governor) in Khurāsān, which was torn by civil war.

---

121. Marwān is generally credited with having replaced the battle lines (ṣufūf) with more mobile cavalry squadrons (karādīs).

This year Abū Ḥamzah the Khārijite met ʿAbdallāh b. Yaḥyā Ṭālib al-Ḥaqq, who summoned him to his way of religion *(madhhab).*[122]

According to ʿAbbās b. ʿĪsā al-ʿUqaylī—Hārūn b. Mūsā al-Farwī[123]—Mūsā b. Kathīr the mawlā of the Sāʿidīs: The beginning of the affair of Abū Ḥamzah who was al-Mukhtār b. ʿAwf al-Azdī al-Salīmī from Baṣrah is as follows. He would go each year to Mecca calling on people to oppose Marwān b. Muḥammad and the Marwānids. He continued to oppose them until ʿAbdallāh b. Yaḥyā came at the end of 128 (August–September 746) and told him, "O Man, listen to a good word. I see that you summon people to what is just, so come with me. I am a man obeyed among my people." ʿAbdallāh then left Mecca and came to Ḥaḍramawt, where Abū Ḥamzah swore allegiance to him as Caliph and preached opposition to Marwān and to the Marwānid house. Muḥammad b. Ḥasan reported that Abū Ḥamzah passed by Maʿdin Banī Sulaym,[124] where the governor was Kathīr b. ʿAbdallāh. He heard some of Abū Ḥamzah's talk, and ordered that he be given seventy lashes. Abū Ḥamzah went on his way to Mecca. Later when he conquered Madīnah, Kathīr hid himself until matters had run their course.

[1943]

---

122. See Ibn Khayyāṭ, I, 406ff, *sub anno* 129; Aghānī, XX, 97–99; Azdī, 77, 101; *FHA*, 168ff. ʿAbdallāh b. Yaḥyā al-Kindī was known as the "Seeker of Justice" (Ṭālib al-Ḥaqq). A devout qāḍī for the governor of Ḥaḍramawt, he had been contacted by the leadership of Ibāḍī Khārijites in Baṣrah. They sent agents such as Abū Ḥamzah to him in order to initiate an Ibāḍī revolt in Ḥaḍramawt and the Yaman. See *EI²* s.v. Ibaḍiyya.

123. The text is Ghazawī; it should be read Farwī, following the Cairo edition.

124. Maʿdin Banī Sulaym was a populated oasis in the district of Madīnah on the road to Najd. See Yāqūt, *Muʿjam*, IV, 572, and III, 565–66, s.v. Farān.

The
Events of The Year

129

(SEPTEMBER 22, 746–SEPTEMBER 10, 747)

One of the events of this year was the death of Shaybān b. ʿAbd al-
ʿAzīz al-Yashkurī, known as Abū al-Dalfāʾ.[125]

The Death of Shaybān b. ʿAbd al-ʿAzīz the Khārijite

When al-Ḍaḥḥāk b. Qays al-Shaybānī the leader of the Khārijites
was slain, and al-Khaybarī after him, those Khārijites who were opposing Marwān b. Muḥammad and making war on him chose Shaybān as their leader and gave him the oath of allegiance. Marwān then
fought them.

Hishām b. Muḥammad and al-Haytham b. ʿAdī reported: When al-
Khaybarī was slain, Sulaymān b. Hishām who was in their camp
told the Khārijites, "What you are doing is not a good idea. If you accept my advice, fine. If you won't, then I'm leaving you." They
asked, "What should we do?" He told them, "If one of you wins a
victory, he then tries to get himself killed, and succeeds. I think we
should leave here in a defensive posture so that we may set up camp
at Mosul and entrench ourselves." They did this, and Marwān pursued them. The Khārijites were on the east bank of the Tigris and

---

125. See Ibn Khayyāṭ, I, 409; *FHA*, 165–66; Yaʿqūbī, *Taʾrīkh*, II, 405.

Marwān was directly opposite them. They then fought each other
for nine months. ʿUmar b. Hubayrah was at Qarqīsiyyah with a large   [1944]
body of troops, men of Syria and of the Jazīrah. Marwān now ordered
him to go to Kūfah, which was then governed by al-Muthannā b.
ʿImrān, a client (ʿāʾidh) of Quraysh and a Khārijite.

According to Aḥmad b. Zuhayr—ʿAbd al-Wahhāb b. Ibrāhīm
—Abū Hāshim Mukhallad b. Muḥammad: Marwān b. Muḥammad
used to fight the Khārijites with the battle line (ṣaff); but when al-
Khaybarī was killed and Shaybān received the oath of allegiance,
Marwān fought them with cavalry squadrons, and discontinued the
battle line from that time forward. The Khārijites also began to form
squadrons like those of Marwān with which to protect themselves
against his squadrons and to fight them. Many of those who followed them for pay now separated from them and deserted,[126] so
there now remained around forty thousand. Sulaymān b. Hishām
advised them to retreat to the city of Mosul and make it a place in
which they could find refuge and ample supplies. They accepted his
advice, and set off by night. Marwān woke the next day and set off
after them. They would hardly leave a place before Marwān would
alight there. They went on to the city of Mosul and camped on the
banks of the Tigris, entrenched their position, and fastened pontoon
bridges between their camp and the city, which was their source of
provisions and facilities. Marwān dug his trench opposite them, and
remained six months sallying forth against them morning and evening.

A son of Sulaymān b. Hishām's brother was brought to Marwān.
He was called Umayyah b. Muʿāwiyah b. Hishām, and had been
with his uncle in the camp of Shaybān at Mosul. He went out to
fight one of Marwān's horsemen in single combat, and the man captured him and brought him in. He told Marwān, "I implore you, for
God and kinship's sake, uncle!" But Marwān replied, "There is no
kinship between me and you this day." He gave the order and, while

---

126. The small dedicated core of the Khārijites were mostly from the Bakr and
Rabīʿah tribes of the Jazīrah. They had been joined by some former followers of Sulaymān b. Hishām and ʿAbdallāh b. ʿUmar. These followers were drawn from the
Yaman. The Khārijites had thus apparently become a large scale movement. They
were the proponents of the equality of all Muslims regardless of genealogy. Marwān's
support came from the Qays of the Jazīrah.

Umayyah's uncle Sulaymān and his brothers looked on, first his hands and then his head were cut off.

[1945]   Marwān wrote to Yazīd b. ʿUmar b. Hubayrah commanding him to march from Qarqīsiyyah with all his troops against ʿUbaydah b. Sawwār, al-Daḥḥāk's deputy in Iraq. He encountered ʿUbaydah's cavalry at ʿAyn Tamr, engaged them, and routed them. Commanding them at that time were al-Muthannā b. ʿImrān, of the clients of Quraysh, and al-Ḥasan b. Yazīd. They then regrouped against him at Nukhaylah[127] by Kūfah, and he put them to flight. Then they gathered at the Ṣarāt Canal, and this time ʿUbaydah was with them. Ibn Hubayrah fought them, and ʿUbaydah was slain. His followers fled, and Ibn Hubayrah plundered their camp. Now they had no one remaining in Iraq, and Ibn Hubayrah took control of the province. Marwān wrote to him from the trenches at Mosul, commanding him to send ʿĀmir b. Ḍubārah al-Murrī to reinforce him, and he sent him with about six or eight thousand men. Word of this reached Shaybān and the Khārijites so they sent two officers at the head of four thousand men against Ibn Ḍubārah. These men were named Ibn Ghawth and al-Jawn. They encountered Ibn Ḍubārah at Sinn[128] outside Mosul, and engaged him in fierce combat, but Ibn Ḍubārah put them to flight. When the defeated Khārijites came back to them, Sulaymān b. Hishām advised them to move from Mosul, telling them that they would have no place to stand if Ibn Ḍubārah came upon them from the rear while Marwān mounted a frontal attack. At this, they moved on, and took the road to Ahwāz and Fārs by way of Ḥulwān.[129] Marwān sent three of his officers with about thirty thousand of his guard (rawābiṭ) to Ibn Ḍubārah. The officers were Muṣʿab b. al-Ṣaḥṣaḥ al-Asadī, Shaqīq, and ʿUṭayf al-Sulamī).[130] Shaqīq was the one of whom the Khārijites said:

> Both your sisters know, O Shaqīq,
>   that you do not recover from your drunkenness.

---

127. The scene of a serious battle against the Khārijites in the time of Muʿāwiyah I. See Yāqūt, *Muʿjam*, IV, 771.

128. For Sinn, see LeStrange, *Lands*, 91.

129. Ḥulwān was on the border between Jibāl and Iraq. It was situated along the great road leading to Khurāsān. See LeStrange, *Lands*, 191.

130. The *nisbah* of al-Sulaymānī is furnished by the Cairo edition.

Marwān wrote to Ibn Dubārah to pursue the Khārijites and not to stop until he had annihilated them. Therefore he did not cease pursuing them until they reached and then left Fārs. During all this time he picked off any of their stragglers whom he encountered. [1946] Then they scattered. Shaybān led one group to Bahrayn and was slain there, and Sulaymān b. Hishām with his mawlās and family embarked on ships for Sind. Marwān returned to his residence in Harrān and stayed there until he set out for the Zāb.

According to Hishām b. Muhammad, Abū Mikhnaf stated: Marwān ordered Yazīd b. Hubayrah, who was at Qarqīsiyyah with many troops from the armies of Syria and the Jazīrah, to march against Kūfah. At that time Kūfah was governed by a Khārijite called al-Muthannā b. 'Imrān al-'Ā'idhī, one of the 'A'idhat Quraysh. Ibn Hubayrah marched along the Euphrates until he came to 'Ayn Tamr; then he moved on and met al-Muthannā at Rawhā'. He came to Kūfah in Ramadān 129 (May 17–June 14, 747), routed the Khārijites and entered the city. Ibn Hubayrah then went to the Sarāt Canal, while Shaybān sent 'Ubaydah b. Sawwār at the head of many cavalry. He camped on the east bank of the Sarāt, while Ibn Hubayrah was on the west side. They joined battle, and 'Ubaydah was slain along with a number of his followers. Mansūr b. Jumhūr was with them at the events on the Sarāt, and he went on from there to gain control of the two Māhs[131] and all the mountain region. Ibn Hubayrah marched now on Wāsit, seized Ibn 'Umar and confined him. He sent Nubātah b. Hanzalah against Sulaymān b. Habīb who was ruling the districts of Ahwāz. Sulaymān sent Dāwud b. Hātim with a force to fight Nubātah, and they encountered each other at Muriyān[132] on the banks of the Kārūn. These people were put to flight, and Dāwud b. Hātim was slain. Concerning this, Khalaf b. Khalīfah said:

---

131. Dīnawar was called Māh al-Kūfah while Nihāwand was known as Māh al-Basrah, because their tax revenues went to the two garrison towns of Iraq in early Islamic times. See LeStrange, *Lands*, 189, 196–97.

132. The vocalization of Muriyān is uncertain. Perhaps this is a variant of, or an error for, Mūriyān, a village in Khūzistān. See Yāqūt, *Mu'jam*, IV, 679. For the Dujayl or the Kārūn which flows in the Ahwāz district of Khūzistān, see LeStrange, *Lands*, 232–36; 245–47.

Would that I'd been a ransom and protection to Dāwud,
when the army surrendered the son of Ḥātim!

He was a Muhallabī, shining of face,
never regretting the favors he'd done.

I asked "Who will let me know the thing as it was
truly [for the ignorant is not like the knowing]."[133]

[1947]

They said, "We beheld him on an outcrop,
attacking like a fierce lion;

Then he doubled over, falling in blood
that flowed over his smooth body,

And the Copts[134] came up [to stand] over his head,
quarrelling over his sword and his ring."

Sulaymān went on until he caught up with Ibn Muʿāwiyah al-Jaʿfarī[135] in Fārs, while Ibn Hubayrah stayed where he was for a month; then he sent ʿĀmir b. Dubārah with Syrian troops to Mosul. ʿĀmir marched until he reached Sinn, where al-Jawn b. Kilāb al-Khārijī encountered him. He put ʿĀmir b. Dubārah to flight, driving him into Sinn, where he fortified himself. Marwān began to send Ibn Dubārah reinforcements. They took the overland route until they came to the Tigris, and then crossed over to him. This continued until their number was great. At the same time, Manṣūr b. Jumhūr was supplying Shaybān with money from the mountain districts. When the troops who followed Ibn Dubārah became numerous, he struck out against al-Jawn b. Kilāb, and al-Jawn was slain. Ibn Dubārah

---

133. This lacuna in the text is filled by the Cairo edition.

134. The text is *al-qibṭ*. It seems very unlikely that Egyptian Christians were in Ibn Hubayrah's army. Probably this should be read *al-qabṭ*, "the group," but the text has been followed in translation.

135. That is ʿAbdallāh b. Muʿāwiyah b. ʿAbdallāh b. Jaʿfar, the great-grandson of ʿAlī b. Abī Ṭālib's brother. ʿAbdallāh revolted in Kūfah in 127. See Ṭabarī, II/3, 1879–87; Ibn Khayyāṭ, I, 394–95; Azdī, 66; Masʿūdī, *Murūj*, VI, 44ff. See also Sharon, *ʿAlīyat*, 194–201; *EI²* s.v. ʿAbd Allāh b. Muʿāwiya. Regarding the incidents recorded here see Ibn Khayyāṭ, II, 409; *FHA*, 162–63; Masʿūdī, 67ff, 169; Azdī, 107 *sub anno* 129; *Akhbār al-Dawlah*, 251. Check also the index to the Aghānī for numerous references to him.

then continued on to Mosul. When news of al-Jawn's death and Ibn Dubārah's approach came to Shaybān, he did not care to stay between the two (Umayyad) armies, so he withdrew with his own troops and the Yamanī cavalry from Syria. Ibn Dubārah proceeded with his men to join Marwān at Mosul. Marwān supplied him with many of his own troops, and commanded him to go against Shaybān. If Shaybān maintained his position, he should do likewise; if he marched, he should march too. He should not initiate a struggle, but if Shaybān attacked him he should fight back. If Shaybān refrained, he should refrain as well, and if Shaybān withdrew, he should follow him. So it was, until Shaybān moved through the mountains and came to Bayḍāʾ of Iṣṭakhr,[136] where ʿAbdallāh b. Muʿāwiyah was with a great body of troops. Matters between him and Ibn Muʿāwiyah had not been settled, so he continued until Jīraft in Kirmān,[137] where he halted. Ibn Dubārah advanced until he was opposite Ibn Muʿāwiyah and halted for several days. Then he set about attacking him, and Ibn Muʿāwiyah ran away, escaping to Harāt. Ibn Dubārah and his troops went on and encountered Shaybān at Jīraft in Kirmān. They fought a violent battle, the Khārijites were put to flight, and their camp was put to auction. Shaybān went on to Sijistān, where he perished in the year 130 (747–748).   [1948]

Abū ʿUbaydah reported: When al-Khaybarī was slain, Shaybān b. ʿAbd al-ʿAzīz al-Yashkurī took command of the Khārijites and made war on Marwān. Their war went on for a long time, but meanwhile at Wāsiṭ Ibn Hubayrah had killed ʿUbaydah b. Sawwār and driven out the Khārijites. He had with him the chief officers of the armies of Syria and the Jazīrah, and he sent ʿĀmir b. Dubārah with four thousand men to reinforce Marwān. He took the route of Madāʾin,[138] and Shaybān learned of his progress. Fearing that Marwān would join forces with Ibn Dubārah's men, he sent al-Jawn b. Kilāb al-Shaybānī to engage Ibn Dubārah. They encountered each other at Sinn, and al-Jawn detained ʿĀmir for several days.

---

136. Bayḍāʾ was the "White City" of Fārs where Arab armies had camped when invading the country. See Yāqūt, *Muʿjam*, I, 791–94. Iṣṭakhr was Persepolis.

137. For Jīraft, see LeStrange, *Lands*, 314. The Shaybān mentioned here may actually be Shaybān b. Salamah. See n. 158.

138. Madāʾin, meaning, "the cities," had a legendary history of settlement by conquerors. The Sasanian capital of Ctesiphon had been situated in this area. See Le-Strange, *Lands*, 33–35.

According to Abū 'Ubaydah—Abū Sa'īd: We covered them, by God, and forced them to fight us. They were already afraid of us and wanted to run away, but we left them no way out. Then 'Āmir told them, "You're dead men; there's no avoiding that, so die with honor." They hit us with a charge nothing would have stood against, and killed our leader, al-Jawn b. Kilāb. We retreated until we joined up with Shaybān, but Ibn Dubārah was following right behind us, until he halted a short way from our camp. We were fighting on two sides: Ibn Dubārah would come down on us from behind, on the Iraq side, and Marwān was in front in the direction of Syria. We were cut off from provisions and supplies, and the prices went high. A round of bread went for a silver piece; then the bread was gone, and nothing could be bought dear or cheap. Ḥabīb b. Khudrah[139] told Shay-

[1949] bān, "Commander of the Faithful, you're in a tight place for subsistence. If only you would move to some other place!" He did, and went to Shahrazūr in the territory of Mosul, but his followers blamed him for it, and there were arguments about it."

One source says that when Shaybān took command of the Khārijites, (he went back with his followers to Mosul),[140] and Marwān followed him, halting when he halted. (Marwān fought him for a month, then)[141] Shaybān fled until he came to Fārs. Marwān sent 'Āmir b. Dubārah after him (and Shaybān crossed over)[142] to the island of Ibn Kāwan (or Kishm)[143] and kept on going until he came to 'Umān, where Julandā b. Mas'ūd b. Jayfar b. Julandā al-Azdī killed him.[144]

In the year 129 (746–747), Ibrāhīm b. Muḥammad b. 'Alī b. 'Abdallāh b. 'Abbās commanded Abū Muslim, who had set forth from Khurāsān to visit him and had reached as far as Qūmis, to go

---

139. The text is Ibn Jadarah. The Cairo edition has Ibn Khudrah (vocalization uncertain), mentioned above as Ḥabīb b. Khudrah, mawlā of the Banū Hilāl, a Khārijite poet.

140. The text is marked by three lacunae. The phrases are supplied from the Cairo edition.

141. See n. 140.

142. See n. 140.

143. This island is known under many names. See LeStrange, *Lands*, 261.

144. The Banū Julandā were the hereditary Azdī princes of 'Umān. Ironically, Ibn Julandā was also a Khārijite imam. He later fought the 'Abbāsids as an Ibāḍī. See *EI*[2] s.v. Ibāḍiyya; *Djulandā*.

back to the ʿAbbāsid Shīʿah in Khurāsān and order them to openly proclaim the revolution and put on the black color.[145]

Abū Muslim Preaches the ʿAbbāsid Revolution in Khurāsān

ʿAlī b. Muḥammad reported the following from his shaykhs: Abū Muslim kept making visits to Khurāsān, until finally the tribal feuds broke out there. Then when the local authority began to unravel, Sulaymān b. Kathīr wrote to Abū Salamah al-Khallāl requesting him to write to Ibrāhīm and ask him to send a man of the people of his House. Abū Salamah thus wrote to Ibrāhīm, and he sent Abū Muslim.[146] In the year 129 (746–747), Ibrāhīm wrote to Abū Muslim asking him to come to him so that he might obtain a report from him. Abū Muslim left halfway through Jumādā II (early March 747) with seventy of the ʿAbbāsid agents (nuqabāʾ).[147] When they had come as far as Dandānqān in Khurāsān,[148] Kāmil—or Abū Kāmil—stopped him and asked where they were going. "On pilgrimage," they said. Then Abū Muslim took him aside and summoned him to their cause. He responded favorably and let them alone. Abū Muslim continued on to Abīward and stayed there some days, and then proceeded to Nasā,[149] where ʿĀṣim b. Qays al-Sulamī was the governor for Naṣr b. Sayyār al-Laythī. As he drew near, he sent al-Faḍl b. Sulaymān al-Ṭūsī with a message to Asīd b. ʿAbdallāh al-Khuzāʿī[150] to inform him that he was coming.

[1950]

---

145. See n. 72 above.

146. See Sharon, ʿAlīyat, 127–38. The *Akhbār al-Dawlah*, 271ff, is particularly rich in its treatment of Abū Muslim's relations with Sulaymān b. Kathīr. See also Ṭabarī, II/3, 1960ff. [J.L.]

147. See *Akhbār al-Dawlah*, 290ff; *FHA*, 176ff. The agents designated as *naqībs* were divided into two groups, a council of twelve which retained primary control, chosen exclusively from agents in Marw, the major revolutionary station in Khurāsān; the individuals were part of a larger group of seventy that included operatives from various regional centers. For details see Sharon, ʿAlīyat, 105–17. [J.L.]

148. Dandānqān was a town southwest of Marw on the road to Sarakhs. See LeStrange, *Lands*, 400.

149. Abīward or Bīward is on the edge of the Marw desert west of Dandānqān off the main road to Sarakhs. Nasā or Nisā is in a fertile valley west of Abīward. See LeStrange, *Lands*, 394. The ʿAbbāsids had *naqībs* in these towns. See *Akhbār al-Dawlah*, 218–19. The text gives a full listing of the ʿAbbāsid agents.

150. Al-Ṭūsī was a *naqīb* from Abīward and Asīd al-Khuzāʿī was the agent from Nasā. See *Akhbār al-Dawlah*, 218–19.

Al-Faḍl went on and stopped at a village of Nasā where he met a man from the Shīʿah who knew him. He asked for Asīd, but the man rebuffed him. Then al-Faḍl said, "O ʿAbdallāh, what is wrong in my asking where is the man's house?" The man replied, "There has been evil in this village. Two men were brought before the governor and slandered. It was said that they were propagandists. They were taken, and al-Aḥjam b. ʿAbdallāh al-Khuzāʿī, Ghaylān b. Faḍālah, Ghālib b. Saʿīd and al-Muhājir b. ʿUthmān were taken too."[151] At this, al-Faḍl went back to Abū Muslim and informed him. He left the road and took another through the villages lower down, and sent Ṭarkhān al-Jammāl to Asīd saying, "Ask him to come to me with as many of the (ʿAbbāsid) Shīʿah as he can, and beware of speaking to anyone you do not know." Ṭarkhān went to Asīd and invited him, and he told him where Abū Muslim was staying. At this, Asīd came to him, and Abū Muslim asked him what had happened. He replied, "Yes, it is true; al-Azhar b. Shuʿayb and ʿAbd al-Malik b. Saʿd came with letters from the Imām for you. They left the letters with me and started back, and they were taken;[152] I do not know who betrayed them. The governor sent them to ʿĀṣim b. Qays, and he had al-Muhājir b. ʿUthmān and other leading men of the Shīʿah beaten." "Where are the letters?" Abū Muslim asked. "At my house," Asīd said. "Bring them to me," said Abū Muslim, (so he brought him the letters and he read them).[153]

Then he went on to Qūmis,[154] which was governed by Bayhas b. Budayl al-ʿIjlī, and Bayhas came to them and said, "Where are you going?" "On pilgrimage," they said. "Do you have a good horse you

[1951]

---

151. Al-Aḥjam and Ghaylān b. Faḍālah were *naqībs*. Al-Muhājir was a lesser functionary, belonging to a group known as the Propagandists of the Propagandists (*duʿāt al-duʿāt*). They seem to have been substitutes for a larger group of seventy known as the *duʿāt*. The *duʿāt* were undoubtedly subordinate to the *naqībs*. Ghālib b. Saʿīd (or Saʿd) was an ʿAbbāsid agent whose function cannot be determined. See *Akhbār al-Dawlah*, 218–19, 222, 291. The account would seem to indicate that the authorities were extremely anxious at this time. This would explain the circuitous routes followed by Abū Muslim and his associates. (J.L.)

152. Al-Azhar b. Shuʿayb was a native of Marw who traveled with Bukayr b. Māhān in the eastern provinces soliciting support and monies for the revolutionary movement. See *Akhbār al-Dawlah*, 223–24. It would appear from this text that he then served as a carrier from the Imām to the revolutionary centers in Khurāsān. (J.L.)

153. These words are missing in the text and are supplied by the Cairo edition.

154. That is to say the small province (or the capital of the province) adjacent to Khurāsān. See LeStrange, *Lands*, 364ff.

would sell?" he asked. "As for selling, no," said Abū Muslim, "but take any of our animals you wish." "Show them to me," he said. They showed them, and he admired a light bay horse. Abū Muslim then said, "It is yours." To this he replied, "No, I'll not accept it without a price." "You be the judge of its worth," Abū Muslim said. "Seven hundred [dirhams]," he said. "It is yours," said Abū Muslim. While Abū Muslim was in Qūmis a letter came from the Imām, and another for Sulaymān b. Kathīr. The one to Abū Muslim said, "I have sent you a flag of victory. Return from wherever my letter finds you, and send me Qaḥṭabah with whatever you have to deliver to me during the Pilgrimage Season." At this, Abū Muslim returned to Khurāsān, and sent Qaḥṭabah to the Imām. When they were in Nasā, the leader of an armed party confronted them in a village, and said, "Who are you?" "We intended to make the Pilgrimage," they said, "and we heard something about the road which frightened us." He brought them to ʿĀṣim b. Qays al-Sulamī who questioned them. They gave him the same answer, and he said, ("Be off." And he ordered)[155] al-Mufaḍḍal b. Sharqī al-Sulamī, who was in charge of security, to expel them from the area. Then Abū Muslim took this man aside and revealed their business to him. He responded favorably and said, "Go at your ease, and do not hurry." He remained with them until they left.

Abū Muslim came to Marw on the first day of Ramaḍān (May 16, 747), and handed the Imām's letter to Sulaymān b. Kathīr. The letter stated, "Proclaim your summons without delay; the time has come." They showed high esteem to Abū Muslim, and said, "He's a man of the People of the House [ahl al-bayt]."[156] They called on people to obey the Banū ʿAbbās, and sent to their partisans whether near or far, commanding them to reveal what was happening, and calling on them for support. Abū Muslim settled in one of the vil-

[1952]

---

155. These words are missing in the text and are supplied by the Cairo edition.

156. *Ahl al-bayt* in pre-Islamic times meant the immediate family of a tribal leader. The term appears twice in the Qur'ān, once in a context which allows one to suppose that the family of the Prophet is indicated (33,33). The Shīʿah of ʿAlī have usually interpreted this through a tradition, the *ḥadīth al-kisāʾ*, which limits it to the family of ʿAlī. The Shīʿah of the ʿAbbāsids used another, the *ḥadīth al-thaqalayn,* whereby "people of the house" is extended to include the family of ʿAbbās, of ʿAlī, and of his two brothers ʿAqil and Jaʿfar, as well as their mawlās. In still another *ḥadīth,* Salmān al-Fārisī, a mawlā of the Prophet, is declared to be of the *ahl al-bayt.* See *EI*[2] s.v. Ahl al-bayt.

lages of the (Arab tribe of) Khuzāʿah called Safīdhanj.[157] At this
time Shaybān[158] and al-Kirmāni were fighting Naṣr b. Sayyār together, so Abū Muslim circulated his summons to people, and his
affair became manifest. The people said, "A man has come from the
Banū Hāshim." They came to him from all directions. On the day of
ʿId al-Fiṭr (ca. June 15, 747), he appeared at the village of Khālid b.
Ibrāhīm.[159] Qāsim b. Mujāshiʿ al-Maraʾī led the people in prayer.
Then Abū Muslim moved and settled at the village of Alīn, also
called Allīn,[160] belonging to the Khuzāʿah. In one day, the people of
sixty villages joined him, and he stayed there forty-two days. Abū
Muslim's first victory[161] was at the hands of Mūsā b. Kaʿb al-
Tamīmī at Abīward while he was occupied with the killing of ʿĀṣim
b. Qays. Then victory came at Marwarrūdh.[162]

[1953]

According to Abū al-Khaṭṭāb : Abū Muslim returned to the terri-
tory of Marw from Qūmis, having first sent Qaḥṭabah b. Shabīb (al-
Ṭāʾī) with the money and other things he had with him for the Imām
Ibrāhīm b. Muḥammad.[163] He arrived on Tuesday, the ninth of
Shaʿbān 129 (April 27, 747), and settled in a village called Fanīn with
Abū al-Ḥakam ʿĪsā b. Aʿyan the naqīb.[164] This was the village of
Abū Dāwud the naqīb. From there he sent Abū Dāwud, accompa-
nied by ʿAmr b. Aʿyan to Ṭukhāristān and the areas this side of

---

157. Safīdhanj, following the text. The reading is problematic. Note the variants in
the apparatus. The Khuzāʿah's origins were disputed, but they were frequently reckoned an offshoot of the Azd. See EI² s.v. Khuzāʿa.

158. Not to be confused with Shaybān b. ʿAbd al-ʿAzīz al-Yashkurī who is mentioned above, this is Shaybān b. Salamah al-Ḥarūrī. See Wellhausen, Arab Kingdom,
395, 490, 498, 529, 537.

159. This is Abū Dāwud Khālid b. Ibrāhīm al-Shaybānī al-Bakrī, one of the ʿAbbāsid
naqībs; see Akhbār al-Dawlah, 216. The village is later identified as Fanīn. See n. 164
below.

160. Yāqūt, Muʿjam, IV, 375 lists Allīn as a village in Marw. There is no entry for
Ālīn or Bālīn. Note Ṭabarī, II/3, 1969, which gives a reading of Ālīn for Abū Muslim's
headquarters and 1965, which gives Bālīn. LeStrange, Lands, 399 refers to a Bālīn
Gate in Marw.

161. Details of Abū Muslim's initial campaign are found in the Akhbār al-Dawlah,
299ff.

162. Not to be confused with Marw, Marwarrūdh was situated about 160 miles
from the former. See LeStrange, Lands, 404.

163. The revolutionaries transferred large sums of money and valuables to the
Imām during their periodic visits with him.

164. A report that Abū Muslim stayed at the house of ʿĪsā b. Aʿyan occurs in the entry on Fanīn in Yāqūt. He indicates that Fanīn was one of the villages of Marw. See
Muʿjam, III, 921.

Balkh, to proclaim publicly the call (to revolution) during the month of Ramaḍān 129 (May 16–June 14, 747). He also sent al-Naḍr b. Ṣubayḥ al-Tamīmī with Sharīk b. Ghaḍī al-Tamīmī[165] to Marwarrūdh to proclaim the propaganda during Ramaḍān, and he sent Abū ʿĀṣim ʿAbd al-Raḥmān b. Sulaym[166] to Ṭālaqān. He sent Abū al-Jahm b. ʿAṭiyyah to ʿAlāʾ b. Ḥurayth[167] in Khwārizm to proclaim the call publicly on the twenty-fourth of Ramaḍān (June 8, 747). If their enemy should move against them before the appointed time, exposing them to injury and suffering, he permitted them to defend themselves and to bare their swords, unsheathing them in struggle against the enemies of God. Those whom the enemy distracted from rising at the appointed time would suffer no harm if they did it at a later time.

Then Abū Muslim moved from the house of Abū al-Ḥakam ʿĪsā b. Aʿyan and stayed with Sulaymān b. Kathīr al-Khuzāʿī in his village, called Safīdhanj in the quarter *(rabʿ)* of Kharqān, on the second night of Ramaḍān (May 17, 747). On Wednesday night, the twenty-fifth of   [1954] Ramaḍān (June 9, 747), he unfurled the banner, sent to him by the Imām and called "The Shadow," on a lance fourteen cubits high, and he fastened the flag, sent by the Imām and called "The Clouds," on a lance thirteen cubits high, reciting the verse, "Permission is given to those who fight because they have been wronged; surely God is able to assist them."[168] Then he and Sulaymān b. Kathīr and Sulaymān's brothers and mawlās and those among the people of Safīdhanj who responded put on black garments. These included Ghaylān b. ʿAbdallāh al-Khuzāʿī, who was Sulaymān's brother-in-law through his sister Umm ʿAmr bt. Kathīr, and Ḥumayd b. Razīn and his brother ʿUthmān b. Razīn.[169] All the Shīʿah from the dis-

---

165. These two were listed as *naqībs*. See *Akhbār al-Dawlah*, 217–18.

166. Perhaps the Abū ʿĀṣim who is listed among the *duʿāt al-duʿāt* in the revolutionary organization. See *Akhbār al-Dawlah*, 223. The *Akhbār*, 221 also lists an ʿAbd al-Raḥmān b. Sulaymān who was a *dāʿī*, hence a member of a more prestigious network of agents. The *duʿāt al-duʿāt* were most likely the substitutes for the *duʿāt* just as the *nuẓarāʾ al-nuqabāʾ* substituted for the *naqībs*. (J.L.)

167. He is listed among the *naqībs*. See *Akhbār al-Dawlah*, 215.

168. Qur. 22:39.

169. Like his brother-in-law, Sulaymān b. Kathīr, Ghaylān al-Khuzāʿī is listed among the *naqībs*. The *Akhbār al-Dawlah* lists an ʿUmayr b. Razīn, the brother of Ḥumayd b. Razīn, the mawlā of the Khuzāʿah. This ʿUmayr was one of the *duʿāt al-duʿāt*. See *Akhbār al-Dawlah*, 218, 222.

trict of Kharqān lit fires that night, which was the prearranged sig-
nal, and they began to gather to Abū Muslim the next morning. The
interpretation of the two names "The Shadow" and "The Clouds"
was: as the clouds cover the earth, so would the 'Abbāsid preaching,
and as the earth is never without a shadow, so it would never be
without an 'Abbāsid caliph to the end of time.

The propagandists *(du'āt)* of Marw came to Abū Muslim with all
those who had answered their call. The first to come were the early
[1955] settlers[170] who were with Abū al-Waddāh al-Hurmuzfarrī 'Isā b.
Shubayl, consisting of nine hundred men and four horsemen.[171]
Among the people of Hurmuzfarrah were Sulaymān b. Hassān with
his brother Yazdān b. Hassān, al-Haytham b. Yazīd b. Kaysān, Bu-
way' the mawlā of Nasr b. Mu'āwiyah, Abū al-Khālid al-Hasan,
Jardā, and Muhammad b. 'Alwān. Then came the early settlers who
were with Abū al-Qāsim Muhriz b. Ibrāhīm al-Jūbānī, with thirteen
hundred men on foot and sixteen horsemen. Also with them were
the propagandists Abū al-'Abbās al-Marwazī, Khidhām b. 'Ammār
and Hamzah b. Rutaym.[172] The early settlers (of the first group) began to shout "God is great!" and those with Muhriz b. Ibrāhīm
would answer from their side, "God is Great!" They kept this up until they entered Abū Muslim's camp at Safīdhanj. This was on Saturday (June 12, 747), two days after Abū Muslim's public proclamation. Abū Muslim gave orders that the fort of Safīdhanj be repaired,
fortified, and set in order. When the 'Id came in Safīdhanj, Abū Muslim told Sulaymān b. Kathīr to lead him and the ('Abbāsid) Shī'ah in
prayer. He set up a minbar for him in the camp, and told him to begin the prayer before the *khutbah* address without the call to prayer
or the *iqamah.*[173] The Umayyads used to begin with the *khutbah*

---

170. The text is *ahl al-Suqādim*; see Ibn al-Athīr, V, 273: *ahl al-taqādum.* Wellhausen, *Arab Kingdom,* 522–23 reads Suqādim, as a place name, though no such
place is known. Shaban, *'Abbāsid Revolution,* 158, reads *taqādum,* to mean "the old
[Arab] settlers in Marw."

171. The early supporters of the 'Abbāsids were not part of the active fighting force
operating in Khurāsān, hence their small number of horsemen. The Arab fighters had
aligned with al-Kirmānī or Nasr b. Sayyār. The later addition of the Arab tribal forces
to the 'Abbāsid camp enabled Abū Muslim to challenge the professional armies of the
Umayyads. (J.L.)

172. The text is Zunaym; read Rutaym, as in the *Akhbār al-Dawlah,* 222, where he
is listed as one of the *du'āt al-du'āt.*

173. The *iqāmah* is the ritual proclamation that the prayer has begun.

and the call to prayer, and then they had the ritual prayer; the *iqā-mah* was added on Friday. On feastdays and Fridays they used to deliver the *khuṭbah* seated in the minbars. But Abū Muslim told Sulaymān b. Kathīr to call "God is Great!" six consecutive times with the first prostration, then to recite (the Qur'ān portions), and afterward to bow down on the seventh "God is Great!" In the second prostration, he was to call it out five consecutive times, then recite, and bow down on the sixth call. He was to begin the *khuṭbah* with "God is Great!" and close it with a recitation from the Qur'ān. The Banū Umayyah used to employ four calls of "God is Great!" in the first prostration on a feast day, and three in the second.

[1956]

When Sulaymān b. Kathīr completed the prayer and the *khuṭbah*, Abū Muslim and the Shīʿah went off to a feast spread for them by Abū Muslim. They feasted rejoicing in anticipation of future success *(mustabshirīn)*.

While Abū Muslim was entrenching himself, he would write to Naṣr b. Sayyār, addressing him as "the Amīr Naṣr." When he had grown powerful by means of the (ʿAbbasid) Shīʿah who gathered in his camp, he disclosed himself and wrote to Naṣr, "As for what follows, truly God, blessed be His names and exalted be His mention, reproaches certain folk in the Qur'ān saying, 'They swore the most binding oaths by God that if a warner came to them they would be more guided than any community, but when a warner came it only increased them in aversion, waxing arrogant in the land and plotting evil; but evil plots encompass only those who make them. Do they expect anything but the way of the ancients? You will find no changing in God's way, nor any evading of the way of God.'"[174]

Naṣr was much astonished at the letter, and that Abū Muslim had shown himself. He closed one eye (and pondered long)[175] and said, "This letter has one answer." When Abū Muslim was settled in his camp at Mākhuwān,[176] he ordered Muḥriz b. Ibrāhīm[177] to dig a defensive trench at Jīranj and gather together his followers with those of the Shīʿah who were so inclined and cut off the communications of Naṣr b. Sayyār with Marwarrūdh, Balkh and the districts of

---

174. Qur. 35:42–43.
175. This phrase is missing in text and is supplied by the Cairo edition.
176. For Mākhuwān, see Yāqūt, *Muʿjam*, IV, 380. Jīranj was a small town *(bulay-dah)* in the vicinity of Marw. See Yāqūt, II, 175.
177. Muḥriz b. Ibrāhīm was a *naqīb*. See *Akhbār al-Dawlah*, 217.

Ṭukhāristān. Muḥriz b. Ibrāhīm did that, and about a thousand men gathered at his camp which was surrounded by a moat. Abū Muslim also ordered Abū Ṣāliḥ Kāmil b. Muẓaffar[178] to send a man to Muḥriz b. Ibrāhīm's camp to review the troops there and enter them in a register with their names, their fathers' names and their villages.[179] He thus sent Abū Ṣāliḥ Ḥumayd al-Azraq to do that. Ḥumayd, who was a scribe, counted 804 able-bodied men in Muḥriz's camp. Among the well-known officers there were Ziyād b. Sayyār al-Azdī in the quarter of Kharqān, from the village called Asbiwādiq; Khidhām b. ʿAmmar al-Kindī of the quarter of the early settlers,[180] from a village called al-Awāyiq; Ḥanīfah b. Qays of the early settlers' quarter, from the village called al-Shanj; ʿAbdawayh al-Jardāmadh b. ʿAbd al-Karīm, of the people of Harāt, who used to bring sheep to Marw; Ḥamzah b. Rutaym[181] al-Bāhilī of the Kharqān quarter, from the village called Mīlādhjird;[182] Abū Hāshim Khalīfah b. Mihrān of the quarter of the early settlers, from the village of Jūbān;[183] Abū Khadījah Jīlān b. al-Sughdī, and Abū Nuʿaym Mūsā b. Ṣubayḥ.[184]

Muḥriz b. Ibrāhīm remained entrenched in his camp until Abū Muslim entered the walls of Marw, vacated the camp at Mākhuwān and camped at Mārsarjas on the way to Naysābūr. Muḥriz b. Ibrāhīm then reinforced Abū Muslim with his troops.

One of the events that occurred while Abū Muslim was at Safīdhanj was that Naṣr b. Sayyār sent a mawlā of his called Yazīd with a large force of cavalry to fight Abū Muslim eighteen days after his public proclamation, and Abū Muslim sent Mālik b. Haytham al-Khuzāʿī together with Muṣʿab b. Qays[185] out against him. They met at the village called Alīn, and Mālik called on them to follow

---

178. Abū Ṣāliḥ was one of the highest ranking operatives in the revolutionary apparatus. See *Akhbār al-Dawlah*, 215.

179. That is, the military roll was based on geographical rather than tribal affiliation, an ʿAbbāsid principle. See n. 217 below.

180. The text is *rabʿ al-Suqādim*; it should be read rabʿ *al-taqādum*, following Ibn Athīr. References to early settlers below are similarly based on this reading. Also, see n. 170 above.

181. The text is Zunaym; it should be read Rutaym. See n. 172 above.

182. The text is Hātladjūr; it should be read Mīlādhjird, as in the Cairo edition.

183. See Yāqūt, *Muʿjam*, II, 139.

184. Vocalization is conjectural here.

185. For Mālik b. Haytham, see the entry in Crone, *Slaves on Horses*, 181–83. Muṣʿab b. Qays was a *naqīb*. See *Akhbār al-Dawlah*, 218.

the Chosen One *(al-Riḍā)* from the family of God's messenger, God bless him and give him peace. They were too haughty for that, so Mālik fought them with a battle line—he had about two hundred men—from daybreak until the time of the afternoon prayer. [1958]

Ṣāliḥ b. Sulaymān al-Ḍabbī,[186] Ibrāhīm b. Yazīd and Ziyād b. ʿĪsā had joined Abū Muslim, so he sent them to Mālik b. Haytham. They came to him at the time of the afternoon prayer, and he was strengthened by their presence. Then Yazīd the mawlā of Naṣr b. Sayyār said to his followers, "If we let them alone this evening, reinforcements will come to them, so attack these people." And they did. Then Abū Naṣr (Mālik b. Haytham) dismounted to fight on foot, and incited his followers saying, "Truly, I trust that God will cut off a part of the unbelievers,[187] so strike them well and truly." Both parties kept on fighting. Thirty-four men of the Marwānid party were killed, and eight were taken prisoner. ʿAbdallāh al-Ṭāʾī attacked Yazīd, the mawlā of Naṣr and the leader of the enemy group; they captured him, and his followers fled. Abū Naṣr sent ʿAbdallāh al-Ṭāʾī and his prisoner with some men of the Shīʿah, along with some prisoners and the heads (of the slain), while he remained in his camp at Safīdhanj. In the delegation were Abū Ḥammād al-Marwazī and Abū ʿAmr al-Aʿjamī. Then Abū Muslim ordered the heads to be displayed on the gate of the wall in his camp. He sent Yazīd al-Aslamī to Abū Isḥāq Khālid b. ʿUthmān and ordered him to treat wounds that Yazīd the mawlā of Naṣr had received, and to treat him with great kindness and consideration. He wrote to Abū Naṣr to come to him. When Naṣr's mawlā Yazīd was healed of his wounds, Abū Muslim called him and said, "If you wish to stay with us and join our cause, then God will have guided you rightly. If you do not, then go back to your master in safety; but give us God's oath not to fight against us or to lie about us, and to say of us [only] what you have seen." Yazīd chose to return to his master, so he sent him on his way. Then Abū Muslim said, "This man will avert from us those [1959] men of piety and morality who assert that we have departed from Islam."

Yazīd came to Naṣr b. Sayyār, who told him, "No welcome to

---

186. A substitute *naqīb* who became one of the great field commanders of the early ʿAbbāsid armies. His family had a long and meritorious role in the affairs of state.

187. Based on Qur. 3:127.

you; by God, I think the enemy only let you live in order to make you an argument against us." "And by God, it's just as you think," said Yazīd. "What's more, they have made me swear not to lie about them, so I'll tell you that they pray the prayers at the proper time, with a call to prayer and *iqāmah*; they recite the Scripture, they make frequent mention of God, and they call men to God's Messenger. I reckon their business will succeed, and were you not my master who freed me from slavery, I'd not have come back to you; I'd have stayed with them." This was the first battle between the (ʿAbbāsid) Shīʿah and the partisans of the Banū Marwān.

In this year, Khāzim b. Khuzaymah[188] prevailed over Marwarrūdh, and Naṣr b. Sayyār's governor there was killed. Khāzim sent a letter with his son Khuzaymah to Abū Muslim announcing the victory.

The Account of Khāzim b. Khuzaymah's Victory Over Marwarrūdh

According to ʿAlī b. Muḥammad—Abū al-Ḥasan al-Jushamī,[189] Zuhayr b. Hunayd and Ḥasan b. Rashīd: When Khāzim b. Khuzaymah was ready to set out for Marwarrūdh, leaders of the Tamīm wanted to prevent him, but he said, "I am a man of your tribe, with Marw as my object. Perhaps I shall be victorious, in which case it will be yours; if I am slain, then you will be done with me." So they let him alone, and he went out and camped in a village called Kanj Rustāh.[190] Then Naḍr b. Ṣubayḥ[191] and Bassām b. Ibrāhīm came to him from Abū Muslim. When it was evening, Khāzim attacked the people of Marwarrūdh by night, and Bishr b. Jaʿfar al-Saʿdī who was Naṣr b. Sayyār's governor in Marwarrūdh was slain. This was in the beginning of Dhū al-Qaʿdah (mid-July 747), and Khāzim sent news of the victory to Abū Muslim by Khuzaymah b. Khāzim, ʿAbdallāh b. Saʿīd and Shabīb b. Wāj.

[1960]

---

188. Khāzim b. Khuzaymah al-Tamīmī was a deputy *naqīb* from Marwarrūdh, an important later general: see Crone, *Slaves on Horses*, 180–81.

189. The text is al-Ḥusmī, emended to al-Jushamī by the Cairo edition.

190. The text gives "Kanj Rustāh," however the textual apparatus lists the variant Kanj Rustaq, and Yāqūt, *Muʿjam*, IV, 308, lists a Kanjrustāq, which LeStrange describes as a district between Bādhghīs and Marwarrūdh.

191. Ibn Ṣubayḥ was a *naqīb*. See *Akhbār al-Dawlah*, 218.

Abū Jaʿfar stated, concerning Abū Muslim's proclamation of revolution, his travels to and from Khurāsān and his return there, a source other than those we have cited gives a differing account: Ibrāhīm the Imām married the daughter of Abū al-Najm to Abū Muslim at the time he sent him to Khurāsān, and sent her dowry with him.[192] Then he wrote to the *naqībs* in Khurāsān, ordering them to listen to Abū Muslim and obey him. According to some assertions, Abū Muslim was from the village of Khuṭarniyyah near Kūfah, and was the steward of Idrīs b. Maʿqil al-ʿIjlī.[193] Then his status changed and he became the mawlā of Muḥammad b. ʿAlī, then of Ibrāhīm b. Muḥammad, and then of the other Imāms who were Muḥammad's sons. He came to Khurāsān while he was still young in years, and Sulaymān b. Kathīr would not accept him. He feared that Abū Muslim would not be strong enough for their task, and fearing for himself and his companions, he sent him away.[194] At this time Abū Dāwud Khālid b. Ibrāhīm was away, beyond the Oxus *(nahr Balkh)*, but when he left there and arrived in Marw, the Imām's letter was read to him, and he asked about the man whom he had sent. They told him that Sulaymān b. Kathīr had sent him away, and so he sent for all of the *naqībs*, who gathered in the house of ʿImrān b. Ismāʿīl.[195] Then Abū Dāwud said to them, "The letter from the Imām came to you with the man he sent while I was absent, and you sent him away. Now what is your case for sending him off?" "His youth," Sulaymān b. Kathīr replied, "and our fear that he would not be able to manage this affair, and our solicitude for him we call men to, and for ourselves, and for those who are answerable

[1961]

---

192. Abū al-Najm was a *naqīb*. The marriage was to establish a tie between Abū Muslim, the Imām's representative, and the Khurāsān apparatus. Despite his *nisbah*, "al-Khurāsānī," Abū Muslim apparently came from Iṣfahān. Note Sulaymān b. Kathīr's initial reaction to Abū Muslim's arrival in the *Akhbār al-Dawlah*, 271–73, and in Ṭabarī below. The relationship of the ʿAbbāsid imāms to the Khurāsān apparatus is a complex problem that has not yet been fully worked out. There is reason to believe that the Khurāsānīs were quite independent until Bukayr b. Māhān's mission to them following the death of Muḥammad b. ʿAlī. See Sharon, *ʿAliyat*, 84–116. (J.L.)

193. The reports of Abū Muslim's origins are marked by considerable confusion. The confusion is perhaps deliberate so as to present Abū Muslim as a man for all peoples and seasons, that is, the ideal picture for a revolutionary operative. A full study of Abū Muslim's origins has been completed by J. Lassner and will appear in a forthcoming festschrift for Franz Rosenthal, edited by Lassner and J.V. Bellamy (J.L.)

194. See n. 192 above.

195. That is, Abū al-Najm.

to us." Then Abū Dāwud said, "Are there any among you who deny that God, blessed be He and exalted, chose Muḥammad, may He bless him and his family and give them peace, and elected him and selected him and sent him with His message to all men? Is there any among you who would deny that?" "No," they said. "Then would you doubt that God, be He exalted, sent down His Book to him, and that Gabriel the trusted spirit came to him making legal what God permits therein, and prohibiting what He forbids, and prescribing what He lays down, and showing His ways, and that he informed him therein of what had been before, and what shall be, up to the Day of Resurrection?" "No," they said. "Then do you doubt that God took His Prophet to Himself after he had delivered the message of his Lord?" "No," they said. "Then," said he, "do you believe that the divine knowledge that was revealed to him was raised [to heaven] with him, or that he left it behind him?" "Of course he left it behind," they said. "Then do you think that he left it behind with those who were not of his family ['itrah], nor people of his house, who were the nearest of the near to him?" "No," they said. "Then," he asked, "would any one of you who had seen this matter progressing, and people receptive to it, see fit to try to turn it all to himself?" "Good God, no!" they replied. "How should that be?" "I do not say that you have done so," he told them, "but sometimes Satan incites great evil concerning what may or may not come to pass. Is there any one of you who would like to transfer control of this matter from the People of the House to some other relatives of the Prophet?" "No," they said. "Then do you doubt that they are the mine of the divine knowledge and keepers of the legacy of the Messenger of God?" "No," they said. "Yet I see," he said, "that you doubted their command, and rejected their knowledge, for had they not known that this was the man who should manage their affairs, they would not have sent him to you. No one has accused him of not being devoted to them, or not being their assistant, or of not standing up for their due."[196]

[1962]

---

196. Possession of esoteric knowledge was one of the qualities of a Shī'ī Imām. There are numerous 'Abbāsid traditions which indicate that this knowledge was passed directly from Muḥammad to the 'Abbāsid line. Other traditions argue that when the Prophet died without leaving any surviving male offspring, his oldest surviving uncle al-'Abbās inherited the Prophet's legacy and passed it to his progeny. The earliest 'Abbāsid claims were based on a transmission of the Imāmate from 'Alī's

At these words from Abū Dāwud, they sent for Abū Muslim and brought him back from Qūmis, accepted him as their leader and listened to him and obeyed him. But there still lingered something in Abū Muslim's soul against Sulaymān b. Kathīr, and he still acknowledged it to Abū Dāwūd.

The *naqībs* and other members of the ('Abbāsid) Shī'ah hearkened to Abū Muslim, obeyed him, deferred to him, and accepted all that came from him. The propagandists spread their word through all the regions of Khurāsān. People joined in droves, their numbers grew, and the propagandists fanned out into all of Khurāsān. Then Ibrāhīm the Imām wrote to Abū Muslim commanding him to come to him during the Pilgrimage that year, that is in 129 (747), so that he could give him his orders for the public proclamation of revolution. He asked him to bring Qaḥṭabah b. Shabīb with him, and whatever monies had been collected. Three hundred and sixty thousand dirhams had been amassed with Abū Muslim, and so he took part of it to buy goods of the stuffs that merchants of Qūh and Marw sell, and sheer and heavy silks. The rest he melted into small ingots of gold and silver and put them in the lining of their cloaks. Then he brought mules and set out midway through Jumādā II (early March 747). Among the *naqībs* who accompanied him were Qaḥṭabah b. Shabīb, Qāsim b. Mujāshi' and Talḥah b. Zurayq, along with forty-one men of the Shī'ah. They outfitted the caravan in the villages of the Khuzā'ah, loading their packs on twenty-one pack mules. An armed man from the Shī'ah was mounted on each mule. They took the desert route, avoiding the armed patrols of Naṣr b. Sayyār, until they came to Abīward.

Abū Muslim wrote to 'Uthmān b. Nahīk[197] and his followers, ordering them to come forward to him. Between them was a distance of five *farsakh*s (30 km). Fifty of their men came to him, and then he journeyed from Abīward, until reaching one of the villages of Nasā called Qāqas. He sent al-Faḍl b. Sulaymān to Andūmān, the village of Asīd, and he met there a man from the Shī'ah and asked him where Asīd was. The man replied, "Why are you asking about him? There has been great evil from the governor today, and he has been

[1963]

---

grandson Abū Hāshim b. Muḥammad b. al-Ḥanafiyyah to the 'Abbāsid Muḥammad b. 'Alī. See, e.g., Omar, *'Abbāsid Caliphate*, 59–67; *EI²* s.v. 'Abbāsids.

197. For 'Uthmān b. Nahīk, who was a *dā'ī* from Abīward, see the entry in Crone, *Slaves on Horses*, 189.

taken, along with al-Aḥjam b. 'Abdallāh,[198] Ghaylān b. Faḍālah, Ghālib b. Sa'īd and Muhājir b. 'Uthmān, to the governor 'Āsim b. Qays b. al-Ḥarūrī, who has imprisoned them." Abū Muslim and his companions moved on to Andūmān, and Abū Mālik (Asīd) and the Shī'ah at Nasā came to him. Abū Mālik informed him that the letter which had been with the Imām's messenger was in his possession, so Abū Muslim told him to bring it to him. He brought him the letter and a banner and a flag. Lo, the letter told him to turn back as soon as he received it and publicly declare the revolution. At this, he fastened the flag that had come to him from the Imām to a lance and the banner as well. The Shī'ah among the people of Nasā gathered to him along with the propagandists and chiefs. He already had the people of Abīward who had come to Nasā with him.

Word of this reached 'Āsim b. Qays al-Ḥarūrī, and he sent (men) to Abū Muslim to question him about his situation. He told him that he was a pilgrim, traveling to the House of God, and that he had with him a number of friends who were merchants. He requested 'Āsim to set free those of his companions whom he had detained, so that they might leave his province. They then demanded that Abū Muslim write a personal contract for them, stating that he would exchange all the slaves, riding animals and weapons that were with him so that his companions, those who had come from the province of the Imām and others, might go their ways. Abū Muslim consented to this, and his friends were set free. He now ordered those of the Shī'ah among his followers to return home. He read the Imām's letter to them, and ordered them to proclaim the revolution publicly. One group of them then went home. Abū Mālik Asīd b. 'Abdallāh al-Khuzā'ī, Zurayq b. Shawdhab[199] and those who had come to him from Abīward continued with him, and he ordered all who turned back to hold themselves in readiness. He went on with those of his companions who had remained, and with Qaḥṭabah b. Shabīb, until they camped at the borders of Jurjān. Abū Muslim then sent

[1964]

---

198. Al-Aḥjam was a *naqīb*. Muhājir b. 'Uthmān was a replacement for a *naqīb*. See *Akhbār al-Dawlah*, 218, 220.

199. Zurayq b. Shawdhab is listed among the *du'āt al-du'āt*. See *Akhbār al-Dawlah*, 222.

word to Khālid b. Barmak and Abū ʿAwn[200] ordering them to bring
whatever funds they had collected from the Shīʿah. They both presented themselves, and he stayed there some days until the caravans
had assembled. He outfitted Qaḥṭabah b. Shabīb and gave him the
money he had with him and the means of transporting it, and sent
him on to Ibrāhīm b. Muḥammad, while Abū Muslim and those
with him went back to Nasā, and from there traveled to Abīward.
From there he traveled on in disguise to Marw, where he stayed at
one of the villages of the Khuzāʿah, called Fanīn. This was on the
twenty-third of Ramaḍān (June 7, 747). He had designated the day of
ʿĪd as the time for his followers to meet him at Marw. He sent Abū
Dāwud and ʿAmr b. Aʿyan to Ṭukhāristān and al-Naḍr b. Ṣubayḥ to
Amul and Bukhārā, with Sharīk b. ʿIsā. Mūsā b. Kaʿb[201] he sent to
Abīward and Nasā, and Khāzim b. Khuzaymah to Marwarrūdh. The
people then came to him, and al-Qāsim b. Mujāshiʿ al-Tamīmī led
them in the prayers on the day of the feast at the prayer-ground
(muṣallā) of the Qanbar family in the village of Abū Dāwud Khālid
b. Ibrāhīm.

This year most of the Arab tribesmen in Khurāsān swore an oath [1965]
and made a compact to fight Abū Muslim. This was at the time his
followers increased and his forces became powerful. Also still in this
year he moved from his camp at Safīdhanj to Mākhuwān.

The Arab Tribesmen of Khurāsān
Ally Against Abū Muslim

According to ʿAlī—al-Ṣabbāḥ the mawlā of Jibrīl—Maslamah b.
Yaḥyā: When Abū Muslim openly proclaimed revolution, people
hastened to join him, and the people of Marw began to come to him.
Naṣr did not prevent them from this nor did he forbid them. Nor did
al-Kirmānī and Shaybān disapprove of Abū Muslim's activities, be-

---

200. For Khālid b. Barmak and his progeny, who later served the ʿAbbāsid house, see
EI² s.v. Barāmika; Lassner, *ʿAbbāsid Rule*, index, 319; Crone, *Slaves on Horses*,
176–77. For Abū ʿAwn, see the entry in Crone, ibid., 174.
201. Mūsā b. Kaʿb al-Tamīmī was one of the highest ranking agents in the ʿAbbāsid
revolutionary apparatus. He later served as a great field commander and security officer. See *Akhbār al-Dawlah*, 215–16; Crone, *Slaves on Horses*, 186.

cause he was calling for deposing Marwān b. Muḥammad. Abū Muslim was staying at a village called Bālīn[202] in a tent, without any guards or doorkeepers. The people magnified his authority and said, "A man from the Banū Hāshim has appeared, endowed with urbanity, gravity and calm." A number of young men from the people of Marw set out, pietists who sought religious insight *(fiqh)* and they came to him at his camp, and asked him about his genealogy.[203] He responded, "What I have to say is better for you than my genealogy." Then they asked him about matters relating to *fiqh*. He told them, "The command to do good and reject what is reprehensible is more important for you than this. We have work to do, and have more need of your assistance than of your questions, so excuse us." They said, "By God, we do not know your genealogy, and we think that it won't be long before you are slain. Nothing is lacking for that except for one of these two to be free."[204] Abū Muslim replied, "On the contrary, it is I who shall slay them both, God willing."

The young men returned and went to Naṣr b. Sayyār and told him (what they had heard). He told them, "May God reward you well; you are the sort to seek him out and learn about him." Then they went to Shaybān and informed him, whereupon he sent a message to Naṣr, "We have each choked the other." Naṣr then wrote to him, "Desist from attacking me so that I can fight him or, if you wish, join me in fighting him until I kill him or drive him away; then we may return to the business we are now engaged in." Shaybān was anxious about what to do, and that became apparent to those in his camp. The spies of Abū Muslim now came to him and informed him of this. Sulaymān said, "What is this matter that has reached them? Have you been talking to somebody?" Abū Muslim then informed him about the young men who had come to him, and Sulaymān said, "Then this is all because of that." They wrote to ʿAlī b. al-Kirmānī saying, "You are a wronged man unable to take revenge. Your father has been murdered.[205] We know that you are not of the

[1966]

---

202. Bāb Bālīn was the northwest gate of Marw. However, the reference to Bālīn here may be an error for "Allīn," one of villages of Marw. See n. 160 above.

203. The name he used, "Father of a Muslim, Khurāsānī," was deliberately ambiguous.

204. That is Naṣr b. Sayyār and Shaybān al-Khārijī.

205. According to Dīnawarī, 362, the death of Judayʿ al-Kirmānī was arranged by Naṣr, who invited him to a parley. Other sources indicate that it was a son of al-

same mind as Shaybān; you are only fighting for revenge, so prevent
Shaybān from a reconciliation with Naṣr." ʿAlī went to Shaybān and
spoke to him, and deterred him from what he intended. Naṣr then
wrote to Shaybān, "Truly you are being deceived, and I swear by
God that this matter is so momentous[206] that by the side of it, you
should find me small."

While they were thus engaged, Abū Muslim sent al-Naḍr b.
Nuʿaym al-Ḍabbī to Harāt, which was governed by ʿIsā b. ʿAqīl al-
Laythī, and al-Naḍr drove him out of Harāt, so that ʿIsā fled to Naṣr
and al-Naḍr took over the city. Then Yaḥyā b. Nuʿaym b. Hubayrah
said (to the Khārijites), "Choose whether you will perish before the
Muḍar, or the Muḍar before you." They asked, "How is that?" He
replied, "This man's affair only surfaced a month ago, but already as
many men as are in your army have joined his army." "What shall
we do?" they asked. "Make peace with Naṣr," he told them, "for if
you have peace with him, these people will fight Naṣr and leave you
alone, because the Muḍar have the government. If you do not make
peace with Naṣr, they will, and they will fight you and it will go
against you." "What shall we do?" they said. "Get ahead of them,"

Ḥārith b. Surayj al-Murjiʾī who killed him. See Ṭabarī II/3, 1975; Yaʿqūbī, *Taʾrīkh,*
408; Ibn Khayyāṭ, I, 410; *FHA,* 188. Judayʿ's son ʿAlī succeeded him as leader of the
Azd.
   206. Naṣr wrote verses in which he urged the Arabs to unite with him to war
against Abū Muslim, as follows:

> Go tell both the Rabīʿah in Marw and the Yamanīs:
>   arouse yourselves, before it will be of no avail;
>
> What are you thinking of, to enkindle the feud between you
>   as if men of wit were absent from your counsels?
>
> You neglect an enemy who has surrounded you,
>   a rabble of no religion or consequence,
>
> Not Arabs like those among men you would know,
>   nor yet true mawlās, if their origins be reckoned;
>
> Who would ask me about the root of their religion?
>   truly, their religion is that the Arabs should perish;
>
> A sect professing doctrines you never heard of
>   from the Prophet, nor brought by the Scriptures.

—Ibn Athīr, v. IV. 304, and also quoted by al-Dīnawarī, 361.

he said, "if by only one hour, and comfort yourselves by their slaying."

[1967]   Then Shaybān sent to Naṣr offering him a truce, and he agreed. Following that, he sent a message to Salm b. Aḥwaz, and between them they concluded an agreement. Shaybān came, with Ibn al-Kirmānī on his right and Yaḥyā b. Nuʿaym on his left, and Salm said to Ibn al-Kirmānī, "One-eyed one, I do not take you to be the one-eyed man at whose hands we are told that the Muḍar will perish."[207] They then made a truce for one year, and put their agreement in writing. This came to Abū Muslim, and he wrote to Shaybān, "We would make a truce with you for some months, so grant us a truce of three months." Then Ibn al-Kirmānī said, "I never made peace with Naṣr; it was Shaybān who did so while I was unwilling. I am a man with blood to avenge, and I will not stop fighting Naṣr." Ibn al-Kirmānī resumed hostilities, but Shaybān refused to help him, saying, "Treachery is not permissible." At this Ibn al-Kirmānī sent a message to Abū Muslim asking his help against Naṣr b. Sayyār. Abū Muslim proceeded to al-Mākhuwān, and sent Shibl b. Ṭahmān[208] to Ibn al-Kirmānī with the message, "I am with you against Naṣr." Ibn al-Kirmānī said, "I should indeed like Abū Muslim to meet me," and Shibl brought word of this. Abū Muslim waited fourteen days, and then he went to Ibn al-Kirmānī, leaving his army behind at al-Mākhuwān. ʿUthmān b. al-Kirmānī met him with cavalry and rode with him until he entered the camp. Then Abū Muslim went to ʿAlī b. al-Kirmānī and stayed mounted outside his chamber. He was asked to dismount, and entered saluting ʿAlī as "Amīr." ʿAlī had prepared a lodging[209] for him in a palace belonging to Makhlad[210] b. Ḥasan al-Azdī. Abū Muslim stayed two days, and then went back to his camp at al-Mākhuwān. This was on the fifth day of Muḥarram, 130 (September 16, 747).

---

207. "One-eyed one" is an insult renderable as "you prick." It is also a reference to the Dajjāl, the one-eyed "great deceiver" who will persecute the faithful and usher in the second coming of Jesus and the Messianic age according to certain *ḥadīths*. Ibn Aḥwaz appears to be saying, "You may be this and that, but you are not the Antichrist who will precede the messianic age and destroy the Muḍar." For al-Dajjāl see *EI*² s.v. ad-Dadjdjāl.

208. Shibl b. Ṭahmān was a *naqīb*. See *Akhbār al-Dawlah*, 216.

209. The text is *qaṣran*, "a palace"; it should be read *manzilan*, "lodging," as in the Cairo edition.

210. According to the Cairo edition, Mukhallad.

Abū al-Khaṭṭāb reported that when the Shīʿah in Abū Muslim's camp became numerous, Safīdhanj was too confining for him, and he desired a more spacious encampment. Al-Mākhuwān answered his need. It was the village of al-ʿAlāʾ b. Ḥurayth, and Abū Isḥāq Khālid b. ʿUthmān, and Abū al-Jahm b. ʿAṭiyyah and his brothers lived there.[211] His stay at Safīdhanj had lasted forty-two days, and from there he went to al-Mākhuwān. He stopped at the house of Abū Isḥāq on Wednesday, the ninth night of Dhū al-Qaʿdah (July 19, 747). He dug a trench around the place, with two entrances to it, and he and the Shīʿah camped there. He put Muṣʿab b. Qays al-Ḥanafī and Bahdal b. Iyās al-Ḍabbī[212] in charge of one entrance, and Abū Sharāhīl and Abū ʿAmr al-Aʿjamī in charge of the other. He appointed Abū Naṣr Mālik b. Haytham in charge of security, and made Abū Isḥāq Khālid b. ʿUthmān captain of the guard. Kāmil b. Muẓaffar Abū Ṣāliḥ was put in charge of the army register, and Aslam b. Ṣubayḥ was in charge of his chancery. Qāsim b. Mujāshiʿ the Tamīmī naqīb he made qāḍī, and he reinforced Mālik b. al-Haytham with Abū al-Waḍḍāḥ and a number of the early settlers.[213] He put the men from the two villages (called) Nawshān—they were eighty-three men—under Abū Isḥāq in the guard.[214]

[1968]

Qāsim b. Mujāshiʿ used to lead the prayers for Abū Muslim in the camp and narrate anecdotes after the afternoon prayer, mentioning the virtues of the Banū Hāshim, and the shameful deeds of the Banū Umayyah. Abū Muslim now settled at the camp at al-Mākhuwān, appearing like any man of the Shīʿah, until ʿAbdallāh b. Bisṭām came to him and brought him tents, pavilions, cooking vessels, nose-bags for the horses and leather troughs for water. The first official that Abū Muslim appointed was Dāwud b. Karrāz.[215] Abū Muslim refused to let the (runaway) slaves join him at his camp, and had an entrenched position dug for them at the village of Shawwāl,[216] putting it in the charge of Dāwud b. Karrāz. When a large number of

[1969]

---

211. It was thus the village of two naqībs and a substitute naqīb. See Akhbār al-Dawlah, 221.

212. Ibn Iyās was one of the duʿāt. See Akhbār al-Dawlah, 221.

213. The text is ahl al-Suqādim.

214. Nawsh was the name of several villages in Marw. The two villages here are not specified. See Yāqūt, Muʿjam, IV, 823–24.

215. Ibn Karrāz was a subsitute naqīb. See Akhbār al-Dawlah, 221.

216. Shawwāl was a village situated three farsakhs (18 km) from Marw. See Yāqūt, Muʿjam, III, 332.

slaves had gathered, he sent them to Mūsā b. Kaʿb at Abīward. He ordered Kāmil b. Muẓaffar to enroll the people at the camp according to their names and their fathers' names and designate them by their villages, recording all that in the register.[217] Kāmil, who was called Abū Ṣāliḥ, did so, and their numbers came to seven thousand men. Their pay was three dirhams per man; then each of them received four at the hands of Abū Ṣāliḥ Kāmil.

At last the tribesmen of the Muḍar, the Rabīʿah and the Qaḥṭān[218] agreed to lay aside their feuds and unite as one in fighting Abū Muslim. Once they had driven him from Marw, they would look to their own affairs and what they had agreed upon. They therefore wrote a carefully worded treaty among themselves, and word of this reached Abū Muslim. It alarmed him, and he took it seriously and reconsidered his situation. Lo, the water supply of Mākhuwān dropped, and he feared that Naṣr b. Sayyār might cut off his water, so he moved to Alīn, the village of Abū Manṣūr Ṭalḥah b. Zurayq[219] the *naqīb*. This was after he had stayed four months at the camp at Mākhuwān, and he settled at Alīn on Thursday the sixth of Dhū al-Ḥijjah 129 (August 14, 747). He dug a trench at Alīn between Alīn and Balāsha Jird.[220] Thus the village was behind the camp, and he (dug so as to) place the house of Muḥtafiz b. ʿUthmān b. Bishr al-Mazanī inside the trench. The inhabitants of Alīn drank the water of a canal called the Kharqān, so Naṣr b. Sayyār could not cut off the drinking-water from Alīn. The Feast of the Day of Sacrifice[221] came, and Qāsim b. Mujāshiʿ led the prayers for Abū Muslim and the Shīʿah at the prayer-ground of Alīn.

[1970]

Naṣr b. Sayyār was camped on the ʿIyāḍ Canal, and he positioned ʿĀṣim b. ʿAmr at Balāsha Jird and Abū al-Dhayyāl at Ṭūsān. Bishr b. Unayf al-Yarbūʿī he placed at Julfar, and he stationed Ḥātim b. al-Ḥārith b. Surayj at Kharaq, seeking to attack Abū Muslim. Abū Dhayyāl quartered his troops with the inhabitants of Ṭūsān while

---

217. That is, they were officially enrolled according to place, not tribe, or origin. This became the standard ʿAbbāsid practice. The advantage was that it played down tribal feelings (ʿaṣabiyyah). See n. 179 above.

218. That is, the Yaman.

219. The text is Ruzayq; read Zurayq, as in textual apparatus variants and *Akhbār al-Dawlah*, 215, 216.

220. The text is Balāsha Jird. Yāqūt, *Muʿjam*, I, 708, lists a Balāshjird which was a village four *farsakh*s (24 km) from Marw.

221. See *EI*[2] s.v. ʿĪd al-Aḍḥā.

Abū Muslim was in his camp, and they injured the people there, treating them like servants, butchering their chickens, cattle and pigeons, and making them bear the cost of their victuals and fodder. The Shīʿah complained of this to Abū Muslim, and he sent some cavalry with them. They encountered Abū Dhayyāl and drove him away, and captured Maymūn al-Aʿsar al-Khwārizmī with about thirty men. Abū Muslim gave them clothing, treated their wounds, and set them free.

In this year, Judayʿ b. ʿAlī al-Kirmānī was slain and crucified.[222]

The Account of the Slaying of Judayʿ b. ʿAlī al-Kirmānī

We have already mentioned the slaying of al-Ḥārith b. Surayj and that al-Kirmānī was the one who killed him. When al-Kirmānī had slain al-Ḥārith, Marw became wholly his, due to that slaying, and Naṣr b. Sayyār removed from Marw to Abrashahr. Al-Kirmānī's rule grew stronger, and according to what is said, Naṣr sent Salm b. Aḥwaz against him. He marched with Naṣr's guards and cavalry until he encountered the followers of al-Kirmānī; he found Yaḥyā b. Nuʿaym al-Maylāʾ stationed at the head of a thousand soldiers of the Rabīʿah, Muḥammad b. al-Muthannā at the head of seven hundred horsemen of the Azd, Ibn al-Ḥasan b. al-Shaykh al-Azdī with one thousand of their young men (fityān), and al-Ḥazmī al-Sughdī with a thousand Abnāʾ of the Yaman.[223] When they stood opposite each other, Salm b. Aḥwaz called to Muḥammad b. al-Muthannā, "O Muḥammad al-Muthannā, get these sailors (i.e., the Azd)[224] to come out against us!" Then Muḥammad said to Salm, "Whoreson, do you say that to Abū ʿAlī?" The two armies moved slowly against each other, and fought with swords. Salm b. Aḥwaz was routed, and over one hundred of his followers were slain, while more than twenty of Muḥammad's followers were killed. Naṣr's men returned to him in disorder, and ʿAqīl b. Maʿqil told him, "Naṣr, you've brought bad luck on the Arabs; when you've gone this far, exert yourself and bare your shank!" Naṣr now sent ʿIṣmah b. ʿAbdallāh al-Asadī, who stood

[1971]

---

222. See n. 205 above.

223. From the context it is not certain whether these *fityān* were Arabs of the Azd or slaves that they had formed into a military contingent. For the Abnāʾ, see *EI*² s.v. Abnāʾ.

224. See n. 113 above.

where Salm b. Aḥwaz had stood. He called out, "O Muḥammad, you know well that a fish can't beat a sea-wolf!" Muḥammad replied, "Then hold on until we get there, you bastard!" He ordered Muḥammad al-Sughdī to go out to him with the Yaman, and they fought a fierce battle. ʿIṣmah fled until he came back to Naṣr b. Sayyār; four hundred of his followers had been slain.

[1972] Naṣr then sent Mālik b. ʿAmr al-Tamīmī, and he advanced with his followers. He called out, "O Ibn Muthannā, come out and fight me, if you're a man!" He answered his challenge, and the Tamīmī struck him between his neck and his shoulder, without effect. Muḥammad b. al-Muthannā struck him in turn with a mace and smashed his head. The fighting became desperate, and they fought a fierce battle, as great a battle as any. Naṣr's followers were routed, and seven hundred of them were slain. Three hundred of al-Kirmānī's followers were killed, and the bad blood between them kept on, so that they all went out to the trenches and fought each other bitterly.

When Abū Muslim was certain that each side had inflicted great losses on the other and would not receive reinforcements, he began to write letters to Shaybān.[225]

Then he would say to the messenger, "Make your way by the Muḍar. They will stop you and take your letters." They would take the letters, and read in them, "I observe that the Yaman will not last, and there is no good in them, so do not rely on them or put trust in them, for I trust that God will show you what you desire, and if He spares me I shall leave them neither hair nor nails." Then he would send another messenger by a different road with a letter in which he mentioned the Muḍar and praised the Yaman in similar terms, so that each party came to favor him. He now began to write to Naṣr b. Sayyār and to al-Kirmānī, "The Imām has recommended you to me, and I shall not act counter to his opinion of you." At the same time he wrote to the districts of the province (telling them) to proclaim the revolution (by showing their colors), and the first one to put on black—it is reported—was Asīd b. ʿAbdallāh at Nasā, who cried, "O Muḥammad! O Manṣūr!"[226] Muqātil b. Ḥakīm and Ibn

---

225. That is, the Khārijite leader operating in Khurāsān.
226. See n. 82 above.

Ghazwān put on black at the same time. So did the people of Abī-ward and Marwarrūdh and those of the villages around Marw.

Abū Muslim advanced to a position midway between the camps [1973] of Naṣr b. Sayyār and that of Judayʿ al-Kirmānī. Both sides came to fear him, and his followers grew in number. Naṣr b. Sayyār wrote to Marwān b. Muḥammad, informing him of Abū Muslim's circumstances and his revolt. He told him of the multitude that were with Abū Muslim and his following, and that he was proclaiming a summons to Ibrāhīm b. Muḥammad. He wrote him some verses of poetry:

> I see among the ashes the flash of live coals,
>   and deem that they will have a kindling;

> A fire may be kindled with two sticks,
>   and a war begin with a few words.

> I say in astonishment "Would that I knew;
>   is [the Clan of] Umayyah awake, or sleeping?"

But Marwān wrote him, "The witness sees what the absent cannot see; cauterize the wart according to your own lights." Then Naṣr exclaimed, "Well, your master has shown us plainly that there is no assistance (naṣr: a pun) with him." He then wrote to Yazīd b. ʿUmar b. Hubayrah the governor of Iraq, requesting aid, and wrote these verses for him:

> Go tell Yazīd—for the best speech is the truest;
>   long since, I saw that there's no good in lying—

> Khurāsān is a land wherein I have seen
>   eggs which, were they to hatch, would astonish you;   [1974

> Chicks two years hatching, and already big,
>   though they haven't yet flown, and are covered with down.

> But should they fly before they are prevented,
>   they will set warfires blazing, wherever fires may blaze.

But Yazīd said, "There's no winning without numbers, and I have not a man." Naṣr then wrote to Marwān informing him about Abū

Muslim and his manifesting a revolution and about his strength, and that he was summoning men to follow Ibrāhīm b. Muḥammad. The letter found Marwān when a messenger from Abū Muslim to Ibrāhīm had already fallen into his hands. The messenger had been returning from Ibrāhīm to Abū Muslim with a letter from Ibrāhīm in answer to one from Abū Muslim. In it he cursed and reviled Abū Muslim for not exploiting his opportunity with Naṣr and al-Kirmānī while he could, and told him not to leave one Arab in Khurāsān unslain.[227] The messenger handed the letter over to Marwān, and Marwān wrote to al-Walīd b. Muʿāwiyah b. ʿAbd al-Malik, his gover-

[1975] nor for Damascus, ordering him to write to the administrator of the Balqāʾ[228] to go to Ḥumaymah Wells, and seize Ibrāhīm b. Muḥammad, bind him securely and send him to him with a mounted escort. Al-Walīd wrote to the governor of the Balqāʾ, and he came upon Ibrāhīm at the mosque in the village. He seized him, tied his hands behind his back, and brought him to al-Walīd. The latter sent him to Marwān, who threw him into a prison.[229]

To return to the account of Naṣr and al-Kirmānī, when their quarrel was at its height, Abū Muslim sent word to al-Kirmānī, "I am with you." Al-Kirmānī accepted this and Abū Muslim joined him, so that matters grew critical for Naṣr. He sent word to al-Kirmānī, "Woe to you! Do not make a mistake! By God, I am fearful for you and your followers from this man. Make a truce with me; we shall enter Marw, and write a treaty of peace between us." He hoped in this way to separate al-Kirmānī from Abū Muslim. Al-Kirmānī then went to his dwelling, and Abū Muslim remained at his camp. Then al-Kirmāni went forth until he halted at the courtyard *(raḥbah)* with one hundred horsemen, wearing a tunic of *khashkashūnah*, and sent

---

227. See n. 116 above on the matter of killing Arabs in Khurāsān. It is, of course, possible that statements of this sort were used by the Umayyads to rally support against the ʿAbbāsids.

228. The Balqāʾ was a name given to all of Transjordan or to the central part of it. See *EI²* s.v. Balḳāʾ. Note *FHA*, 189, reads "Kirār and al-Ḥumaymah," indicating two distinct places.

229. It is highly unlikely that Ibrāhīm al-Imām would have been identified in correspondence. His true identity would have been known only to the inner circles of the movement and they were enjoined not to risk exposing him. This tradition would appear to be part of the ʿAbbāsid historiography which describes various members of the Banū ʿAbbās as martyrs. There is reason to doubt that he was "imprisoned" because the Umayyads became fully aware of his activities, or that they had him murdered. For a detailed exposition see Sharon, *ʿAlīyat*, 237–61. (J.L.)

word to Naṣr, "Come out, so we may write that treaty between us."
Naṣr perceived deceit in him, and sent the son of al-Ḥārith b. Surayj
against him with about three hundred horsemen. They clashed in
the courtyard and fought each other for a long time. Finally al-Kirmānī was speared in his side and fell from his horse. His followers
protected him until they were overwhelmed. Naṣr then had al-
Kirmānī killed and crucified the body with a fish[230] beside it. Al-
Kirmānī's son ʿAlī now advanced; he had gone to Abū Muslim and
had gathered a large force which he led against Naṣr b. Sayyār. He
fought him until he drove him from the governor's palace, whereupon Naṣr went to one of the mansions in Marw. Then Abū Muslim   [1976]
entered Marw, and ʿAlī b. Judayʿ al-Kirmānī came to meet him. Abū
Muslim saluted him with the title of "Amīr" and informed him of
his support, saying, "Give me your orders." ʿAlī then told him, "Do
just what you are doing until I have some other order to give you."

In this year ʿAbdallāh b. Muʿāwiyah b. ʿAbdallāh b. Jaʿfar b. Abī
Ṭālib gained control of Fārs.[231]

ʿAbdallāh b. Muʿāwiyah al-Jaʿfarī Gains Control of Fārs

According to ʿAlī b. Muḥammad—ʿĀṣim b. Ḥafṣ al-Tamīmī and
others: When ʿAbdallāh b. Muʿāwiyah b. ʿAbdallāh Jaʿfar b. Abī
Ṭālib was driven out of Kūfah, he went to Madāʾin,[232] where the
people swore allegiance to him, and a group from Kūfah joined him.
He then went to Jibāl and seized control there as well as in Ḥulwān,
Qūmis, Iṣbahān and Rayy. The slaves of the Kūfans ran away to join
him. When he had prevailed, he resided at Iṣbahān.

Muḥārib b. Mūsā, a mawlā of the Banū Yashkur, had been very
powerful in Fārs, and he came walking in his sandals to the Govern-

---

230. A contemptuous symbol for the Azd.

231. The revolt of ʿAbdallāh b. Muʿāwiyah, the Jaʿfarid, represented a great threat to
the ʿAbbāsids. Their own revolution was predicted in the collapse of the ʿAlid movement of Zayd b. ʿAlī. They assumed that they could attract his following. The movement of the Jaʿfarid pretender thus threatened to undercut ʿAbbāsid support at a critical moment. Ibn Muʿāwiyah attracted support and initially met with success in battle. The ʿAbbāsids at first supported the revolt in order to show the solidarity of the
Banū Hāshim, but they were ready to abandon him at first opportunity. They later
had him killed. For a detailed treatment of his revolt, see Sharon, ʿAlīyat, 154–205.
(J.L.)

232. Meaning "the cities." The Arab name of the site of Ctesiphon-Seleucia, the
Persian capitals on the Tigris just to the south of later Baghdad. See LeStrange, Lands,
33–35.

ment House of Iṣṭakhr (Persepolis) and expelled the governor appointed by Ibn ʿUmar (b. ʿAbd al- ʿAzīz) and said to a man whose name was ʿUmārah, "Have the people swear allegiance." The inhabitants said, "On what?" He then said, "On what you love and hate." They then swore allegiance to Ibn Muʿāwiyah. Then Muḥārib went to Kirmān and raided there, and on his raid he took some camels belonging to Thaʿlabah b. Ḥassān al-Māzinī and drove them back with him. Thaʿlabah then went out looking for his camels at a village of his called Ashhar. With Thaʿlabah was a mawlā of his, who asked him, "Why don't we murder Muḥārib? If you like, you can strike him down while I keep his people busy, or if you like I'll kill him while you keep them busy." Thaʿlabah replied, "Alas! Would you commit murder [and the camels get away from us, when we didn't even meet][233] the man?" Then he went in to see Muḥārib, who welcomed him, and said, "What would you ask of me?" "My camels," he told him. "[Yes", he said, "I took them][234] not knowing whose they were. Now I know, and here are your camels." Then Thaʿlabah took them and said to his mawlā, ["This is better. And what was it you wanted?"][235] The mawlā replied, "Something which, if we had taken it, would have been even more useful."

[1977]

Muḥārib was joined by officers and commanders of the Syrian army, and he moved against Muslim b. Musayyab who was governing Shīrāz for Ibn ʿUmar, and slew him in the year 128 (745–746), and then went up to Iṣbahān. ʿAbdallāh b. Muʿāwiyah then moved to Iṣṭakhr, appointing his brother Ḥasan to govern Jibāl. Then he settled at a monastery one mile *(mīl)* away from Iṣṭakhr. He appointed his brother Yazīd to rule Fārs, and remained where he was. People came to him, members of the Banū Hāshim and others. He collected taxes, and sent out governors. With him were Manṣūr b. Jumhūr, Sulaymān b. Hishām b. ʿAbd al-Malik, and Shaybān b. al-Ḥils b. ʿAbd al-ʿAzīz al-Shaybānī the Khārijite. Abū Jaʿfar ʿAbdallāh and ʿAbdallāh and ʿĪsā b. ʿAlī came to him as well.[236]

Yazīd b. ʿUmar b. Hubayrah then came as governor of Iraq, and sent Nubātah b. Ḥanẓalah al-Kilābī against ʿAbdallāh b. Muʿāwiyah.

---

233. The text has three lacunae here. The Cairo edition supplies the missing phrases from manuscripts not available to the earlier editors.

234. See n. 233 above.

235. See n. 233 above.

236. That is, the future Caliph al-Manṣūr and two of his paternal uncles.

Sulaymān b. Ḥabīb learned that Ibn Hubayrah had made Nubātah governor of Ahwāz, and he dispatched Dāwud b. Ḥatim, who stationed himself at Kurbuj Dīnār[237] to keep Nubātah out of Ahwāz. Then Nubātah advanced and fought him and Dāwud was killed. Sulaymān fled to Sābūr,[238] where the Kurds had seized control and driven out al-Masīḥ b. al-Ḥawārī.[239] Sulaymān fought them and drove them out. He then wrote to ʿAbdallāh b. Muʿāwiyah swearing allegiance to him, but ʿAbd al-Raḥmān b. Yazīd b. al-Muhallab said, "He will not keep faith with you; he only wants to keep you away from him and devour Sābūr. Write to him and have him come before you, if he is sincere." He wrote to him, and Sulaymān came. But he told his followers, "Come in with me, and if anyone tries to prevent you, fight him." Then they went in, and he told Ibn Muʿāwiyah, "I am the most obedient of men to you." Ibn Muʿāwiyah told him, "Return to your position." And he went back.

Then Muḥārib b. Mūsā broke with Ibn Muʿāwiyah. He gathered a force and marched on Sābūr. His son Mukhallad[240] b. Muḥārib was detained at Sābūr, for Yazīd b. Muʿāwiyah, brother of ʿAbdallāh, had seized him and put him in prison. Someone told Muḥārib, "Your son is in this man's hands, and you make war on him! Aren't you afraid that he'll kill your son?" But he replied, "May God put him far away!" Yazīd fought him, and Muḥārib was put to flight. He went to Kirmān where he stayed until Muḥammad b. al-Ashʿath approached, whereupon he went with him. But he broke with Ibn al-Ashʿath, who killed him and twenty-four of his sons. ʿAbdallāh b. Muʿāwiyah remained at Iṣṭakhr, until Ibn Dubārah came against him with Dāwud, the son of Yazīd b. ʿUmar b. Hubayrah. Ibn Muʿāwiyah gave orders to cut the (pontoon) bridge at Kūfah, so Ibn Hubayrah sent Maʿn b. Zāʾidah from the other side. Sulaymān then said to Abān b. Muʿāwiyah b. Hishām, "The enemy has come against you." And he replied, "I was not commanded to fight them." Sulaymān said, "And by God, you'll never get any orders about

[1978]

---

237. The text is Kurbukh Dīnār; it should be read Kurbuj Dīnār, which was a place near Ahwāz. See Yāqūt, *Muʿjam*, IV, 249.

238. Sābūr of Bīshāpūr had been a Sasanian royal residence, and was one of the five great districts (*kūrah*) of Fārs. See LeStrange, *Lands*, 248.

239. A curious name; "Messiah son of Disciple." The Cairo edition gives al-Ḥimārī.

240. Vocalization is conjectural.

them, either!" Maʿn came and fought them by Marw al-Shādhān,[241] and recited this *rajaz*:

[1979]   The Prince of the enemy is not the great deceiver;
                         he fled from death, and fell into death.

Both Ibn al-Muqaffaʿ and another authority give: "He fled from death, and in it he fell." (Maʿn) called out, "A stay? I told you, I've done." Then Ibn Muʿāwiyah fled, and Maʿn did not pursue them. In the battle, a man from the family of Abū Lahab was killed.[242] It had been predicted that a man of the Banū Hāshim would be slain in Marw al-Shādhān. Many prisoners were taken, and Ibn Ḍubārah put a large number of them to death. It is said that among those killed that day was Ḥakīm al-Fard, Abū al-Majd. But it is also said that he was killed at Ahwāz, by Nubātah.

When Ibn Muʿāwiyah fled, Shaybān fled to the island of Ibn Kā-wān, and Manṣūr b. Jumhūr to Sind. ʿAbd al-Raḥmān b. Yazīd ran away to ʿUmān, and ʿAmr b. Sahl b. ʿAbd al-ʿAzīz escaped to Egypt. The remainder of the prisoners were sent to Ibn Hubayrah.

Ḥumayd al-Ṭawīl reported: He set those prisoners free, and none of them were put to death except Ḥusayn b. Waʿlah al-Sadūsī. When Ibn Hubayrah ordered him slain, Ḥusayn said, "I alone am to be killed, among all these prisoners?" "Yes," he said, "you are a poly-theist, for you composed the verse:

And were I to command the sun, it would not rise.

Ibn Muʿāwiyah went directly to Sijistān; then he came to Khu-rāsān and Manṣūr b. Jumhūr went to Sind. Maʿn b. Zāʾidah went in search of him along with ʿAṭiyyah al-Thaʿlabī and others of the Banū
[1980]   Thaʿlabah, but they could not catch him and turned back. Ḥusayn b. Waʿlah al-Sadūsī had been with Yazīd b. Muʿāwiyah, who then aban-doned him, [and he joined up with ʿAbdallāh b. Muʿāwiyah.][243]

---

241. That is the Marw of Fārs which was originally a quarter of Iṣṭakhr. Perhaps it had already become the separate village it was in later times. See LeStrange, *Lands*, 280.

242. Abū Lahab was an uncle of the Prophet; in his position of leadership of the Banū Hāshim following the death of Abū Ṭālib, he cooperated with the Prophet's ene-mies. See *EI*[2] s.v. Abū Lahab.

243. These passages in parenthesis are given in the Cairo edition and fill in the la-cunae of the text.

Muwwari' al-Sulamī [captured Ḥusayn].[244] He had seen him go inside a thicket and seized him and brought him [to Ma'n b.
Zā'idah][245] who sent him to Ibn Dubārah, and he sent him to Wāsiṭ.
Ibn Dubārah marched against 'Abdallāh b. Mu'āwiyah at Iṣṭakhr,
and settled down opposite the city along the river of Iṣṭakhr.[246]
Then Ibn al-Ṣaḥṣaḥ crossed the river with a thousand men. Abān b.
Mu'āwiyah b. Hishām and his Syrian troops, followers of 'Abdallāh
b. Mu'āwiyah who had once supported Sulaymān b. Hishām, met
this force and they engaged in battle. Ibn Nubātah made for the
bridge, and those of the Khārijites who followed Ibn Mu'āwiyah engaged his force. Abān and the Khārijites were routed and a thousand
of them were captured and brought to Ibn Dubārah, who let them
go.[247]

One who was taken that day was 'Abdallāh b. 'Alī b. 'Abdallāh b.
'Abbās. Ibn Dubārah learned his genealogy, and said, "What brought
you to Ibn Mu'āwiyah, when you knew that he was opposing the
Commander of the Faithful?" He replied, "I had a debt, and I paid
it." Then Ḥarb b. Qaṭan al-Kinānī spoke on his behalf, saying, "He is
our sister's son!"[248] Ibn Dubārah gave 'Abdallāh to him, and said, "I
wouldn't have proceeded against a man of Quraysh." Then Ibn Dubārah said, "The man you were with is charged with certain of-
fenses; do you have any knowledge of them?" "Yes," he said, and he
reproached Ibn Mu'āwiyah and accused his friends of sodomy. They
brought Ibn Dubārah youths who were wearing bright mantles dyed
in different colors, more than a hundred boys, and Ibn Dubārah
stood them before the people, so that they might look upon them.
Then Ibn Dubārah sent 'Abdallāh b. 'Alī by post-horse to Ibn Hubay-   [1981]
rah so he might give him his information. Ibn Hubayrah sent him
with Syrian troops to Marwān, and he used to reproach him.

At this time, Ibn Dubārah was in the Kirmān desert pursuing
'Abdallāh b. Mu'āwiyah. Word of Nubātah's death[249] had reached

---

244. See n. 243 above.

245. See n. 243 above.

246. That is, the Pulwār. See LeStrange, *Lands,* 275–77.

247. This was a departure from the usual practice with these intransigents. Ibn
Dubārah seems to have dealt mildly with all the vanquished that day.

248. That is, there were blood relations between them. The Quraysh are a subgroup
of the Kinānah.

249. Nubātah was not killed until 130 (September 11, 747–August 30, 748). See
Ṭabarī, II/3, 2003 *sub anno* 130, and III/1, 4ff *sub anno* 131. The revolt of 'Abdallāh b.

Ibn Hubayrah. He sent Kurab b. Maṣqalah, al-Ḥakam b. Abī Abyaḍ al-ʿAbsī and Ibn Muḥammad al-Sakūnī, all of whom were eloquent speakers, and they spoke in praise of Ibn Ḍubārah. Ibn Hubayrah also wrote to Ibn Ḍubārah to march with his troops to Fārs; then there came a letter from him ordering him to march to Iṣbahān.

In this year Abū Ḥamzah al-Khārijī led the Pilgrimage acting on behalf of ʿAbdallāh b. Yaḥyā Ṭālib al-Ḥaqq, and as a Khārijite manifesting open opposition to Marwān b. Muḥammad.[250]

How Abū Ḥamzah the Khārijite Led the Pilgrimage

According to al-ʿAbbās b. ʿIsā al-ʿUqaylī—Hārūn b. Mūsā al-Farwī—Mūsā b. Kathīr the mawlā of the Sāʿidīs: At the end of 129 (August 747), the pilgrims had not yet gone to ʿArafah[251] when standards appeared (in Mecca) made of black turbans of *ḥirqānī* stuff fixed to the heads of lances, carried by seven hundred men. The people were frightened as soon as they saw them, and asked, "What are you doing, and what do you want?" The men then told them of their opposition to Marwān and the Marwānids, and their disavowal of him. ʿAbd al-Wāḥid b. Sulaymān, who was at that time governor of Madīnah and Mecca,[252] sent messages to them under the truce (of the Pilgrimage), and they replied, "Our minds are resolved upon our pilgrimage, and we begrudge any other business." He made a peace agreement with them on the condition that each party should guarantee the other's safety until the last pilgrims returned from Minā.[253] However, they rose early on the morrow and took their stance as a separate group on Mt. ʿArafah,[254] and ʿAbd al-Wāḥid b.

[1982]

Muʿāwiyah extended over several years. He was ultimately killed by the ʿAbbāsids. See n. 231 above.

250. See Ṭabarī, II/3, 1942, 1943 and 2006–2014; III/1, 11; *FHA*, 168ff; Yaʿqūbī, *Taʾrīkh*, 406, 417.

251. The assembly on Mt. ʿArafah on the ninth day of the Month of Pilgrimage from noon to sunset is the central rite of the pilgrimage. See *EI²* s.v. ʿArafa and Ḥadjdj.

252. His father Sulaymān was the son of the Umayyad Caliph ʿAbd al-Malik.

253. The three days at Minā conclude the pilgrimage season in a mood of celebration and festivity from the 11th to the 13th of the month. See *EI²* s.v. Ḥadjdj. The text then has *yaṣbaḥū*, "they rise at morning," corrected by the Cairo edition to *aṣbaḥū*.

254. As followers of a different caliph, the Khārijites could not follow the rites of Marwān's appointee.

Sulaymān b. ʿAbd al-Malik b. Marwān was pushed aside with the people. When the pilgrims were at Minā, people reproached ʿAbd al-Wāḥid and said, "You made a mistake with them. Had you incited the pilgrims against them, they'd have been no more than an itch on your head." Abū Ḥamzah stayed at Qurayn al-Thaʿālib,[255] and ʿAbd al-Wāḥid at the governor's residence *(manzil al-sulṭān)*. Then ʿAbd al-Wāḥid sent ʿAbdallāh b. al-Ḥasan b. al-Ḥasan b. ʿAlī, Muḥammad b. ʿAbdallāh b. ʿAmr b. ʿUthmān, ʿAbd al-Raḥmān b. al-Qāsim b. Muḥammad b. Abī Bakr and ʿUbaydallāh b. ʿUmar b. Ḥafṣ b. ʿĀṣim b. ʿUmar b. al-Khaṭṭāb as well as Rabīʿah b. ʿAbd al-Raḥmān and such (notables) to visit Abū Ḥamzah. They found him wearing a rough cotton waist-wrapper. ʿAbdallāh b. al-Ḥasan (the ʿAlawī) and Muḥammad b. ʿAbdallāh (the ʿUthmānī) presented them to him, and he asked for their own genealogies, so they traced their lineage for him. He looked sternly into their faces and showed his aversion.[256] He then asked ʿAbd al-Raḥmān b. Qāsim (the Bakrī) and ʿUbaydallāh b. ʿUmar (the ʿUmarī), and they traced their lineage for him. He was cheerful toward them, and smiling in their faces, he said, "By God, we only became Khārijites that we might follow the course of both your forefathers!" At this, ʿAbdallāh b. Ḥasan (the ʿAlawī) told him, "And by God, we didn't come out so that you could show your favor to some of our forefathers; the amīr sent us to you with a message, and Rabīʿah will inform you of it!"

When Rabīʿah mentioned "breach of agreement," Balj and Abrahah, who were two of his officers, said, "Now! Now!" But Abū Ḥamzah turned to them and said, "God forbid that we should break our agreement or detain you. By God, I would not do it, though this neck of mine were to be cut. However, you are breaking the truce that is between us and you." When he had refused them, they left and informed ʿAbd al-Wāḥid. When the pilgrims left Minā, ʿAbd al-Wāḥid was in the first party. He left Mecca to Abū Ḥamzah, who entered it without a fight. [1983]

ʿAbbās—Hārūn—Yaʿqūb b. Ṭalḥah al-Laythī recited some verses in which ʿAbd al-Wāḥid was satirized. He said, "They are by some poet whose name I don't remember:"

---

255. For Qurayn al-Thaʿālib, see Azraqī, I, 410, 414.

256. The Khārijites regarded both ʿUthmān and ʿAlī as grave sinners. For them, only Abū Bakr and ʿUmar among the first four caliphs were "rightly guided shaykhs."

> There visited the pilgrims a gang who contravened
> God's own religion, so ʿAbd al-Wāḥid fled.
>
> He left his women and his amirate running,
> striking the ground like a runaway camel.
>
> Had his father stripped his bone of flesh,
> his origin had been purer, due the father's root.

Then ʿAbd al-Wāḥid went on until he entered Madīnah and called for the registry *(dīwān)*. He called up the people in a levy, and gave each of them a ten dirham increase in their pay. According to ʿAbbās—Hārūn—Abū Ḍamrah Anas b. ʿIyāḍ: He was among those who were registered, but then his name was erased. He also said, "More than one of our companions told me that ʿAbd al-Wāḥid appointed ʿAbd al-ʿAzīz b. ʿAbdallāh b. ʿAmr b. ʿUthmān to lead the people, and they went out. When they were at the Ḥarrah[257] they came upon slaughtered camels, and passed on."

[1984] ʿAbd al-Wāḥid b. Sulaymān b. ʿAbd al-Malik b. Marwān led the Pilgrimage this year, according to Aḥmad b. Thābit—someone—Isḥāq b. ʿĪsā—Abū Maʿshar al-Sindī. Muḥammad b. ʿUmar al-Wāqidī and others say the same. ʿAbd al-Wāḥid was governor of Mecca and Madīnah. The governor of Iraq was Yazīd b. ʿUmar b. Hubayrah. According to what is mentioned, al-Ḥajjāj b. ʿĀṣim al-Muḥāribī was in charge of the judiciary at Kūfah, while at Baṣrah it was ʿAbbād b. Manṣūr. Khurāsān was ruled by Naṣr b. Sayyār, and there was civil war.

---

257. The basalt desert outside of Madīnah. See *EI²* s.v. al-Ḥarra.

The
Events of the Year

130

(SEPTEMBER 11, 747–AUGUST 30, 748)

Among the events of this year was Abū Muslim's entry into the walled city of Marw and his occupation of the Government House (Dār al-Imārah) there, and the agreement of ʿAlī b. Judayʿ al-Kirmānī to join him in fighting Naṣr b. Sayyār.[258]

How Abū Muslim Entered the Walled City of Marw

Abū al-Khaṭṭāb reported:[259] Abū Muslim's entrance into the walled city of Marw and his occupation of the Government House where the governors of Khurāsān reside occurred on Thursday, the ninth of Jumādā II 130 (February 14, 748). The reason for ʿAlī b. Judayʿ al-Kirmānī's move to Abū Muslim was as follows. Sulaymān b. Kathīr was camped opposite ʿAlī b. Kirmānī when the latter made a pact with Naṣr to fight Abū Muslim. Sulaymān b. Kathīr said to ʿAlī, "Abū Muslim says, 'Aren't you reluctant to make up with Naṣr b. Sayyār, when only yesterday he killed your father and crucified him? I had not reckoned you would join with Naṣr b. Sayyār [even] to pray in one mosque with him.'" At this, ʿAlī b. al-Kirmānī's zeal

[1985]

---

258. See *Akhbār al-Dawlah,* 310ff; Ibn Khayyāṭ, I, 412.
259. That is Ḥamzah b. ʿAlī b. Muḥfiz al-Rāwī. See index to Cairo edition, X, 230.

was stirred, and he went back on his decision; the truce of the Arabs thus came apart.

When the truce came apart, Naṣr sent to Abū Muslim asking him to come in on the side of the Muḍar, while the Rabīʿah and the Qaḥṭān sent similar requests on their own behalf. They had exchanged messages on this for some days, when Abū Muslim told them to let delegations from both factions come to him so that he might choose one or the other. They did so. But Abū Muslim ordered the (ʿAbbāsid) Shīʿah to choose the Rabīʿah and the Qaḥṭān, since authority *(sulṭān)* was vested in Muḍar and it was they who were governing for Marwān al-Jaʿdī[260] and the murderers of Yaḥyā b. Zayd.[261] The two delegations then appeared. In the delegation of Muḍar there were ʿAqīl b. Maʿqil b. Ḥassān al-Laythī, ʿUbaydallāh b. ʿAbd Rabbihi al-Laythī, al-Khaṭṭāb b. Muḥriz al-Sulamī and others among their leading men. The delegation of Qaḥṭān were ʿUthmān b. al-Kirmānī, Muḥammad b. al-Muthannā, Sawrah b. Muḥammad b. ʿAzīz al-Kindī and other leading men of theirs. Abū Muslim told ʿUthmān b. al-Kirmānī and his companions to go into the orchard of al-Muḥtafiz where carpets and cushions were spread for them. They seated themselves there while Abū Muslim took his place in a room of the house of al-Muḥtafiz. Permission was given to ʿAqīl b. Maʿqil and his companions from the delegation of Muḍar, and they entered. There were seventy men of the Shīʿah[262] in the room with Abū Muslim. He read aloud a document he had written for the Shīʿah, that said they should choose one side or the other. When he had finished reading the document, Sulaymān b. Kathīr rose and spoke. He was an eloquent orator, and he chose ʿAlī b. al-Kirmānī and his followers. Then Abū Manṣūr Ṭalḥah b. Zurayq the *naqīb* stood up. He was also an accomplished speaker, and he said much the same as Sulaymān b. Kathīr. Mazyad b. Shaqīq al-Sulamī[263] then rose and

[1986]

---

260. That is, the Caliph. The name "Jaʿdī" can mean "curly-haired." This is most often used to discredit Marwān.

261. Yaḥyā b. Zayd b. ʿAlī b. Ḥusayn b. ʿAlī was the son of the Zayd from whom the Zaydī Shīʿah take their name, who had been killed in an uprising in Kūfah in 122(740). Yaḥyā fled to Khurāsān and hid in Balkh for three years and was slain in 126 (744). His death aroused great sympathy in Khurāsān. There had been links between him and the ʿAbbāsids, and Abū Muslim's acting as his avenger was a popular move. See Wellhausen, *Arab Kingdom*, 338.

262. Presumably the seventy *naqībs* and *duʿāt*.

263. Mazyad b. Shaqīq was a *naqīb*. See *Akhbār al-Dawlah*, 217.

said, "Muḍar are the slayers of the Prophet's family, the supporters of the Banū Umayyah and the party of Marwān al-Jaʿdī. Our blood is on their necks, our possessions are in their hands, and the consequences (of their acts) await them. Naṣr b. Sayyār is Marwān's governor for Khurāsān, who carries out his orders, and calls for allegiance to him in his minbar, and calls him 'Commander of the Faithful.' Before God, we are innocent of all that, or that Marwān should command the Faithful or that Naṣr should judge what is guidance or right behavior. We have chosen ʿAlī b. al-Kirmānī and his followers from the Qaḥṭān and the Rabīʿah." Then the seventy who had gathered in the room agreed with the words of Mazyad b. Shaqīq.

The delegation of Muḍar then got up humiliated and distressed, and Abū Muslim sent al-Qāsim b. Mujāshiʿ with horsemen to escort them back to where they were safe, while the delegation of ʿAlī b. al-Kirmānī returned full of joy and triumph. Abū Muslim stayed at Alīn for twenty-nine days, and from there went back to his camp at Mākhuwān. He told the Shīʿah to build dwellings for themselves and to lay in supplies for the winter, since God had spared them from a united Arab front against them, and at their hands, had led the Arabs to disunity, as He had preordained in His might. After journeying from Alīn, Abū Muslim entered Mākhuwān on Thursday, midway through Ṣafar 130 (October 25, 747). He stayed at Mākhuwān three months, or ninety days, and entered the walled city of Marw on Thursday, the ninth night of Jumādā I that same year (January 26, 748).

The walled city of Marw was then held by Naṣr b. Sayyār, since he was the governor of Khurāsān. ʿAlī b. al-Kirmānī now sent a message to Abū Muslim, "Enter the walled city and my tribe with me will also enter, and thus we shall gain control of the walled town." Abū Muslim sent this reply, "I fear that you will join with Naṣr b. Sayyār to fight me, but go on; enter and engage him and his followers in combat." ʿAlī b. al-Kirmānī did so, and Abū Muslim sent Abū ʿAlī Shibl b. Ṭahmān the *naqīb* with a force. They came inside the walled city, settled in the palace of the Bukhārakhudā and sent word to Abū Muslim to come. Abū Muslim came into the city from the camp at Mākhuwān. Over his vanguard he put Asīd b. ʿAbdallāh al-Khuzāʿī, Mālik b. Haytham al-Khuzāʿī led the right flank, and al-Qāsim b. Mujāshiʿ al-Tamīmī the left. He proceeded until he was in-

[1987]

side the walls, where the two factions were fighting each other. He then ordered them to desist, reciting the words from God's Book, "And he entered the city at a time when its people were careless, and found there two men fighting; the one was of his own Shīʿah, and the other was one of his enemies."[264] Abū Muslim then went on to the Government Palace of Marw, where the governors of Khurāsān stayed. This was on Thursday, the ninth of Jumādā I (January 27, 748).

The next day, Friday, the tenth of Jumādā (January 28, 748), Naṣr b. Sayyār fled Marw, leaving the city to Abū Muslim. When he entered the walled city of Marw, Abū Muslim ordered Abū Manṣūr Ṭalḥah b. Zurayq to administer the oath of allegiance to the forces of the Hāshimiyyah.[265] Abū Manṣūr was an eloquent man of noble mien, skilled in speech, and learned in the polemics of the Hāshimiyyah and their esoteric doctrines. He was one of the twelve *na-qībs* whom Muḥammad b. ʿAlī had selected from among the seventy who had responded favorably to him when he sent his emissary to Khurāsān in 103 or 104 (721 or 722). Muḥammad b. ʿAlī had instructed the emissary to have them swear allegiance to the Chosen One *(al-Riḍā)* but not to specify anyone by name.

[1988]

He set patterns of action for his emissary, and described what justice should be like. The latter then went out to them and propagandized secretly, and people responded to him. When their numbers reached seventy, he took twelve of them as *naqībs*. From the Khuzāʿah, Sulaymān b. Kathīr, Mālik b. al-Haytham, Ziyād b. Ṣāliḥ, Ṭalḥah b. Zurayq and ʿAmr b. Aʿyān. From the Ṭayyʾ, Qaḥṭabah whose name was Ziyād b. Shabīb b. Khālid b. Maʿdān. From the Tamīm, Mūsā b. Kaʿb called Abū ʿUyaynah, Lāhiz b. Qurayẓ and al-Qāsim b. Mujashiʿ, all from the Banū Imruʾ al-Qays, and Aslam b. Sallām, called Abū Sallām.[266] From Bakr b. Wāʾil there were Abū Dāwud

---

264. Qur. 18:15.

265. The Hāshimiyyah in Khurāsān are almost certainly to be identified with the Rāwandiyyah. They believed that Abū Hāshim b. Muḥammad b. ʿAlī b. Abī Ṭalib at his death, ca. 98 (716-717) had transferred the Imāmate to Muḥammad b. ʿAlī the ʿAbbāsid. Most of his following, based in Iraq, had transferred their allegiance to the ʿAbbāsids. This Iraqī group represented only one part of the ʿAbbāsid Shīʿah but it was the inner core, in which the Khurāsānī following was subsumed. See *EI²* s.v. Hāshimiyya.

266. The *Akhbār al-Dawlah*, 282, 288, 291, mentions an Aslam b. Abī Sallām who was active in the ʿAbbāsid cause. He is, however, not listed among the *naqībs*.

Khālid b. Ibrāhīm, the brother of Sadūs, of the Banū ʿAmr b. Shaybān
and Abū ʿAlī al-Harawī. Elsewhere it is stated that Shibl b. Ṭahmān
was in place of ʿAmr b. Aʿyan, and that ʿIsā b. Kaʿb or Abū al-Najm
ʿImrān b. Ismaʿīl was in the place of Abū ʿAlī al-Harawī, who was a
relative of Abū Muslim's wife.[267]

The only one of the *naqībs* whose father was still alive was Abū
Manṣūr Ṭalḥah b. Zurayq b. Asʿad known as Abū Zaynab al-Khuzāʿī.
He had seen the campaign of ʿAbd al-Raḥmān b. Muḥammad b. al-
Ashʿath, and had been a comrade of al-Muhallab b. Abī Ṣufrah in
frontier raids *(maghāzī)*. Abū Muslim used to consult him on matters, and ask him about his experiences in wars and raids. He would
call him by his *kunyā* of Abū Manṣūr, and would say, "Abū Manṣūr,
what do you say? What do you think?"

Abū al-Khaṭṭāb reported: One who was there when Abū Manṣūr   [1989]
administered the oath of allegiance to the Hāshimiyyah told us he
said, "I ask you for allegiance to the Book of God, may He be exalted
and glorified, and to the *sunnah* of His prophet, God bless him and
give him peace, and to obey the Chosen One from the family of
God's messenger. You must swear to do this by solemn oath and
covenant with God, that [otherwise] your wives will be divorced and
your slaves set free and you must go on foot to the House of God.
Pledge that you will not ask for wage or pay until your superiors
[*wulāt*] initiate it for you. Even if the enemy of one of you should be
beneath his foot, you will not stir up strife except by the order of
your superiors." When Abū Muslim had imprisoned Salm b. Aḥwaz,
Yūnus b. ʿAbd Rabbihi, ʿAqīl b. Maʿqil and Manṣūr b. Abī al-Khirqāʾ
and his companions, he consulted Abū Manṣūr. He told him, "Make

---

267. If one substitutes the replacements indicated by Ṭabarī, his list is identical to
that of the *Akhbār al-ʿAbbās*, 215ff. This list, as it stands in this text of Ṭabarī, is
identical to the first group of *naqībs* allegedly formed at the turn of the first Islamic
century. See Ṭabarī, II/3, 1358 *sub anno* 100. The earlier account of Ṭabarī is apparently recalled here. This would imply that there were two lists of *naqībs*: one drawn
up in 100 (718-719) and the other drawn up by Bukayr b. Māhān after the death of
Muḥammad b. ʿAlī in 125 (November 4, 742-October 23, 743). It would have been re-
markable that so many *naqībs* of the Khurāsān apparatus continued to be active in
their positions thirty years after their initial recruitment to the ʿAbbāsid cause. It
may well be that the early list mentioned by Ṭabarī *sub anno* 100 (August 3, 718-July
23, 719) is a backformation to give the ʿAbbāsids an active revolutionary presence in
that region from almost the beginning of Muḥammad b. ʿAlī's imāmate, and that the
likes of Sulaymān b. Kathīr, Qaḥṭabah b. Shabīb and the others only later became part
of a formal revolutionary organization. (J.L.)

your whip the sword, and your prison the grave." So Abū Muslim brought them out and killed them. Their number was twenty-four men.

According to 'Alī b. Muḥammad—al-Ṣabbaḥ the mawlā of Jibrīl—Maslamah b. Yaḥyā: Abū Muslim appointed Khālid b. 'Uthmān chief of his guard; Mālik b. al-Haytham was made chief of security; al-Qāsim b. Mujāshi' was put in charge of the judiciary; and Kāmil b. Muẓaffar was in charge of the registry (dīwān).[268] He gave each man a salary (rizq) of four thousand dirhams. Abū Muslim stayed in his camp at Mākhuwān for three months and then marched by night with a large force for the camp of Ibn al-Kirmānī. Lāhiz b. Qurayẓ had command of his right, al-Qāsim b. Mujāshi' had the left, and Abū Naṣr Mālik b. al-Haytham commanded the vanguard. He left Abū 'Abd al-Raḥmān al-Mākhuwānī in charge of his fortified camp. By the early morning, Abū Muslim was in the camp of Shaybān, so Naṣr feared that Abū Muslim and Ibn al-Kirmānī would join together to fight him. He therefore sent a message to Abū Muslim proposing that the latter enter the city of Marw and he would be reconciled with him. Abū Muslim responded favorably, so Naṣr was reconciled toward Abū Muslim. All that same day, Naṣr had exchanged messages with Ibn Aḥwaz, while Abū Muslim was in the camp of Shaybān. The next morning Naṣr and Ibn al-Kirmānī engaged in combat, and Abū Muslim came up to enter the city of Marw. He warded off Naṣr's cavalry as well as that of Ibn al-Kirmānī, and entered the city on the seventh or ninth of Rabī' II 130 (January 12 or 14, 748) reciting the verse, "And he entered the city, at a time when its people were careless, and found there two men fighting; the one was of his own Shī'ah, and the other was one of his enemies. Then the one that was of his Shī'ah cried to him to aid him against the one that was of his enemies; so Moses struck him and killed him, and said, 'This is of Satan's doing; surely he is a misleading and manifest enemy!' "[269]

According to 'Alī—Abū al-Dhayyāl and Mufaḍḍal al-Ḍabbī:

[1990]

---

268. That is, Abū Muslim created elements of a shadow government even before he displaced the Umayyads from rule in Khurāsān. The expanded shadow governments in Khurāsān and Iraq (under Abū Salamah) then became the 'Abbāsid government in place and tended to ease the transition between the end of the Umayyads and the establishment of their successors. See Sharon, 'Alīyat, 176–84. (J.L.)

269. Qur. 28:15.

When Abū Muslim entered the city of Marw, Naṣr told his follow-ers, "I see that this man's strength has grown and that the people have come running to him. I have made a truce with him, and what he wants will be, so let us get out of this city and leave him here." Then they differed, some saying "yes" and some "no". At last he said, "You will surely remember what I said." He told his particular friends among the Muḍar, "Go off to Abū Muslim, meet him, and obtain whatever terms you can from him." Abū Muslim sent Lāhiz b. Qurayz to Naṣr to summon him, and Lāhiz quoted the Qur'ānic verse, "The Council are conspiring to kill you."[270] He recited the verses before that as well. Naṣr understood, and he told his slave, "Prepare my ablution for me." He rose as if he were going to make his ablutions, went into an orchard, slipped out of it and mounted a horse and fled.[271]

According to ʿAlī—Abū al-Dhayyāl—Iyās b. Ṭalḥah b. Ṭalḥah: I was with my father, and my paternal uncle had gone to Abū Muslim to offer him his allegiance but had delayed until I prayed the after-noon prayer. There was little daylight left and we were waiting for him. We had prepared dinner for him, and I was sitting with my fa-ther, when Naṣr suddenly passed by us on a horse which I knew was the best in his palace. With him were his chamberlain and al-Ḥakam b. Numaylah al-Numayrī. My father said, "Surely he's fleeing; no one is with him, and there is no spear or banner carried before him." He passed by us and barely saluted us. When he'd gone past, he struck his horse, and al-Ḥakam b. Numaylah called to his slaves, and they mounted and followed him.

According to ʿAlī—Abū al-Dhayyāl—Iyās: Our place was four farsakhs (24 km) from Marw, and Naṣr passed by us after dark. The people of the village began to clamor and ran away. My family and my brothers said, "Get out, don't be killed!" They wept, so I left with my father's brother, al-Muhallab b. Iyās, and we caught up with Naṣr after part of the night had passed. He had forty men with him. His horse had stopped, and he had dismounted from it. Bishr b. Bisṭam b. ʿImrān b. al-Faḍl al-Burjumī put him on his own horse. Then Naṣr said, "I don't feel safe from pursuit. Who's going to lead

[1991]

---

270. Qur. 28:20.
271. Dīnawarī, 363, indicates that Naṣr had agreed to join Abū Muslim and had in fact been given a surety. Nevertheless, he fled.

us?" ʿAbdallāh b. ʿArʿarah al-Ḍabbī said, "I'll lead you." "You're the man to do it," Naṣr told him. He hurried us through that night, until we stopped at dawn at a well in the desert twenty *farsakh*s (120 km) or so away. We were six hundred now, and we traveled all day and dismounted at the afternoon prayer within sight of the houses and strongholds of Sarakhs. By now we were fifteen hundred. I went off with my uncle to a friend of ours from the Banū Ḥanīfah called Miskīn, and we slept through the night there without eating anything. We woke up next morning and he brought us a dish of gruel of which we ate. We were very hungry, not having eaten for a day and a night. Then the people gathered together, and they had become three thousand. We stopped at Sarakhs two days, and when no one came after us, Naṣr went on to Ṭūs and told them the news about Abū Muslim. He stopped there for fifteen days, and then moved on, as did we, to Naysābūr and stayed there.

Now Abū Muslim had settled in the governor's palace after Naṣr [1992] fled Marw. Ibn al-Kirmānī had come and had entered Marw when Abū Muslim did. Abū Muslim said when Naṣr escaped, "Naṣr considers me a wizard, but by God, he's one."

Another source that I have not mentioned says this on the matter of Naṣr and Ibn al-Kirmānī and Shaybān al-Ḥarūrī: Abū Muslim moved in 130 (747–748) from his camp at the village of Sulaymān b. Kathīr to a village called Mākhuwān and camped there. He sought the aid of ʿAlī b. Judayʿ al-Kirmānī and his Yamanī followers, and he also sought help from Naṣr b. Sayyār and his followers. He sent messages to both sides, showing each of them that he was prepared to make peace with them and come to an agreement with them, and ready to obey them. ʿAlī b. Judayʿ accepted this, and acted as Abū Muslim wanted him to by entering into a pact with him. When Abū Muslim was assured by ʿAli b. Judayʿ's pledge to him, he wrote to Naṣr b. Sayyār to send a delegation to be present when he and his companions discussed the promise he had made to side with Naṣr. He sent a similar message to ʿAlī b. Judayʿ. This source describes how the leaders of the Shīʿah chose the Yaman over the Muḍar, much as it is described by the man whose account we have mentioned above in this book, and he observes that when Abū Muslim sent Shibl b. Ṭahmān with others to Marw to occupy the palace of the Bukhārākhudāh, he only sent him as a reinforcement for ʿAlī b. Al-Kirmānī. He says (that) Abū Muslim and all his followers went

from his fortified camp at Mākhuwān to ʿAlī b. Judayʿ. The chief
men *(ashrāf)* of the Yaman were there with ʿAlī and his brother
ʿUthmān, as well as their allies of the Rabīʿah. When Abū Muslim
was opposite the walled city of Marw, ʿUthmān b. Judayʿ and the
chief men of the Yaman and Rabīʿah received him with a great body
of horsemen. He entered the camp of ʿAlī b. al-Kirmānī and Shaybān   [1993]
b. Salamah al-Ḥarūrī along with the *naqībs*, and waited at ʿAlī b.
Judayʿ's chamber. ʿAlī entered and agreed to (the alliance), and gave
him and all those with him guarantees of safety. They then went together to the chamber of Shaybān, who was saluted in those days as
Commander of the Faithful (that is, Caliph). Abū Muslim told ʿAlī
to go sit beside Shaybān, informing ʿAlī that it was not lawful for
him to salute Shaybān (in this way). Abū Muslim wanted to greet
ʿAlī as "Amīr," so that Shaybān would think that he was saluting
Shaybān. ʿAlī did this, and then Abū Muslim went in and said,
"Peace be to you, Amīr." He was gracious to Shaybān and made
much of him. Then Abū Muslim took his leave and stayed two
nights at the palace of Muḥammad b. al-Ḥasan al-Azdī. He then returned to his entrenched camp at Mākhuwān and stayed there three
months. He moved from Mākhuwān to Marw on the seventh of
Rabīʿ II 130 (January 12, 748) leaving Abū ʿAbd al-Karīm al-
Mākhuwānī behind in charge of his army. Abū Muslim appointed
Lāhiz b. Qurayẓ to command his right wing, Qāsim b. al-Mujāshiʿ
his left, and Mālik b. al-Haytham over his vanguard. Marching by
night, he came early in the morning to the gates of Marw, and sent
word to ʿAlī b. Judayʿ to send his cavalry. When he came to the gate
of the governor's palace, he found the two factions engaged in a violent battle within the walled city. He sent messengers to them to
cease fighting and each go to their own camp, and they complied. He
then sent Lāhiz b. Qurayẓ, Quraysh b. Shaqīq, ʿAbdallāh b. al-Bakhtarī and Dāwud b. Karrāz to Naṣr, summoning him to the Book of
God and obedience to the Chosen One, from the family of
Muḥammad. When Naṣr saw what the Yaman and the Rabīʿah and
the non-Arabs were doing, and that he was powerless against them,
he saw no way out but to show his acceptance of the message sent   [1994]
him, that is, to come to Abū Muslim and pay his allegiance. He delayed until evening, due to the thoughts of faithlessness and of flight
which troubled him. He then ordered his followers to leave that
night for a place where they would be safe. However, it was not easy

for them to leave that night and Salm b. Aḥwaz told him, "It is not feasible for us to leave tonight, but we shall leave the next." When dawn came, Abū Muslim began to array his cavalry squadrons, and kept at this into the afternoon. He sent Lāhiz b. Qurayẓ, Quraysh b. Shaqīq, ʿAbdallāh b. al-Bakhtarī, Dāwud b. Karrāz and a number of the non-Arabs of the Shīʿah to Naṣr. They went in to see him, and Naṣr said, "How evil is what you return for." Lāhiz replied, "There is no way out of this for you." Then Naṣr said, "Well then, if there is no way out, I shall make my ablutions and go out to him. I shall send a messenger to Abū Muslim, and if this is his idea and his command I shall go to him, and may it be pleasant in his sight. I shall ready myself until my messenger returns." Then Naṣr stood, and when he stood, Lāhiz recited this verse of the Qurʾān, "The council are conspiring to kill you; depart, for I am one of your sincere advisers."[272] Naṣr went into his dwelling and told them he would wait for his messenger's return from Abū Muslim. As soon as night fell, he slipped out from behind his chamber with Tamīm his son and al-Ḥakam b. Numaylah al-Numayrī, his chamberlain, and his wife, and they fled. When Lāhiz and his companions missed him, they entered his dwelling and discovered that he had left. When this came to (the ears of) Abū Muslim, he went to the camp of Naṣr and took his trusted followers and their chief men and tied their hands behind their backs. One of these was Salm b. Aḥwaz, Naṣr's chief of security. The others were al-Bakhtarī his secretary, and two of his sons; Yūnus b. ʿAbd Rabbihi, Muḥammad b. Qaṭan, Mujāhid b. Yaḥyā b. Ḥuḍayn, [Naṣr b. Idrīs, Manṣūr b. ʿUmar b. Alī al-Khirqāʾ, ʿAqīl b. Maʿqil al-Laythī, Sayyār b. ʿUmar al-Sulamī, and leading men of the Muḍar]. He put them in irons [and put ʿIsā b. Aʿyan in charge of them].[273] They stayed in confinement with him until Abū Muslim ordered them all put to death.

[1995]

Naṣr stopped at Sarakhs with the Muḍar who had followed him, who numbered three thousand. Abū Muslim and ʿAlī b. Judayʿ set out in pursuit of him, and followed him all that night, until at daybreak they came to a village called Naṣrāniyyah. They found that

---

272. Qur. 28:20.
273. These passages in brackets are taken from the Cairo edition and replace lacunae in the text.

Naṣr had left his wife, al-Marzubānah, behind in the village and (thus) saved himself.

Abū Muslim and ʿAlī went back to Marw, and Abū Muslim asked those whom he had sent to Naṣr, "What made him suspicious of you?" "We do not know," they replied. "Did one of you say anything?" he asked. They replied, "Lāhiz recited this verse of the Qurʾān, 'The council are conspiring to kill you.'" "That is what put him to flight," Abū Muslim said. Then he asked, "Lāhiz, would you corrupt religion?" and cut off his head.

This year Shaybān b. Salamah al-Ḥarūrī was killed.

The Death of Shaybān b. Salamah the Khārijite and the Reason for It

According to what has been reported the reason for his death is as follows. ʿAlī b. Judayʿ and Shaybān had joined forces to fight Naṣr b. Sayyār because of Shaybān's hostility to Naṣr. This was because he was one of Marwān b. Muḥammad's governors, while Shaybān held the opinions of the Khārijites. ʿAlī b. Judayʿ was opposed to Naṣr because ʿAlī was a Yamanī and Naṣr was a Muḍarī and (because) Naṣr had killed ʿAlī's father and crucified him, and because of the tribal feeling (ʿaṣabiyyah) that separated the two factions, Yaman and Muḍar. When ʿAlī b. al-Kirmānī entered an agreement with Abū Muslim and Shaybān abandoned them, Shaybān left Marw, since he knew he could not fight Abū Muslim and ʿAlī (combined against him). Meanwhile Naṣr had fled Marw (and gone to Sarakhs).[274]

[1996]

According to [ʿAlī b. Muḥammad—Abū Ḥafṣ and] al-Ḥa [san b. Rashīd and Abū al-Dhayyāl]: When [the period of truce between Abū Muslim and Shaybān][275] was over, Abū Muslim sent to Shaybān asking him for his allegiance. Shaybān said, "It is I who call on you for allegiance." Abū Muslim then sent him this message, "If you will not live under our rule, then leave the place where you are dwelling." At this, Shaybān sent to ʿAlī al-Kirmānī asking for help, but he refused to give it. Shaybān thus went to Sarakhs, where a large number of the Bakr b. Wāʾil joined him. Abū Muslim sent him

---

274. See n. 273 above.
275. See n. 273 above.

nine men of the tribe of Azd, among them al-Muntajiʿ b. al-Zubayr, calling on him to join their movement and asking him to stop what he was doing. Shaybān sent back an answer, and then arrested Abū Muslim's messengers and put them in prison. At this, Abū Muslim wrote to Bassām b. Ibrāhīm, the mawlā of the Banū Layth at Abīward, ordering him to march against Shaybān and fight him. Bassām did so, and put him to flight and pursued him into the town. Shaybān was killed along with a number of the Bakr b. Wāʾil. Someone told Abū Muslim, "Bassām is taking revenge for his father, and slays the innocent with the guilty." Abū Muslim wrote him to come to Marw, and he did, leaving a man behind in charge of his forces.

[1997] According to ʿAlī—al-Mufaḍḍal: When Shaybān was killed, a man of Bakr b. Wāʾil called Khafāf came upon the messengers whom Abū Muslim had sent to Shaybān. They were imprisoned in a house, and he took them out and killed them. It is also said that Abū Muslim sent a force on his behalf against Shaybān, headed by Khuzaymah b. Khāzim and Bassām b. Ibrāhīm.

In this year Abū Muslim killed ʿAlī and ʿUthmān the sons of Judayʿ al-Kirmānī.

Why Abū Muslim Killed the Sons of Judayʿ al-Kirmānī

The reason for this, according to what is said is that Abū Muslim had sent Mūsā b. Kaʿb against Abīward. He captured the city, wrote of this to Abū Muslim, and sent Abū Dāwūd to Balkh, where Ziyād b. ʿAbd al-Raḥmān al-Qushayrī was. When word that Abū Dāwūd was making for Balkh reached Ziyād, he left there for Jūzjān together with troops of Balkh, Tirmidh, and others from the districts of Ṭukhāristan. When Abū Dāwud drew near, they fled back to Tirmidh, and Abū Dāwud entered the city of Balkh. Abū Muslim wrote Abū Dāwud ordering him to come to him, and sent Yaḥyā b. Nuʿaym Abū al-Maylāʾ to replace him [at Balkh. Abū Dāwud left][276] and a letter from Abū Muslim came to him on the way, ordering him to turn back. He did, and Abū al-Maylāʾ advanced toward him. Yaḥyā b. Nuʿaym al-Maylāʾ then wrote to Ziyād b. ʿAbd al-Raḥmān al-Qushayrī that they should join forces, and Ziyād responded favorably. Ziyād then returned, with Muslim b. ʿAbd al-

---

276. This passage is taken from the Cairo edition and replaces a lacuna in the text.

Rahmān b. Muslim al-Bāhilī, 'Īsā b. Zur'ah al-Sulamī and the inhabitants of Balkh and Tirmidh and the kings of Ṭukhāristan and the districts on both sides of the river (Oxus). Ziyād and his followers camped one *farsakh* (6 km) from the city of Balkh. Yaḥyā b. Nu'aym Abū Maylā' came out to him with his own followers, and they joined forces. In full accord, the Muḍar, the Yaman, the Rabī'ah and the non-Arabs with them, as well, agreed to fight the black-clad warriors. They gave the command to Muqātil b. Ḥayyān al-Nabaṭī, disliking that it should go to anyone from the three tribal divisions. Abū Muslim now ordered Abū Dāwud to al-'Ūd,[277] and Abū Dāwud proceeded together with his men until they gathered at the river Sarjanān. Ziyād b. 'Abd al-Raḥmān and his men had already sent Abū Sa'īd al-Qurashī as a lookout in the area between 'Ūd and a village called Amadiyān, lest the followers of Abū Dāwud come upon them from the rear, and Abū Sa'īd's flags and banners were the ('Abbāsid) black. [1998]

When Abū Dāwud and Ziyād gathered with their followers in battle formation, Abū Sa'īd al-Qurashī ordered his own men to join Ziyād and his followers from their rear. They turned and came out behind them from the road to 'Ūd with black banners, so Ziyād's men supposed that this was a surprise attack from Abū Dāwud's side. The battle between the two factions had already been joined, and Ziyād and his followers fled, while Abū Dāwud pursued them. Most of Ziyād's followers plunged into the river Sarjanān, while the majority of his men who stayed behind were killed. Abū Dāwud settled at their camp, taking possession of all that was in it. He did not follow Ziyād or [his followers. Most of those who did pursue them were the forward units of the vanguard][278] of Abū Dāwūd's cavalry, but [only as far] as the city [of Balkh].[279] Ziyād and Yaḥyā and those with them went on to Tirmidh, while Abū Dāwud stayed all that day and part of the next where he was and did not enter the city of Balkh, plundering the goods of those killed at the Sarjanān and of the Arabs and others who had fled. Balkh was now secure for Abū Dāwud. [1999]

Abū Muslim then wrote Abū Dāwud ordering him to come to

---

277. A large village three *farsakh*s (18 km) from Balkh. See text apparatus n. C.
278. See n. 276 above.
279. See n. 276 above.

him, and sent al-Naḍr b. Ṣubayḥ al-Murrī to govern Balkh. Abū Dāwud came, and he and Abū Muslim agreed to separate ʿAlī and ʿUthmān the two sons of al-Kirmānī. Abū Muslim thus sent ʿUthmān to serve as governor of Balkh, and when he got there he appointed al-Furāfiṣah b. Zuhayr al-ʿAbsī as his deputy in the city. Meanwhile the Muḍar advanced from Tirmidh, under the command of Muslim b. ʿAbd al-Raḥmān al-Bāhilī. The forces confronted each other, while ʿUthmān's followers were at a village between Barūqān and Dastajird.[280] They fought each other in a violent battle, and ʿUthmān b. Judayʿ's followers were routed while the Muḍar and Muslim b. ʿAbd al-Raḥmān took possession of the city of Balkh, driving out al-Furāfiṣah. The news reached ʿUthmān b. Judayʿ and al-Naḍr b. Ṣubayḥ while they were at Marwarrudh, so they marched against them. Word of their approach reached Ziyād b. ʿAbd al-Raḥmān's men, and they fled that night. Al-Naḍr was slow to pursue them, hoping they would get away. ʿUthmān b. Judayʿ's men then encountered them, and they engaged in a violent battle. ʿUthmān's forces were routed, many of his men were killed, and the Muḍar made their way to their friends.

Abū Dāwud returned from Marw to Balkh, and Abū Muslim, accompanied by ʿAlī b. Judayʿ, went to Naysābūr. Abū Muslim had agreed with Abū Dāwud that he would kill ʿAlī while Abū Dāwud would kill ʿUthmān on the same day. So, when Abū Dāwud arrived at Balkh, he sent ʿUthmān as governor to Khuttal,[281] along with his [2000] troops from the Yaman and Rabīʿah of Marw and of Balkh. When he left Balkh, Abū Dāwud left [in pursuit of him, and caught up with him on the banks of the Wakhshāb at Wakhsh][282] in the land of Khuttal. Abū Dāwud then fell upon ʿUthmān and his followers. He imprisoned them all, and bound them and beheaded them. Abū Muslim killed ʿAlī b. al-Kirmānī that same day. He had already told ʿAlī to name for him his special friends, so that he might award

---

280. These were villages in the vicinity of Balkh. Dastajird was probably the village known as Dastajird Jumūkiyān. See Yāqūt, *Muʿjam*, I, 597; II, 573.

281. Khuttal was the region between the Wakhsh river on the west and the Upper Oxus river, or Jaryāb, on the east. To the south, Khuttal was bounded by the Oxus, or Amū Daryā. See LeStrange, *Lands*, 437–38.

282. This passage is taken from the Cairo edition and fills in a lacuna in the text. For the Wakhshāb and Wakhsh, see LeStrange, *Lands*, 434–35.

them positions of trust and give them presents and raiment. ʿAlī had given him the names, so he now put all of them to death.

In this year, Qaḥṭabah b. Shabīb came to Abū Muslim in Khurāsān from Ibrāhīm b. Muḥammad b. ʿAlī. Qaḥṭabah brought the standard which had been given to him by Ibrāhīm, and as soon as he arrived, Abū Muslim put him in charge of his vanguard. He put troops under Qaḥṭabah's command and granted him the power to remove and appoint officers. Abū Muslim then wrote to the army to pay heed to Qaḥṭabah and obey him.

He sent Qaḥṭabah this same year to Naysābūr to encounter Naṣr. According to ʿAlī b. Muḥammad—Abū Dhayyāl, al-Ḥasan b. Rashīd and Abū al-Ḥasan al-Jushamī: When Shaybān b. Salamah al-Ḥarūrī was killed, his followers joined Naṣr who was at Naysābur. Al-Nābī b. Suwayd al-ʿIjlī wrote to Naṣr asking for aid, and Naṣr sent him his son Tamīm b. Naṣr with two thousand men. Meanwhile, Naṣr was preparing to go to Ṭūs. Abū Muslim then sent Qaḥṭabah b. Shabīb with other officers, including al-Qāsim b. Mujāshiʿ and Jahwar b. Marrār. Al-Qāsim went by way of Sarakhs, while Jahwar went by way of Abīward. Tamīm sent ʿĀṣim b. ʿUmayr al-Sughdī against Jahwar, who was nearest to him, and ʿĀṣim b. ʿUmayr drove him off. Jahwar then entrenched himself at Kubādqān. Qaḥṭabah and al-Qāsim drew near where al-Nābī was, so Tamīm sent word to ʿĀṣim, "Turn away from Jahwar and confront them." He did, and Qaḥṭabah fought his men.

Abu Jaʿfar reported from another source than those from whom ʿAlī b. Muḥammad received the information we have cited about Qaḥṭabah and how Abū Muslim sent him against Naṣr and his followers: When Abū Muslim had killed Shaybān al-Khārijī and the sons of al-Kirmānī, driven Naṣr out of Marw and gained the upper hand in all of Khurāsān, he sent his governors to all its territories. He appointed Sibāʿ b. al-Nuʿmān al-Azdī for Samarqand and Abū Dāwūd Khālid b. Ibrāhīm for Ṭukharistān. He sent Muḥammad b. al-Ashʿath to the two Ṭabases and Fāris[283] and set Mālik b. al-Haytham over his security forces. Qaḥṭabah he sent to Ṭūs with a number of officers, including Abū ʿAwn ʿAbd al-Malik Ibn Yazīd, Mu-

[2001]

---

283. Ṭabas al-ʿUnnāb, Ṭabas al-Tamr and Fāris were the chief towns of the province south of Nīshāpūr (Naysābur). See Yāqūt, *Muʿjam*, III, 513; LeStrange, *Lands*, 352ff.

qātil b. Ḥakīm al-ʿAkkī, Khālid b. Barmak, Khāzim b. Khuzaymah, Mundhir b. ʿAbd al-Raḥmān, ʿUthmān b. Nahīk, Jahwar b. Marrār al-ʿIjlī, Abū al-ʿAbbās al-Ṭūsī, ʿAbdallāh b. ʿUthmān al-Ṭāʾī, Salamah b. Muḥammad, Abū Ghānim ʿAbd al-Ḥamīd b. Ribʿī, Abū Ḥumayd, Abū al-Jahm, whom Abū Muslim appointed as army secretary for Qaḥṭabah, ʿĀmir b. Ismāʿīl, and Muḥriz b. Ibrāhīm, who had with him a number of officers. They engaged the forces at Ṭūs, who were put to flight; the number of those who were trampled to death in the rout was greater than those who were slain in combat. The total number killed that day was about ten thousand.

[2002]   Abū Muslim sent al-Qāsim b. Mujāshiʿ to Naysābūr along the main road, and wrote to Qaḥṭabah ordering him to engage Tamīm b. Naṣr b. Sayyār and al-Nābī b. Suwayd and those Khurasānīs who were attached to them. He also ordered him to send Mūsā b. Kaʿb to him from Abīward. When Qaḥṭabah arrived at Abīward, he sent Mūsā to Abū Muslim and wrote to Muqātil b. Ḥakīm ordering him to send a man to Naysābūr to relieve Qāsim b. Mujāshiʿ. Abū Muslim sent ʿAlī b. Maʿqil with ten thousand men against Tamīm b. Naṣr, ordering him to go to Qaḥṭabah with his men, so that [when Qaḥṭabah entered][284] Ṭūs they could reinforce him. ʿAlī b. Maʿqil went on to camp at a village called Ḥulwān. Word reached Qaḥṭabah of ʿAlī's march and the position he had taken, so he hastened to march to Sūdhqān, the camp of Tamīm b. Naṣr and al-Nābī b. Suwayd. He sent his vanguard with Asīd b. ʿAbdallāh al-Khuzāʿī commanding [three thousand men of the Shīʿah] from Nasā and Abīward, and Asīd marched to camp at a village called [Ḥabūsān as Tamīm and al-Nābī prepared] to do battle with him. Asīd then wrote Qaḥṭabah informing him [of their resolve to do battle, and that if][285] Qaḥṭabah did not come to him soon, he would be summoning Asīd's men to the judgment of God. He informed him, as well, that these two commanded thirty thousand of the best Khurasānī troops and their cavalry. Qaḥṭabah then sent Muqātil b. Ḥakīm al-ʿAkkī

---

284. The phrase in parentheses is taken from the Cairo edition and replaces the lacuna in the text.

285. The passages in parentheses are taken from the Cairo edition and replace lacunae in the text.

with a thousand men and Khālid b. Barmak[286] with another thousand. They went to join Asīd, but word reached Tamīm and al-Nābī,
who drove them off. Then Qaḥṭabah and his followers came up and
prepared to do battle with Tamīm. Qaḥṭabah put Muqātil b. Ḥakīm,
Abū ʿAwn ʿAbd al-Malik b. Yazīd and Khālid b. Barmak in charge of
his right wing, and Asīd b. ʿAbdallāh al-Khuzāʿī, al-Ḥasan b.   [2003]
Qaḥṭabah, al-Musayyab b. Zuhayr and ʿAbd al-Jabbār b. ʿAbd al-Raḥmān in charge of his left, while he himself took the center. He then
moved slowly toward the enemy, and called on them to obey the
Book of God and the *sunnah* of His Prophet, as well as the Chosen
One from the family of Muḥammad. However, they did not respond
affirmatively. With that, he ordered his right and left wings to attack, and the two forces fought a violent battle, as violent as it could
be. Tamīm b. Naṣr was killed in the fighting, and there was great
slaughter of his men. Their camp was overrun. Al-Nābī took flight
with a number of others, and they locked themselves up in the
town. The soldiers then laid siege to the town, breached the wall
and entered it, and al-Nābī and those with him were slain. ʿĀṣim b.
ʿUmayr al-Samarqandī and Sālim b. Rāwiyah al-Saʿīdī fled to Naṣr b.
Sayyār at Naysābūr and told him how his son, Tamīm, and al-Nābī
had been slain, along with their followers.

When Qaḥṭabah gained possession of their camp and all that was
in it, he placed it in the charge of Khālid b. Barmak and sent Muqātil
b. Ḥakīm al-ʿAkkī in command of his vanguard to Naysābūr. News
of this reached Naṣr b. Sayyār and he set out, fleeing after the people
of Abrashahr. He camped in Qūmis, where his followers left him to
join Nubātah b. Ḥanzalah in Jurjān. Meanwhile Qaḥṭabah advanced
on Naysābūr with his troops.

This same year Nubātah b. Ḥanzalah, governor of Jurjān for Yazīd
b. ʿUmar b. Hubayrah (the Umayyad governor of Iraq) was slain.[287]

---

286. The ancestor of the Barmakī family of wazīrs. He was son of the last *Parmak*
or hereditary high priest of the Nawbahār Buddhist temple near Balkh, and he was active in the Hāshimiyyah movement. *EI*[2] s.v. Barāmika.

289. See *Akhbār al-Dawlah*, 328–31; Ibn Khayyāṭ, II, 413ff; Yaʿqūbī, *Taʾrīkh*, II,
410; *FHA*, 193.

The Slaying of the Governor of Jurjan

[2004] According to ʿAlī b. Muḥammad—Zuhayr b. Hunayd, Abū al-Ḥasan al-Jushamī, Jabalah b. Farrūkh and Abū ʿAbd al-Raḥmān al-Iṣbahānī: Yazīd b. ʿUmar b. Hubayrah sent Nubātah b. Ḥanẓalah al-Kilābī to Naṣr. He went to Fārs and Iṣbahān and then marched to Rayy and on to Jurjān, but he did not reinforce Naṣr b. Sayyār. At this the Qays told Naṣr, "You'll not take us to Qūmis." They then went off to Jurjān. Nubātah dug a defensive trench. When it ran through the habitation of a particular group, they would bribe him and he would put it off. His trench extended for about a *farsakh* (6 km).

Qaḥṭabah came into Jurjān in Dhū al-Qaʿdah 130 (July 748), with Asīd b. ʿAbdallāh al-Khuzāʿī, Khālid b. Barmak, Abū ʿAwn ʿAbd al-Malik b. Yazīd, Mūsā b. Kaʿb al-Maraʾī, al-Musayyab b. Zuhayr, and ʿAbd al-Jabbār b. ʿAbd al-Raḥmān al-Azdī. Mūsā b. Kaʿb commanded his right wing, Asīd b. ʿAbdallāh his left, and al-Ḥasan b. Qaḥṭabah led the vanguard. Qaḥṭabah addressed (his forces), "Men of Khurāsān, do you know against whom you are marching and with whom you will do battle? You are going to fight with the remnants of those who burned the House of God, Mighty and Glorified be He."[288]

Al-Ḥasan went forward with the vanguard to the borders of Khurāsān and camped. He sent out ʿUthmān b. Rufayʿ, Nāfiʿ al-Marwazī, Abū Khālid al-Marwarrūdhī and Masʿadah al-Ṭāʾī against an armed party of Nubātah headed by a man called Dhuʿayb. They attacked him by night, killing Dhuʿayb and seventy of his men, and then returned to al-Ḥasan's camp. Qaḥṭabah now arrived and camped opposite Nubātah. The Syrians appeared in greater number than people had ever seen, so that upon beholding them the Khurasānīs were awed and spoke openly to this effect. This reached Qaḥṭabah, and he addressed them saying, "Men of Khurāsān, this land belonged to

[2005] your forefathers before you, and they were given victory over their enemies because they were just and behaved rightly, until they changed and behaved unjustly. God the Mighty and Glorious was then angered with them. Their authority was taken from them, and the humblest people [ummah] to share the earth with them was given power over them and took their land and their women and en-

---

288. The reference is to the Syrian troops of the Umayyads who had ravaged Mecca in 64 (683) and 74 (694). See *EI²* s.v. Kaʿba, history.

slaved their children. Yet this people ruled justly withal and kept
their word and succored the oppressed. Then they changed and al-
tered; they went astray in their governance, and people of probity
and piety came to fear from the race of God's Apostle, may God's
benediction be on him, and peace! Thus God has empowered you
against them in order that revenge be enacted through you, that you
should be their greatest punishment, for you have sought them out
for vengeance. The Imam has sworn to me that you would encounter them in numbers great as these, but that God would give you victory over them, and you will rout and slay them."[289]

Qaḥṭabah had a letter from Abū Muslim read out loud: "From
Abū Muslim to Qaḥṭabah, in the Name of God, the Merciful, the
Compassionate. Rise up against your enemy, for God the Mighty
and Glorified is your helper. And when you prevail against them, let
the slaughter be great."

They clashed on a Friday, the first night of Dhū al-Ḥijjah 130
(about June 29, 748), and Qaḥṭabah said, "Men of Khurāsān,
God—blessed and glorified be He—has preferred this day above all
days, when deeds are increased manifold above all days. This is a
great month, wherein is the greatest of your feasts in the sight of
God. The Imām has already informed us that you will win a victory
on this day of this month against your enemy, so meet him firmly
and steadfastly, reckoning on God's reward, for truly, God is with
those who persevere."

Qaḥṭabah set off against them with al-Ḥasan b. Qaḥṭabah commanding his right wing and Khālid b. Barmak and Muqātil b. Ḥakīm
al-ʿAkkī commanding his left. The armies engaged in combat, each
persevering against the other. Nubātah was slain, the Syrians were
put to flight, and ten thousand of them were killed. Qaḥṭabah then
sent Abū Muslim the head of Nubātah and that of his son Ḥayyah.   [2006]

According to an elder of the Banū ʿAdī—his father: Sālim b. Rāwiyah al-Tamīmī was one of those who had fled from Abū Muslim
and left with Naṣr. Then he was with Nubātah and fought against
Qaḥṭabah in Jurjān. When the army fled, he stayed on fighting by
himself. ʿAbdallāh al-Ṭāʾī, who was one of Qaḥṭabah's cavalrymen,
attacked him, and Sālim b. Rāwiyah struck him in the face, putting

---

289. This speech, if it is authentic, would seem to show that the majority of Qaḥṭabah's "Men of Khurāsān" were non-Arab Muslims: a disputed question.

out his eye. Sālim continued to fight until he was pushed back to the mosque. He went in, and his opponents followed him. Everywhere he attacked them, he made them scatter. He then began shouting, "Give me a waterjug, and by God I'll really give them trouble this day!" They set fire to the roof of the mosque and threw stones at him until they killed him. They brought his head to Qaḥṭabah; there was not a single unmarked spot on the head or the face, so that Qaḥṭabah said, "I've never seen anything like this."

In this year the battle at Qudayd between Abū Ḥamzah the Khā-rijite and the people of Madīnah[290] took place.

Abū Ḥamzah's Battle with the Madīnans at Qudayd

According to al-ʿAbbās b. ʿIsā al-ʿUqaylī—Hārūn b. Mūsā al-Far-wī—more than one source: ʿAbd al-Wahīd b. Sulaymān (b. ʿAbd al-Malik) appointed ʿAbd al-ʿAzīz b. ʿAbdallāh b. ʿAmr b. ʿUthmān to lead the people, and they went out (from Madīnah). When they were at the Ḥarrah,[291] they came upon slaughtered camels, and went on. When they were at ʿAqīq[292] their banner caught on a thorn tree, and the pole broke. They thought this beginning boded ill, but kept go-ing until they halted at Qudayd for the night. The village of Qudayd was in the vicinity of the castle which is standing there today; the water-tanks were in that place. They made a camp close together, being no warriors, and no one paid attention to them but a group who came out to them from the castle.[293]

[2007]

Some have asserted that it was the tribe of Khuzāʿah who showed Abū Ḥamzah their exposed situation, and who led them to the Khā-rijites who slew them. The killing was at the expense of the Quraysh, they being most of the people, the ones with effective power (al-shawkah); a great number of them were slain.

According to ʿAbbās—Hārūn—one of his informants: A man of the Quraysh saw a man from the Yaman who was saying, "Praise be

---

290. See Ibn Khayyāṭ, I 413ff; FHA, 168–70; Azdī, 108–110; Yaʿqūbī, Taʾrīkh, II, 406. Qudayd was a place between Mecca and Madīnah. See Yāqūt, Muʿjam, IV, 42.

291. See EI² s.v. al-Ḥarra.

292. The "blessed valley" west of Madīnah, where according to tradition the Prophet was once told to pray by an angel. See EI² s.v. al-ʿAḳīḳ.

293. The reading al-qaṣr is from the Cairo edition, emending al-faḍl in the text.

to God, who has cooled my eye with the slaughter of Quraysh!"[294]
Then he said to his son, "My boy, begin with this one." And it was
one of the men of Madīnah. His son came up near him and cut off
the man's head. Then the father would say to his son, "Come lad, up
this way." And so they fought, until they both were killed. The sur-
vivors fled back to Madīnah, and the people mourned their slain.
Women grieved at great length for their relatives and would not
leave until news about their men arrived. Then the women went
out, one after another, each going to her relative, until not one
woman remained.

Abū Ḍamrah recited these verses to me concerning his kinsmen
slain at Qudayd; one of their comrades lamented them, and said:

> What a loss for me; and a loss, no mistake,
>   for the riders in the dry gulch on the uplands;

> There is ʿAmr, and ʿAmr, and ʿAbdallāh among them,
>   and both their sons—five, and al-Ḥārith makes six.

In this year, Abū Ḥamzah the Khārijite entered Madīnah, city of
the Messenger of God, may God bless him and give him peace, and
ʿAbd al-Waḥīd b. Sulaymān b. ʿAbd al-Malik fled to Syria.

Abū Ḥamzah's Entry into Madīnah   [2008]
and What Came of It

According to ʿAbbās b. ʿIsā—Hārūn b. Mūsā al-Farwī—Mūsā b.
Kathīr: Abū Ḥamzah entered Madīnah in the year 130 (747–748), as
ʿAbd al-Waḥīd b. Sulaymān b. ʿAbd al-Malik fled to Syria. Abū Ḥamzah ascended the *minbar*,[295] praised God and eulogised Him, and
said, "People of Madīnah, we have asked you about these rulers of

---

294. To the Khārijites, who recognized "no genealogy [*nasab*] in religion," the
Quraysh were the subverters of the Prophetic community.

295. The *minbar* was the governor's throne in a mosque at this time, and this particular minbar had been the pulpit of the Prophet. Abū Ḥamzah's addresses from this
pulpit were considered models of excellent rhetoric and are preserved in a number of
collections dealing with Arab eloquence. Parts of the addresses are translated in various editions of Williams, *Islam* s.v. The Khārijīs. See also Ibn Khayyaṭ, I, 407ff *sub
anno* 129; Azdī, 106; Ibn ʿAbd Rabbihi, IV, 144ff; al-Jaḥiẓ, *Bayān*, II, 124ff; Ibn
Qutaybah, ʿ*Uyūn*, II, 249ff.

yours, and as God lives, what you had to say of them was bad. We asked you, 'Did they put people to death on suspicion?' You told us, 'Yes.' We asked you, 'Did they take, as lawful, wealth and women that are forbidden to them?' You replied, 'Yes.' So we said to you, 'Come, let us go together and ask them in God's name to turn away from you and from us.' You said, 'They will not do it.' Then we told you, 'Come, let us go and fight them together, and if we prevail, we shall bring those who will establish among us the Book of God, and the *(sunnah)* tradition of His Prophet Muḥammad, God's blessing and peace be upon him.' You said, 'We are not strong.' Then we told you, 'Then leave us and them alone. And if we are victorious, we shall be fair in our judgments towards you, and rely with you on the *sunnah* of your Prophet, and divide your *fay'* among you'.[296] Yet you refused, and fought us without them, and we therefore killed you. May God keep you from good and from prosperity!"

According to Muḥammad b. ʿUmar[297]—Ḥizām b. Hishām: The Khārijites numbered four hundred. One group was headed by al-Ḥā-rith, and one group by Bakkār b. Muḥammad al-ʿAdawī (that is, the) ʿAdī of Quraysh, and another was led by Abū Ḥamzah. They clashed with the people of Madīnah after the latter had made ready to fight them after pleas from the Khārijites to desist. These told them, "By God, we have no need to fight you. Let us go on against our ene-mies." But the men of Madīnah refused. They met in battle on Thursday, after the seventh night of Ṣafar 130 (October 19, 747), and the men of Madīnah were massacred. None escaped but those who ran away. Their commander ʿAbd al-ʿAzīz b. ʿAbdallāh was slain, and the Quraysh suspected that the Khuzāʿah had betrayed them with the Khārijites. Ḥizām told me (Muḥammad b. ʿUmar), "By God, I gave shelter to some men from Quraysh until people were given a guarantee of safety. Balj had charge of the vanguard, and the

[2009]

---

296. *Fay'* was revenue of properties taken in conquest. The disposition of these rev-enues by the second and third caliphs was a sore topic. ʿUmar and ʿUthmān had in ef-fect held the properties in trust and used the revenues for the community. ʿAlī and his followers, and the later Khārijites, were known to favor dividing the *fay'* among the victors. ʿUmar had not permitted Arabs to farm land outside the Arabian Peninsula. This especially offended the Yamanīs, who had old agricultural traditions. See *EI²* s.v. Fay'.

297. That is, Muḥammad b. ʿUmar al-Wāqidī, a historian of Madīnah whose works reflect the traditions of the city. He was, however, a beneficiary of the ʿAbbāsids, and careful not to offend his patrons. See Petersen, *ʿAlī and Muʿāwiya*, 83–93.

Khārijites advanced on Madīnah on the 19th night of Safar [October 31, 747]."

According to ʿAbbās b. ʿIsā—Hārūn b. Mūsā—some of their shaykhs: When Abū Ḥamzah entered Madīnah, he stood up and delivered an address, saying, "People of Madīnah, I passed among you in the time of the squint-eyed Hishām b. ʿAbd al-Malik, when a blight had struck your dates. You wrote to him requesting him to lower the tax on them, and he wrote back lowering it for you. The rich became richer, and the poor became poorer, but you said, 'May God reward you with good!' May God reward neither you nor him with good!"

According to ʿAbbās—Hārūn—Yaḥyā b. Zakariyyāʾ: Abū Ḥamzah gave the following address; he went up into the minbar, praised God and lauded Him, and then said,

Know, O people of Madīnah that we did not leave our homes and our possessions lightly or carelessly, or to no avail, nor to overthrow a kingdom wishing to immerse ourselves in government, nor for revenge for an old grievance that touched our honor; but when we saw the lamps of truth had been neglected, and the speaker of truth was upbraided, and that he who stood up for justice was slain, then the earth in all its width became narrow for us, and we heard a herald [dāʿī] calling us to obey the Merciful Lord and the rule of the Qurʾān. We responded to the summoner of God, "And he who answers not God's summoner shall not frustrate God's plan on earth."[298] We came forward from scattered tribes, a group of us on one camel carrying ourselves and our supplies, sharing one blanket among ourselves, little people, held as weak on earth; and He received us and aided us by His succor, and we all became brothers to each other, by God, through His grace. Then we met your men at Qudayd, and we summoned them to obey the Merciful Lord and the rule of the Qurʾān. But they summoned us to obey Satan and the judgment of the family of Marwān. And by God's life, far apart are guidance and error! They scurried forward hastening, for Satan had struck in them his partners; his cauldrons boiled with their blood, and his supposition about them was con-

[2010]

---

298. Qur. 46:32.

firmed. But the helpers of God, Mighty and Majestic, came forward in small bands and in squadrons, with every sharpened blade gleaming; and our coil turned, and their coil twisted away, with a blow from which triflers recoil. As for you, O people of Madīnah, if you aid Marwān and the family of Marwān, the God of might and majesty shall destroy you with punishment delivered by Himself or at our hands, and the breasts of faithful folk will recover health. O people of Madīnah, the first among you were the very best, and the last among you are the very worst. O people of Madīnah, the people are of us, and we are of them, unless it be a polytheist who worships idols, or a polytheist among the People of the Book,[299] or an imām who acts unjustly. O People of Madīnah, if anyone asserts that God the Mighty, the Majestic, charges any soul with what is beyond its power or asks of it more than is given to it, then he is an enemy of God, and we have war. O People of Madīnah, they have told me that there are eight divisions of the *zakāt*[300] which God has ordained upon strong and weak alike in his Book. Now a ninth has come, due no part of it, not one portion, and takes all of it for himself, arrogant in opposition to his Lord!

O People of Madīnah, it has reached me that you belittle my comrades. You say they are callow young men, barefoot bedouins. Alas for you, O people of Madīnah! What were the followers of the Messenger of God, God bless him and give him peace, but callow young men? Youths, by God, who were fully mature in their youth—youths whose eyes were closed to evil and whose feet were slow to approach wrongdoing; exchanging with God the life that dies for the life that dies not, they mingled all that was theirs with their fatigue, and rose at night to watch and pray after fasting all the day. They bent their backs over portions of the Qurʾān, and so oft as they came upon a verse [of fear,

[2011]

---

299. "People of the Book," e.g., Jews and Christians who possessed revealed scriptures, are often accused of having "associated" lesser being with God, thereby becoming guilty of idolatry, the worst of sins. See *EI²* s.v. Ahl al-Kitāb.

300. The *zakāt* is a tax imposed on all, as it says in Qurʾān 10:60, for carefully defined community purposes. The eight legal beneficiaries are the poor, needy, collectors of the tax, "those whose hearts are to be reconciled," slaves to be ransomed, debtors, "those in God's Way," and travelers. The abbreviated form in which this address is cast, even omitting the proof-text as the speaker would not have done, demonstrates that we have here only a sketch of the main points.

they were racked with terror of the Fire, and when they came upon a verse][301] of desire they were racked with longing for Paradise. When they looked to swords drawn against them, lances pointed at them, arrows notched for them, when a detachment of cavalry thundered at them with bolts of death, they made little account of the threat of that detachment beside the threat of God. They did not take God's threat lightly beside the threat of a detachment; so blessed were they, and fair the place where they returned! And how many an eye which had overflowed long in the depth of night from fear of God met the beak of a bird! How many a hand left its wrist whereon its owner long supported himself [in his prostration to God! How many an excellent cheek and fine forehead was cleft by maces of iron! God have mercy upon those bodies, and make their souls to enter His gardens].[302] I say my say, and I ask God to forgive our deficiencies, for there is no success for me but in God; in Him have I put my trust, to Him shall I repair.

According to 'Abbās—Hārūn—his grandfather Abū 'Alqamah: I heard Abū Ḥamzah on the minbar of God's messenger saying, "Whoever fornicates is an infidel; whoever doubts it is an infidel. Whoever steals is an infidel; whoever doubts that he is an infidel is also an infidel."

According to 'Abbās—Hārūn—his grandfather: He had conducted himself so well among the people of Madīnah that people inclined to him even when they heard him say, "Whoever fornicates is an infidel."

According to 'Abbās—Hārūn—one of his companions: When he ascended the minbar he said, "The concealed has been revealed, wherever you may be taken. Whoever fornicates is an infidel; whoever steals is an infidel." Hārūn also said that someone recited these verses about the Battle of Qudayd:

What's wrong with Time, and wrong with me, ah—[303]   [2012]
   Qudayd has destroyed my menfolk, ah—

---

301. This phrase is missing in the text and is added from the Cairo edition.
302. See n. 301 above.
303. Read *mā li-l-zamān* with the Cairo edition and *al-Aghānī*; the text has *mā li-Qudayd*.

> Then let me weep by all means secretly;
> and surely I shall weep in public, ah—
>
> I'll weep until I gasp,[304]
> like the dogs that bark, ah—

Abū Ḥamzah and his men entered Madīnah on the 17th of Ṣafar (October 29, 747). The authorities differ about how long they remained there: al-Wāqidī says it was three months. Another says they stayed there for the rest of Ṣafar, the two months of Rabīʿ, and part of Jumādā I (i.e., into January 748). The number of the people from Madīnah who were slain at Qudayd according to al-Wāqidī was seven hundred.

It is mentioned that Abū Ḥamzah sent ahead a group of his men commanded by Abū Bakr b. Muḥammad b. ʿAbdallāh b. ʿUmar al-Qurashī. After him, it was one of the Banū ʿAdī b. Kaʿb, then Balj b. ʿUyaynah b. al-Hayṣam al-Asadī, a man of Baṣrah. Marwān b. Muḥammad sent ʿAbd al-Malik b. Muḥammad b. ʿAṭiyyah, one of the Banū Saʿd, from Syria with a Syrian contingent.

According to ʿAbbās b. ʿĪsā—Hārūn b. Mūsā—Mūsā b. Kathīr: Abū Ḥamzah went out from Madīnah, leaving one of his followers in charge, and went on until he halted at the Wādī.[305]

According to ʿAbbās—Hārūn—a companion from whom Abū Yaḥyā al-Zuhrī used to recite traditions: Marwān picked four thousand men of his army, put Ibn ʿAṭiyyah in command, and ordered him to move resolutely. He gave each man a hundred gold dīnārs, an Arab horse, and a mule for his baggage. He ordered Ibn ʿAṭiyyah to go engage them, and if he was victorious, to go on to the Yaman and fight ʿAbdallāh b. Yaḥyā and his followers. Ibn ʿAṭiyyah went out and halted at ʿUlā.[306] A man from Madīnah called al-ʿAlāʾ b. Aflaḥ

[2013]

---

304. Read *shajītu*, "I gasp," with the Cairo edition; the text has *shahantu*, "I chase in vain."

305. Presumably the Wādī al-Qurā, a long valley of many villages which was the gateway from the Ḥijāz to Syria. Whoever controlled this Wādī could exert great pressure on the Ḥijāz by cutting off supplies from the north. See Yāqūt, *Muʿjam*, IV, 81, 878; Lassner, *ʿAbbāsid Rule*, 71, 264, n. 44. For this account see Ibn Khayyāt I, 416ff; Azdī, 110ff; *FHA*, 181–85; Masʿūdī, *Murūj*, IV, 66ff. (J.L.)

306. ʿUlā is the biblical Dedan, an oasis town on the incense road in the north Ḥijāz with extensive remains of an advanced pre-Islamic civilization. See Yāqūt, *Muʿjam*, III, 709.

the mawlā of Abū al-Ghayth used to say, "I was a boy at that time, and one of Ibn ʿAṭiyyah's men met me and asked, 'What's your name, boy?' I told him, 'al-ʿAlā.' 'Son of whom?' he asked. 'Son of Aflaḥ,' I told him. 'Mawlā of whom?' he asked. 'Mawlā of Abū al-Ghayth,' I told him. 'Where are we?' he asked. 'At ʿUlā,' I told him. 'And where shall we be tomorrow?' said he. 'At Ghālib,'[307] I told him. He said nothing, but mounted me behind him and rode off taking me to Ibn ʿAṭiyyah. 'Ask this boy his name,' he said. He asked me the questions and I answered as before. He was pleased at that, and gave me several dirhams."

According to ʿAbbās—Hārūn—ʿAbd al-Malik b. al-Mājashūn: When Abū Ḥamzah and Ibn ʿAṭiyyah encountered each other, Abū Ḥamzah told his people, "Don't engage them until you are informed about them." They called out to Ibn ʿAṭiyyah's men, "What do you say about the Qurʾān, and doing as it says?" Ibn ʿAṭiyyah shouted back, "We put it in a bag." They called, "What do you say about the property of the orphan?" He replied, "Let's consume the property and commit debauchery with his mother!" These are only some of the things I have heard that they questioned them about. When they had heard their answers, they fought with them until evening. Then they called, "Woe to you, Ibn ʿAṭiyyah; God has made the night for repose;[308] so you repose and we'll repose!" But he refused, and fought them until he killed them.

According to ʿAbbās—Hārūn: When Abū Ḥamzah went out, he took leave of the people of Madīnah saying, "O people of Madīnah, we are going out against Marwān. If we prevail, we will be fair in ruling you, and treat you in accord with the *sunnah* of your Prophet Muḥammad, and divide fairly your *fayʾ* among you. If it goes as they wish, 'those who have done wrong shall learn by what an overturning they will be overturned.'"[309]   [2014]

According to ʿAbbās—Hārūn—one of his companions: "When the news of Abū Ḥamzah's death came to the people [of Madīnah], they fell upon his followers and slew them."

---

307. Ghālib was a place in the Ḥijāz near Madīnah; see Yāqūt, *Muʿjam*, III, 869. There is a play on *ghālib* here, which means "a winner," as well as on other words in the responses with fortunate connotations.
308. Qur. 6:96.
309. Qur. 26:227.

Muḥammad b. ʿUmar reported that Abū Ḥamzah and his followers marched against Marwān, and his cavalry, led by Ibn ʿAṭiyyah al-Saʿdī of Qays, met them in Wādī al-Qurā and attacked them. They returned in flight to Madīnah, and the people of Madīnah met them and killed them. He continues: The commander of Marwān's army, ʿAbd al-Malik b. Muḥammad b. ʿAṭiyyah al-Saʿdī, that is, Saʿd of Hawāzin,[310] came on to Madīnah at the head of four thousand Arab horsemen. Each had a mule, and some wore two breastplates, or one breastplate and armor[311] and coats of mail and other equipment the likes of which had not been seen at that time. They then went on to Mecca.

Another source reports that when Ibn ʿAṭiyyah entered Madīnah, he stayed there for a month, and then went on to Mecca. He appointed as his deputy in Madīnah al-Walīd b. ʿUrwah b. Muḥammad b. ʿAṭiyyah and continued on to Mecca and the Yaman. He appointed as his deputy in Mecca Ibn Māʿiz, from the Syrian army. Ibn ʿAṭiyyah went on; word reached ʿAbdallāh b. Yaḥyā at Ṣanʿāʾ that he was coming against him, so he advanced against him with his supporters. The two forces clashed, and Ibn ʿAṭiyyah killed ʿAbdallāh b. Yaḥyā, and sent his son Bashīr to Marwān. Ibn ʿAṭiyyah went on to enter Ṣanʿāʾ, and then sent ʿAbdallāh b. Yaḥyā's head to Marwān.[312] Then Marwān wrote Ibn ʿAṭiyyah, ordering him to march posthaste and lead the Pilgrimage at Mecca. According to al-ʿAbbās b. ʿIsā—Hārūn: He left leading a small group of his men, until they camped at Jurf,[313] as ʿAbbās has it. This attracted the attention of some of the people of the village, who said, "He's running away, by God!" Then they started to attack him. He told them, "Woe betide you! This is the leader of the Pilgrimage! By God, the Commander of the Faithful has written to me!"

According to Muḥammad b. ʿUmar—Abū al-Zubayr b. ʿAbd al-Raḥmān: I went out along with twelve other men with Ibn ʿAṭiyyah

[2015]

---

310. The Saʿd b. Bakr were a subtribe of the Hawāzin, a large North Arabian group of tribes of Qays ʿAylān, which was mostly of Ḥijāzi origin. See *EI²* s.v. Hawāzin.

311. Read *sannawar* with the Cairo edition, emending the text which has *tannūr*.

312. The head would have been taken first to Ṣanʿāʾ to show people there the proof that ʿAbdallāh b. Yaḥyā's reign was over.

313. Yāqūt, *Muʿjam*, II, 63, lists a place called al-Jurf in the Yaman. However Azdī, 113, and Masʿūdī, *Murūj*, IV, 67, say the place was al-Jurash. Yāqūt, 59, describes Jurash as both a province of the Yaman and a place where a great city had flourished.

al-Saʿdī, who had Marwān's deed of appointment for the Pilgrimage. He had forty thousand dīnārs in his saddlebag. His army and cavalry were behind at Ṣanʿāʾ, and until he camped at Jurf making for the Pilgrimage, by God, we felt secure and confident. Then I overheard a woman saying, "God smite both the sons of Jumānah! How grim-faced[314] they are!" I stood up as if I were going for water, and went up on a hillock. And lo, there was a band of men with swords, horses, and slings. Then the aforementioned sons of Jumānah were standing over us; we were surrounded on every side. We said, "What do you want?" They then said, "You're robbers!" Ibn ʿAṭiyyah took out his document and said, "This is the letter of the Commander of the Faithful, and his deed of appointment for the Pilgrimage. I am Ibn ʿAṭiyyah." But they said, "This is no good; you are robbers!" At this, we foresaw evil, and al-Ṣafar b. Ḥabīb mounted his horse, and fought well until he was slain. Ibn ʿAṭiyyah got on his horse, and fought until he too was killed. Then all those who were with us were killed, and I remained. They said, "Who are you?" "A man of Hamdān,"[315] I replied. "What Hamdān are you from?" they said. I traced back a lineage to one of their sub-groups, since I knew the sub-groups of Hamdān, and they let me alone. They told me, "Your life is safe, and everything that is yours in this place you can take." If I had claimed all of the money, they'd have given it to me. Then they sent some riders with me as far as Ṣaʿdah, and I was safe and went on until I came to Mecca.

In this year the summer campaign against the Byzantines was led by al-Walīd b. Hishām. He went down to ʿAmq and built the citadel of Marʿash.[316]

This year the plague broke out at Baṣrah.

This year Qaḥṭabah b. Shabīb killed many of the people of Jurjān;   [2016]
some say it was as many as thirty thousand. A version coming from people of Jurjān has it that after the slaying of Nubātah b. Ḥanẓalah

---

315. The Hamdān were a large tribe of northern Yaman, whose range was between Ṣanʿāʾ and Saʿdah. The western moiety, the Hāshid, are still active there. Historically, they have been mostly Shīʿīs. See *EI*² s.v. Hamdān. Saʿdah is a district some 60 *farsakh*s (360 km) from Ṣanʿāʾ. See Yāqūt, *Muʿjam*, III, 388.

314. The text is *mā ashtam*; the Cairo edition has *mā ashʿam*, "how inauspicious."

316. ʿAmq is the alluvial plain of Cilicia, situated northeast of Antioch. See *EI*² s.v. al-ʿAmḳ. The Marwānid construction of the citadel of Marʿash is confirmed by Yāqūt, *Muʿjam*, IV, 498. See also LeStrange, *Lands*, 128–29.

they all decided to fight Qaḥṭabah. When word reached Qaḥṭabah of this, he went in and indiscriminately killed those whom I have mentioned.

When Naṣr b. Sayyār learned that Qaḥṭabah had killed Nubātah and a number of people of Jurjān, he was in Qūmis. He then moved to Khuwār of Rayy.[317]

Naṣr's reason for camping at Rayy according to 'Alī b. Muḥammad—Abū Dhayyāl, Ḥasan b. Rashīd and Abū al-Ḥasan al-Jushamī: Abū Muslim sent a letter with al-Minhāl b. Fattān to Ziyād b. Zurārah al-Qushayrī with a deed of appointment to govern Naysābūr, after Tamīm b. Naṣr and al-Nābī b. Suwayd al-'Ijlī were killed. He also wrote to Qaḥṭabah ordering him to pursue Naṣr. Qaḥṭabah then sent al-'Akkī with his vanguard, while he went to Naysābūr and stayed there for the months of Ramaḍān and Shawwāl 130 (early May to end of June 748). He was there while Naṣr was staying at a village in Qūmis called Badhash.[318] The Qaysīs with him stayed in

[2017]   another village, called Mumidd.[319] Naṣr then wrote to Ibn Hubayrah at Wāsiṭ asking him for aid, and sent the message with notables of Khurāsān to stress the importance of the matter. But Ibn Hubayrah threw his messengers in prison. Naṣr then wrote to Marwān, "I have sent some of the leading men of Khurāsān to Ibn Hubayrah to inform him on our behalf of the situation of the people there and to ask him for reinforcements. He has imprisoned my messengers and has not reinforced me with a single man. My situation is that of a man driven from his bedroom to his chamber, and from his chamber to his sitting-room, and from the sitting-room to the courtyard. If someone will come to him and help him, he may perhaps return to his house and it will remain his; but if he is driven from the house to the street, he will have neither house nor courtyard." Marwān wrote to Ibn Hubayrah ordering him to assist Naṣr, informing him of that. Naṣr then sent a letter to Ibn Hubayrah with Khālid the mawlā of the Banū Layth, asking him to send the army to

---

317. Khuwār of Rayy was the westernmost town of Qūmis, on the road from Khurāsān, and the first important town east of Rayy. See Yāqūt, *Mu'jam*, II, 479; also LeStrange, *Lands*, 367.

318. Badhash was the first village inside Jurjān on the post-road from Nīshāpūr (Naysābūr). Yāqūt states that it was two *farsakh*s (12 km) from Bisṭām. See also LeStrange, *Lands*, 368.

319. The text is al-Maydā, corrected by the Cairo edition. The vocalization is uncertain.

him quickly, "For I have lied to the people of Khurāsān until not a man among them will believe a word I say; so reinforce me with ten thousand men before you have to reinforce me with a hundred thousand, and after that nothing will be of use."

In this year Muḥammad b. ʿAbd al-Malik b. Marwān led the Pilgrimage. That is what is related by Aḥmad b. Thābit—someone—Ishāq b. ʿIsā—Abū Maʿshar (al-Sindī).

Muḥammad b. ʿAbd al-Malik was governor of Mecca, Madīnah and Ṭāʾif.

Iraq was governed by Yazīd b. ʿUmar b. Hubayrah.

Al-Ḥajjāj b. ʿĀṣim al-Muḥāribī was in charge of the judiciary at Kūfah, and ʿAbbād b. Manṣūr at Baṣrah.

Naṣr b. Sayyār was governor of Khurāsān, but matters there were as we have mentioned.

The
Events of the Year

131

(AUGUST 31, 748–AUGUST 19, 749)

One of the events of this year was that Qaḥṭabah sent his son al-Ḥasan to Naṣr while he was in Qūmis.[320]

According to ʿAlī b. Muḥammad—Zuhayr b. Hunayd, al-Ḥasan b. Rashīd and Jabalah b. Farrūkh al-Tājī: When Nubātah was killed, Naṣr moved from Badhash and entered Khuwār, whose governor was Abū Bakr al-ʿUqaylī. Qaḥṭabah sent his son al-Ḥasan to Qūmis in Muḥarram 131 (September 748), and after that he sent Abū Kāmil, Abū al-Qāsim Muḥriz b. Ibrāhīm, and Abū al-ʿAbbās al-Marwazī to Ḥasan with seven hundred men. When they were close to him, Abū Kāmil ran away from them, left his camp, and went over to Naṣr informing him of the whereabouts of the officer who was leading them. Naṣr then sent troops against them and besieged them in the walled town where they were. Jamīl b. Mihrān then pierced the wall and fled with his followers, leaving part of their equipment which Naṣr's followers seized, and which Naṣr sent to Ibn Hubayrah. ʿUṭayf[321] interfered in this at Rayy; he took Naṣr's letter and the

[2]

---

320. See *Akhbār al-Dawlah*, 331ff; Ibn Khayyāṭ, II, 419; Dīnawarī, 362; Yaʿqūbī, *Taʾrīkh*, II, 410; Ibn Qutaybah, *Maʿāriff*, 370.

321. Probably ʿUṭayf al-Sulamī sent by Marwān to join Ibn Hubayrah. See Ṭabarī, II/3, 1945. He was now following the orders of Ibn Hubayrah, who would not help Naṣr.

booty from the messenger, and sent them on to Ibn Hubayrah. At this Naṣr was furious, and said, "Does Ibn Hubayrah want to play with me? Is he stirring up all the good-for-nothings of Qays against me? By God, I will surely have nothing to do with him. Let him fully understand that he is nothing, and neither is his son from whom great things are expected." He went on and stopped at Rayy, which was being governed by Ḥabīb b. Budayl al-Nahshalī. ʿUṭayf left Rayy as soon as Naṣr came there, for Hamadhān. Mālik b. Adham b. Muḥriz al-Bāhilī was at Hamadhān commanding the Ṣaḥṣaḥiyyah corps,[322] so when ʿUṭayf saw that Mālik was at Hamadhān, he turned away from there and went to ʿĀmir b. Ḍubārah at Iṣbahān. ʿUṭayf had three thousand men with him, and Ibn Hubayrah sent him to Naṣr at Rayy. ʿUṭayf went to Rayy and stayed there, but did not go to see Naṣr. Naṣr stayed a couple of days at Rayy; then he fell ill and had to be carried on a litter until he reached Sāwah, near Hamadhān, and there he expired. When he died, his followers went on into Hamadhān. It is said that his death occurred on the twelfth of Rabīʿ I 131 (November 9, 748), when he was eighty-five years old.

It is also said that when Naṣr set out from Khuwār towards Rayy, he did not enter Rayy but stayed in the desert between Rayy and Hamadhān, and died there.

Returning to what ʿAlī (al-Madāʾinī) was told by his shaykhs: When Naṣr died, Qaḥṭabah's son al-Ḥasan sent Khāzim b. Khuzaymah to a village called Simnān[323] while Qaḥṭabah came up from Jurjān sending Ziyād b. Zurārah al-Qushayrī ahead of him. Ziyād regretted having followed Abū Muslim, and deserted Qaḥṭabah. He took the road to Iṣbahān, wishing to join ʿĀmir b. Ḍubārah, but Qaḥṭabah sent al-Musayyab b. Zuhayr al-Ḍabbī after him, who caught up with him the next afternoon and fought him. Ziyād fled, and most of his followers were killed. Musayyab then returned to Qaḥṭabah and Qaḥṭabah went to Qūmis where his son al-Ḥasan was. Khāzim came forward from the direction in which al-Ḥasan had sent him, and Qaḥṭabah had his son advance to Rayy. News of

[3]

---

322. This was apparently a regiment organized along the lines of the Dhakwāniyyah, perhaps by Muṣʿab b. Ṣaḥṣaḥ (see Ṭabarī, II/3, 1945, 1980). They were Marwān's own men and ʿUṭayf was avoiding them as part of Ibn Hubayrah's plan to appear to be helping Naṣr without doing so.

323. Simnān later became an important town. It was situated on the Khurāsān road east of Khuwār. See LeStrange, *Lands*, 366.

al-Ḥasan's march reached Ḥabīb b. Budayl al-Nahshalī and the Syrian troops who were with him, so they left Rayy. Al-Ḥasan then entered the city and stayed there until his father joined him. Upon ar-
riving at Rayy, Qaḥṭabah wrote to Abū Muslim, informing him that
he was encamped there.

In the same year, Abū Muslim moved from Marw to Naysābūr
and camped there.

Qaḥṭabah at Rayy and Abū Muslim at Naysābūr

When Qaḥṭabah wrote to Abū Muslim that he was encamped at
Rayy, the latter left Marw, as we have mentioned, and settled at
Naysābūr, where he dug a defensive trench. Qaḥṭabah sent his son
al-Ḥasan on to Hamadhān three days after he himself had entered
Rayy.

ʿAlī reports the following from his shaykhs and other authorities.
When al-Ḥasan b. Qaḥṭabah set out for Hamadhān, Mālik b. Adham
and the Syrians and Khurāsānīs who were with him there left for
Nihāwand. Mālik summoned them to take their allowances, saying,
"Let everyone who is registered in a *diwān* take his pay." At this, a
great number of people left their registries and went away. Mālik positioned himself with those who stayed with him, Syrians and Khurāsānīs who had been with Naṣr b. Sayyār. Meanwhile al-Ḥasan
marched from Hamadhān to Nihāwand and camped four *farsakh*s
(24 km) from the city. Qaḥṭabah then reinforced him with Abū Jahm
[4]   b. ʿAṭiyyah the mawlā of the (tribe of) Bāhilah and seven hundred
men, so that he was now able to surround the city and lay siege to
it.[324]

In this year ʿĀmir b. Ḍubārah was slain.

The Death of ʿĀmir b. Ḍubārah and the Reason For It

The reason for his slaying was that ʿAbdallāh b. Muʿāwiyah b. ʿAbdallāh b. Jaʿfar fled toward Khurāsān when he was put to flight by
Ibn Ḍubārah. He took his route by way of Kirmān, and ʿAmir b.
Ḍubārah set off in pursuit of him. Meanwhile word reached Yazīd b.
ʿUmar of Nubātah b. Ḥanẓalah's death in Jurjān.

---

324. For these events, see *Akhbār al-Dawlah*, 333–39.

According to ʿAlī b. Muḥammad—Abū al-Sarī al-Marwazī, Abū al-Ḥasan al-Jushamī, al-Ḥasan b. Rashīd, Jabalah b. Farrūkh and Ḥafṣ b. Shabīb: When Nubātah was killed, Ibn Hubayrah wrote to ʿĀmir b. Ḍubārah and to his son Dāwud b. Yazīd b. ʿUmar to march against Qaḥṭabah; they were both in Kirmān. They went with fifty thousand men and halted in (the oasis of) Iṣbahān at the city of Jayy.[325] People used to call Ibn Ḍubārah's army "the army of armies." Qaḥṭabah sent Muqātil (al-ʿAkkī) against him with Abū Ḥafṣ al-Muhallabī, Abū Ḥammad al-Marwazī the mawlā of the Banū Sulaym, Mūsā b. ʿAqīl, Aslam b. Ḥassān, Dhuʿayb b. al-Ashʿath, Kulthūm b. Shabīb, Mālik b. Ṭarīf, al-Mukhāriq b. Ghifar and al-Haytham b. Ziyād, with al-ʿAkkī in command. They marched to Qumm and halted there. Word reached Ibn Ḍubārah that al-Ḥasan b. Qaḥṭabah had camped among the people of Nihāwand, and he wanted to go to them and aid them. News of this reached al-ʿAkkī so he sent to inform Qaḥṭabah of it. Qaḥṭabah then dispatched Zuhayr b. Muḥammad to Qāshān[326] while al-ʿAkkī quit Qumm, leaving behind Ṭarīf b. Ghaylān. However, Qaḥṭabah wrote to al-ʿAkkī ordering him to wait until he could catch up with him and to then return to Qumm. Qaḥṭabah joined the latter's forces to his own. Then ʿĀmir b. Ḍubārah came against them—the distance between him and Qaḥṭabah's force was one *farsakh* (6km). ʿĀmir stayed there some days, and then Qaḥṭabah marched against his forces and the two armies met in battle.[327] Al-ʿAkkī, who had Khālid b. al-Barmak with him, commanded Qaḥṭabah's right wing, and ʿAbd al-Ḥamīd b. Ribʿī al-Ṭāʾī, assisted by Mālik b. Ṭarīf, commanded the left wing. Qaḥṭabah had twenty thousand men and Ibn Ḍubārah a hundred thousand—it is even said he had a hundred and fifty thousand. Qaḥṭabah gave orders for a copy of the Qurʾān, which was fixed on a lance, and then proclaimed, "Men of Syria, we would call you to what is in this Book!" They then reviled him with foul language, so Qaḥṭabah sent the order, "Attack them!" Al-ʿAkkī attacked the Syrians and the forces rushed into combat. There was not much fighting before the Syrians were routed, suffering extensive casualties.

[5]

---

325. For this city, see LeStrange, *Lands,* 203.

326. See LeStrange, *Lands,* 209.

327. That is, at the battle of Jābalq, a place in the district of Iṣfahān (Iṣbahān). See Yāqūt, *Muʿjam,* II, 2. For the battle, perhaps the most important of the ʿAbbāsid revolution, see *Akhbār al-Dawlah,* 343ff; Ibn Khayyāṭ, II, 418ff; Azdī, 116.

Qaḥṭabah's forces took possession of their camp and obtained quantities of weapons, equipment and slaves that could not be reckoned. Qaḥṭabah sent word of the victory by Shurayḥ b. ʿAbdallāh to his son al-Ḥasan.

ʿAlī reported the following from Abū al-Dhayyāl: When Qaḥṭabah met ʿĀmir b. Ḍubārah (in battle) the latter had with him leading men from Khurāsān, including Ṣāliḥ b. al-Ḥajjāj al-Numayrī, Bishr b. Bisṭām b. ʿImrān b. al-Faḍl al-Burjumī, and ʿAbd al-ʿAzīz b. Shammās al-Māzinī. Ibn Ḍubārah was commanding only cavalry while Qaḥṭabah had both horse and foot soldiers, so his men shot arrows at the horses, and Ibn Ḍubārah fled back into his camp. Qaḥṭabah pursued him, so Ibn Ḍubārah quit his camp and gave the call, "To me!" Nonetheless, his people fled and he was killed.

[6]   ʿAlī reported the following from al-Mufaḍḍal b. Muḥammad al-Ḍabbī: When Qaḥṭabah met Ibn Ḍubārah, Dāwud b. Yazīd b. ʿUmar fled. ʿĀmir asked about him and was told, "He's fled." At this, ʿĀmir exclaimed, "God has cursed our wickedness with this reversal!" Then he fought on until he was killed.

According to ʿAlī—Ḥafṣ b. Shabīb—an eyewitness with Qaḥṭabah: I've never seen any army that collected what the Syrians had collected at Iṣbahān in the way of horses, weapons and slaves. It was as if we had conquered a city. We obtained more guitars *(barābiṭ)*, drums and flutes than one might count. There was not a tent or shelter that we entered in which we did not find a wineskin, be it large or small. Thus one of the poets said:

> When we overthrew the chiefs of Muḍar,[328]
> Qaḥṭabah cut them up a dry fare;
>
> They called on Marwān as one calls on the Lord.

In this year befell Qaḥṭabah's battle at Nihāwand with the troops of Marwān b. Muḥammad who had taken refuge there. Also, it is said that the battle at Jābalq in Iṣbahān occurred on Saturday, the twenty-third of Rajab 131 (March 18, 749).

---

328. A line is missing in the text and is supplied by the Cairo edition.

Qaḥṭabah's Battle at Nihāward

'Alī reported the following from al-Ḥasan b. Rashīd and Zuhayr b.
al-Hunayd: When Ibn Ḍubārah was killed, Qaḥṭabah wrote of it to
his son al-Ḥasan[329] (at Nihāwand). When the letter arrived, he
cried, "Allāhu Akbar!" and so did all his army. Then they shouted
that Ibn Ḍubārah had been killed. At this, 'Āṣim b. 'Umayr al-
Sughdī said, "These people would never shout about killing Ibn Ḍubārah unless it were true, so go out to Ḥasan b. Qaḥṭabah and his followers and don't stand about for them; leave any way you please
before his father comes to him or sends him reinforcements." At
this, the footsoldiers said, "You'll go out as cavaliers on horseback
and then run off and leave us!" Then Mālik b. Adham al-Bāhilī said,
"Ibn Hubayrah has written to me. I will not retreat until he comes   [7]
to me." At this, they stayed where they were, and Qaḥṭabah stayed
at Iṣbahān for twenty days. He then moved to join al-Ḥasan at Nihāwand, where he besieged the city for some months. Then he offered
the defenders a safe-conduct, but they rejected it, so he set up mangonels against them. When Mālik saw that, he sought a guarantee
for himself and the Syrian troops, unbeknownst to the Khurāsānīs
(in his forces). Qaḥṭabah gave him his guarantee, and kept his word.
Not one of these men was killed, but all the men of Khurāsān who
were in Nihāwand were slain except al-Ḥakam b. Thābit b. Abī
Mas'ar al-Ḥanafī. Among the people of Khurāsān who were killed
were Abū Kāmil, Ḥātim b. al-Ḥārith b. Shurayḥ, the son of Naṣr b.
Sayyār, 'Āṣim b. 'Umayr, 'Alī b. 'Aqīl and Bayhas b. Budayl of the
Banū Sulaym of the people of the Jazīrah, and a man of Quraysh
known as al-Bukhturī who was a descendant of 'Umar b. al-
Khaṭṭāb—some assert that the family of al-Kaṭṭāb do not recognize
him—and Qaṭan b. Ḥarb al-Hilālī.

According to 'Alī—Yaḥyā b. al-Ḥakam al-Hamadhanī—one of
their mawlās: When Mālik b. Adham made terms with Qaḥṭabah,
Bayhas b. Budayl said, "Ibn Adham has made peace at our expense,
and by God we will surely murder him." The attackers from Khurāsān found that the gates had been opened for them, and they entered

---

329. See *Akhbār al-Dawlah*, 336–38, 353–56.

the city. One of the Khurāsānīs with Qaḥṭabah then let him in through a protective wall.

[8]

Other sources say that Qaḥṭabah sent to the Khurāsānīs inside Nihāwand inviting them to come out to him, and offered them a guarantee of safeconduct, but they refused. He then sent the same offer to the Syrian troops there, who accepted. They entered an agreement after they had been besieged for three months: Shaʿbān, Ramaḍān, and Shawwāl (April, May and June 749). The Syrians sent word to Qaḥṭabah, requesting him to keep the people of the city occupied so that they might open the gate unperceived.

Qaḥṭabah did this, keeping the people of the city busy in combat. Then the Syrians opened the gate that they were defending. When the Khurāsānī troops who were inside the city saw the Syrians going out, they asked what they were doing. The Syrians told them, "We have made terms for ourselves and for you." The Khurāsānī leaders (inside the city) went out to Qaḥṭabah, who put each one of them in the care of an officer from Khurāsān. Later he ordered his herald to proclaim, "Let everyone who has a prisoner from those who came out to us from the city cut off his head and bring it to me." They acted accordingly, and not one of those who had fled from Abū Muslim to the walled city remained alive, except for the Syrians. These he set free, exacting their promise not to conspire with the enemy against him.

Returning to the account of ʿAlī on the authority of his shaykhs: When the Syrians and Khurāsānīs who were in Nihāwand had let Qaḥṭabah inside the walls, ʿĀṣim b. ʿUmayr told them, "Woe to you! Now they enter the walls!" ʿĀṣim then went out. He had already put on his breastplate and a black garment he had. He was met by a Shākirī trooper who had been attached to him in Khurāsān, who recognized him and said, "You're wearing black now?" "Yes," he replied. At this, the Shākirī brought him to an underground conduit, and told a slave of his, "Watch over him, and let no one come upon him here." Then Qaḥṭabah ordered, "Whoever has a prisoner with him, bring him to me." At this the slave who was entrusted with ʿĀṣim said, "I have a prisoner that I fear will be taken from me by force." A man from the Yamanī troops heard this and said, "Let me see him." The slave showed ʿĀṣim to the Yamanī, and he recognized him. He went off to Qaḥṭabah and informed him, saying, "Here is one head of the tyrants!" Then Qaḥṭabah sent for ʿĀṣim and put him to death. But he kept his word to the men of Syria so that not a single one of them was killed.

According to ʿAlī—Abū al-Ḥasan al-Khurāsānī and Jabalah b. Far-rūkh: When Qaḥṭabah came to Nihāwand and al-Ḥasan was laying siege to it, Qaḥṭabah took charge and sent al-Ḥasan to Marj al-Qalʿah.[330] Al-Ḥasan sent Khāzim b. Khuzaymah on to Ḥulwān where ʿAbdallāh b. al-ʿAlāʾ al-Kindī was governing, and ʿAbdallāh fled the city leaving it unprotected. [9]

ʿAlī reported the following from Muḥriz b. Ibrāhīm: When Qaḥṭa-bah conquered Nihāwand, people wanted to write to Marwān using Qaḥṭabah's name, and they said, "This is an abominable name; turn it around." It then came out "Habathaq." At this they said, "The first name, awful as it is, is easier than that." Hence they changed it back to Qaḥṭabah.[331]

Abū ʿAwn's Battle at Shahrazūr

In this year occurred Abū ʿAwn's battle at Shahrazūr. ʿAlī reported the following from Abū al-Ḥasan and Jabalah b. Farrūkh: Qaḥṭabah sent Abū ʿAwn ʿAbd al-Malik b. Yazīd al-Khurāsānī and Mālik b. Ṭarīf[332] al-Khurāsānī with four thousand men to Shahrazūr, where ʿUthmān b. Sufyān commanded the advance forces of ʿAbdallāh b. Marwān. Abū ʿAwn and Mālik came up and camped two *farsakh*s (12 km) from Shahrazūr. They held their positions for a day and a night, and then fought ʿUthmān b. Sufyān on the twentieth of Dhū al-Ḥijjah 131 (August 10, 749). ʿUthmān b. Sufyān was killed, and Abū ʿAwn sent Ismāʿīl b. al-Mutawakkil with the good news. Abū ʿAwn then stayed in the area of Mosul.

Some say that ʿUthmān b. Sufyān was not killed but fled to ʿAb-dallāh b. Marwān, while Abū ʿAwn decimated his army and killed an enormous number of his followers after a violent battle. It is said that Qaḥṭabah sent Abū ʿAwn to Shahrazūr with thirty thousand men at the order of Abū Muslim himself. They also say that when news of Abū ʿAwn's victory came to Marwān at Ḥarrān, he set out [10]

---

330. Marj al-Qalʿah (Castle Meadow) was two days travel from Ḥulwān on the way to Hamadān, in Jibāl. By the tenth century, it was a large and fine walled town. See LeStrange, *Lands*, 192.

331. His name was actually Ziyād. See *EI*[2] s.v. Ḳaḥṭaba b. Shabīb.

332. Ibn Athīr has "Ṭarāfah."

from there with the troops of Syria, the Jazīrah and Mosul. The
Umayyad family rallied their Abnā' to Marwān as he moved to meet
Abū 'Awn, until he reached Mosul. He then began to dig a network
of trenches, until he was encamped at the Greater Zāb river. Abū
'Awn stayed at Shahrazūr for the rest of the month of Dhū al-Ḥijjah
131 and Muḥarram 132 (August and early September 749), and he
gave military pay to five thousand men.

Other Events

[11] This year Qaḥṭabah marched against Ibn Hubayrah. According to
'Alī—Abū al-Ḥasan, Zuhayr b. Hunayd, Ismā'īl b. Abī Ismā'īl and
Jabalah b. Farrūkh: When Ibn Hubayrah's son fled to him from Ḥulwān, Ibn Hubayrah came out and gave battle to Qaḥṭabah. With him
he had a great number of men that could not be reckoned, as well as
Ḥawtharah b. Suhayl al-Bāhilī whom Marwān had sent to reinforce
him. Putting Ziyād b. Sahl al-Ghaṭafānī in charge of his rear guard,
Yazīd b. 'Umar b. Hubayrah marched until he came to the battle-
ground of Jalūlā'.[333] He dug in there, clearing out the old trench dug
by the Persians at the Battle of Jalūlā'. Qaḥṭabah advanced until he
came to Qirmāsīn.[334] He then marched to Ḥulwān and stopped in
Khāniqīn. Then he left Khāniqīn, and Ibn Hubayrah left his position,
returning to Daskarah.

Hishām reported the following from Abū Mikhnaf: Qaḥṭabah advanced, while Ibn Hubayrah was entrenching himself at Jalūlā', and
then went up to 'Ukbarā' and crossed the Tigris, moving on until he
stopped at Dimimmā below Anbār on the Euphrates.[335] Ibn Hubayrah and those with him then left to get to Kūfah before Qaḥṭabah.
He stopped on the east bank of the Euphrates and sent on Ḥawtharah with fifteen thousand men to Kūfah (on the west bank and to
the south). Qaḥṭabah crossed the Euphrates at Dimimmā so that he
was on the west side and marched for Kūfah, until he reached the
place where Ibn Hubayrah was.

This year the Pilgrimage was led by al-Walīd b. 'Urwah b. Muḥam-

---

333. A district and town in the Sawād of Iraq between Daskarah and Khānaqīn. It
was famous as the site of a great battle won by the Muslims in 16 (637) against the
Sasanians. See LeStrange, *Lands*, 62; *EI*² s.v. Djalūlā'.
334. See LeStrange, *Lands*, 186–87.
335. See LeStrange, *Lands*, 50; 65–66.

mad b. ʿAṭiyyah al-Saʿdī, of the Saʿd division of the tribe of Hawāzin, who was brother's son to ʿAbd al-Malik b. Muḥammad b. ʿAṭiyyah who killed Abū Ḥamzah al-Khārijī. Al-Walīd was governor of Madīnah on behalf of his uncle, as I have been told by Aḥmad b. Thābit—Isḥāq b. ʿĪsā—Abū Maʿshar. Al-Wāqidī and others report the same.

It has also been reported that al-Walīd b. ʿUrwah was just outside Madīnah when Marwān wrote to al-Walīd's uncle ʿAbd al-Malik ordering him to lead the Pilgrimage though he was in the Yaman, busied as we have mentioned elsewhere.[336] When his uncle was detained, al-Walīd forged a letter from him deputing him to lead the Pilgrimage, and then led it. It has been mentioned that word reached al-Walīd b. ʿUrwah that his uncle ʿAbd al-Malik had been killed, whereupon al-Walīd went against those who had killed his uncle and slew a great number of them. He ripped open the bellies of their women and slew the male children, burning in fires all those who fell into his hands.

Al-Walīd b. ʿUrwah al-Saʿdī was governor of Mecca, Madīnah and Ṭāʾif this year in place of his uncle ʿAbd al-Malik b. Muḥammad. The governor of Iraq was Yazīd b. ʿUmar b. Hubayrah, while in Kūfah al-Ḥajjāj b. ʿĀṣim al-Muḥāribī was in charge of the judiciary. ʿAbbād b. Manṣūr al-Nājī was in charge of the judiciary in Baṣrah.

---

336. See Ṭabarī, II/3, 2014 *sub anno* 130. For his activities in the Yaman see *FHA*, 175ff.

The
Events of the Year

132

(AUGUST 20, 749–AUGUST 8, 750)

[12]   One of the events of this year was the death of Qaḥṭabah b. Shabīb.[337]

The Death of Qaḥṭabah and the Reasons For It

The reason is as follows. When Qaḥṭabah stopped at Khāniqīn en route to Ibn Hubayrah, who was at Jalūlāʾ, the latter moved from Jalūlāʾ to Daskarah. According to what is mentioned, Qaḥṭabah sent his son al-Ḥasan as a scout to learn news of Ibn Hubayrah. Ibn Hubayrah was returning to his trench at Jalūlāʾ, and al-Ḥasan found him there, so he returned to his father and told him of Ibn Hubayrah's whereabouts.

According to ʿAlī b. Muḥammad—Zuhayr b. Hunayd, Jabalah b. Farrūkh, Ismāʿīl b. Abī Ismāʿīl and al-Ḥasan b. Rashīd: When al-Ḥasan returned and informed his father concerning Ibn Hubayrah's activities, Qaḥṭabah asked his companions, "Do you know a road that will bring us to Kūfah bypassing Ibn Hubayrah?" Khalaf b. Muwarriʿ al-Hamadhānī, one of the Banū Tamīm, replied, "Yes, I will

---

337. See *Akhbār al-Dawlah*, 369–71; Ibn Khayyāṭ, II, 422ff; Azdī, 118ff; *FHA*, 194-95; Yaʿqūbī, *Taʾrīkh,*, II, 412; Dīnawarī, 368; Masʿūdī, *Murūj*, VI, 73.

guide you." Qaḥṭabah crossed the Tāmarrā with him at Rūstuqbādh and took the main road until he halted at Buzurg Sābūr. Then he came to 'Ukbarā' and crossed the Tigris to Awānā.[338]

According to 'Alī—Ibrāhīm b. Yazīd al-Khurāsānī: Qaḥṭabah camped at Khāniqīn when Ibn Hubayrah was at Jalūlā' with a distance of five *farsakh*s (30 km) between them. Qaḥṭabah sent out his scouts to gain information about Ibn Hubayrah, and they returned and informed him that Ibn Hubayrah had taken up a position. Qaḥṭabah then ordered Khāzim b. Khuzaymah to cross the Tigris.   [13]
Khāzim crossed over and proceeded between the Tigris and the Dujayl until he came to Karnabā.[339] Qaḥṭabah now wrote to Khāzim ordering him to march to Anbār (on the Euphrates) and send down to him whatever boats and craft he could find to cross with. Qaḥṭabah would then meet him at Dimimmā. He crossed the Euphrates in Muḥarram 132 (August–September 749). He sent the baggage into the open country while the horsemen proceeded with him along the bank of the Euphrates. Ibn Hubayrah now camped in the area of Upper Fallūjah[340] at the mouth of the Euphrates, twenty-three *farsakh*s (138 km) from Kūfah. Ibn Ḍubārah's fleeing men had gathered there with him and Marwān had reinforced him with Ḥawtharah b. Suhayl al-Bāhilī at the head of twenty thousand Syrian troops.

'Alī reported the following from al-Ḥasan b. Rashīd and Jabalah b. Farrūkh: When Qaḥṭabah left Ibn Hubayrah and marched on Kūfah, Ḥawtharah b. Suhayl al-Bāhilī and chiefs of the Syrian army told Ibn Hubayrah, "Qaḥṭabah has turned toward Kūfah. So you set out for Khurāsān and leave him to Marwān, and you'll break him; or more likely, he'll follow you." But Ibn Hubayrah replied, "That's not how I see it. He won't follow me and leave Kūfah, so the best thing is to beat him to Kūfah."

When Qaḥṭabah had crossed the Euphrates and marched along the

---

338. See Yāqūt, *Mu'jam*, I, 604 lists a Buzurjsābūr as one of the districts (*tassūj*) of Baghdad. Rustuqbādh was a district of Kūfah, see Yāqūt, II, 733–34. For 'Ukbarā', see LeStrange, *Lands*, 50. The course of his travels was northwest.

339. The Dujayl or "little Tigris" was also known as the Karun. See LeStrange, *Lands*, 232ff. The text has Kūthbā; read Karnabā as in Ms. B. See Yāqūt, *Mu'jam*, IV, 268.

340. Upper and Lower Fallūjah were districts between the main stream of the Euphrates on the west and the Sūrā Canal on the east, after it bifurcated below the ruins of Babylon. See LeStrange, *Lands*, 74.

river bank, Ibn Hubayrah moved from his camp in the Fallūjah district. He put Ḥawtharah b. Suhayl in charge of his vanguard, ordering him to march to Kūfah, so both groups were marching along the banks of the Euphrates—Ibn Hubayrah between the Euphrates and the Sūrā branch, and Qaḥṭabah to the west, adjacent to the open country. Qaḥṭabah halted, and a bedouin crossed over to him in a skiff and greeted him peaceably. Qaḥṭabah asked, "What tribe are you from?" "From Ṭayyʾ," he replied. Then the bedouin said to Qaḥṭabah, "Drink of this water, and give me what you leave over to drink." Qaḥṭabah filled a bowl and drank, and gave the bedouin to [14] drink. Then the bedouin said, "Praise be to God, who has delayed my death until I beheld this army drink of this water!" "Is your thirst quenched now?" asked Qaḥṭabah. "Yes," replied the bedouin. "Then who are you from?" Qaḥṭabah asked him. "Of Ṭayyʾ," said the bedouin, "One of the Banū Nabhān." Qaḥṭabah then exclaimed, "My Imām has spoken truthfully. He said that I shall fight a battle on this river and have the victory. Brother of the Banū Nabhān, is there a ford in this place?" "There is, but I don't know it," said the bedouin. "I can show you who does: al-Sindī b. ʿAṣamm." Qaḥṭabah sent for this man, who came with his father and with help, and they showed him the ford. That evening they came against Ibn Hubayrah's vanguard, twenty thousand men led by Ḥawtharah.

ʿAlī reported the following from Shihāb al-ʿAbdī: Qaḥṭabah camped at Jabbāriyyah,[341] and he said, "The Imām has spoken truthfully to me. He informed me that the victory would occur in this place." He then paid the troops their allowances. The paymaster gave him back sixteen thousand dirhams, more or less, and said, "You'll do fine, as long as you're like this." The Syrian cavalry met him, and the bedouins had already showed him the ford, so he said, "I only wait for a holy month and the eve of ʿĀshūrāʾ."[342] This was the year 132 (749–750).

As for Hishām b. Muḥammad—Abū Mikhnaf: Qaḥṭabah reached the site of a ford which had been mentioned to him at sundown on the night of Wednesday, the eighth of Muḥarram 132 (August 28, 749). When he came to the ford he rushed blindly forward with some

---

341. The text is unclear. The Cairo edition gives "al-Jabbāriyyah."
342. *ʿĀshūrāʾ*, the tenth of the "holy month" of Muḥarram, marked the anniversary of the slaying of the Prophet's grandson al-Ḥusayn by the Umayyad governor of Iraq at the Euphrates in the vicinity of Kūfah. See *EI²* s.v. ʿĀshūrāʾ and al-Ḥusayn b. ʿAlī.

of his men to attack Ibn Hubayrah, whose men turned and fled. Then they dismounted at the mouth of the Nīl Canal, while Hawtharah continued until he stopped at Qaṣr Ibn Hubayrah.[343] At dawn the Khurāsānīs found that their commander was missing and reconciled themselves, and al-Ḥasan b. Qaḥṭabah took command of the army.

Going back to the account of ʿAlī—Shihāb al-ʿAbdī: As for Qaḥṭa- [15] bah's personal standard-bearer, his mawlā Khayrān or Yasār, Qaḥṭa- bah told him, "Cross over!" He said the same to his flag-bearer Masʿūd b. ʿIlāj who was from the Bakr b. Wāʾil. To his chief of secur- ity ʿAbd al-Ḥamīd b. Ribʿī, called Abū Ghānim, a man of the Banū Nabhān of Ṭayyʾ, he called out, "Cross over, Abū Ghānim, and bring us good news of the plunder!" A group crossed over until they num- bered four hundred, whereupon they fought Hawtharah's troops un- til they denied them access to the water. They met with Muḥam- mad b. Nubātah's forces and fought them. They raised their torches, and the Syrian troops fled. The ʿAbbāsid forces then found that Qaḥṭabah was missing, and they reluctantly acclaimed Ḥumayd b. Qaḥṭabah as their leader. They appointed a man called Abū Naḍr with two hundred men to see after the baggage, and Ḥumayd pressed on until he came to Karbalāʾ, then to Dayr al-Aʿwar, then to ʿAbbāsiyyah.[344]

According to ʿAlī—Khālid b. al-Aṣfaḥ and Abū al-Dhayyāl: Qaḥṭa- bah was found, and Abū al-Jahm buried him. Then a prominent man said, "If anyone knows of some testament of Qaḥṭabah, then let him inform us of it." Muqātil b. Mālik al-ʿAkkī said, "I heard Qaḥṭabah say, 'If anything happens to me, then al-Ḥasan is the army's com- mander.'" The army then gave its allegiance to Ḥumayd who ac- cepted on behalf of al-Ḥasan, and they sent word to al-Ḥasan. The messenger caught up with him outside the village of Shāhī,[345] and al-Ḥasan came back. Abū al-Jahm gave him Qaḥṭabah's seal, and the

---

343. The government complex near the Sūrā Bridge midway between Kūfah and Baghdad. It is frequently confused with Madīnat Ibn Hubayrah. See Lassner, *Abbāsid Rule*, 283, n. 41.

344. Yāqūt, *Muʿjam*, II, 644, lists Dayr al-Aʿwar as a place adjacent to Kūfah. There were several places of that name, but none conveniently fit the topographical setting here. See Yāqūt, III, 600ff for Karbalāʾ, the site of al-Ḥusayn b. ʿAlī's death. See *EI²* s.v. Karbalāʾ.

345. A place near Qādisiyyah. See Yāqūt, *Muʿjam*, III, 246.

army swore allegiance to him. Al-Ḥasan said, "If Qaḥṭabah is dead, I am Qaḥṭabah's son." On this night were slain Ibn Nabhān al-Sadūsī, Ḥarb b. Salm b. Aḥwaz and 'Isā b. Iyās al-'Adawī and a man of the Asāwira[346] called Muṣ'ab. Those who claimed to have killed Qaḥṭabah were Ma'n b. Zā'idah and Yaḥyā b. Ḥudayn.

'Alī reported the following from Abū Dhayyāl: They found Qaḥṭabah slain in a ditch, with Ḥarb b. Salm b. Aḥwaz slain beside him, and they supposed that they had killed each other.

'Alī gives the following from 'Abdallāh b. Badr: I was with Ibn Hubayrah on the night Qaḥṭabah attacked. They crossed over to us and fought us on a quay on which were five horsemen. Ibn Hubayrah sent Muḥammad b. Nubātah who engaged them in combat and we pushed them back some distance. Then Ma'n b. Zā'idah struck Qaḥṭabah on the tendon of his shoulder, and the sword went deep. Qaḥṭabah fell into the water, and they pulled him out. He said, "Tie up my arm," and they tied it up in a turban. Then he said, "If I die, throw me into the water so that no one will know I've been killed." Then the Khurāsānīs returned the charge, and Ibn Nubātah and the Syrians were surrounded. They pursued us—one of the patrols on the flank had already been taken. A group of Khurāsānīs caught up with us, and we fought them a long time. Had it not been for two soldiers of the Syrian army who put up a terrific struggle on our behalf, we would not have been saved. Then one of the Khurāsānīs said in Persian, "Leave these dogs!" At this, they went away from us. Qaḥṭabah died, but before dying he said, "When you get to Kūfah, the Imām's wazīr is Abū Salamah. Put yourselves at his disposal." After that, Ibn Hubayrah went back to Wāsiṭ.

Other reports have been given of Qaḥṭabah's death than those we have mentioned from 'Alī b. Muḥammad's shaykhs. One such account states that when Qaḥṭabah came up opposite Ibn Hubayrah on the west side of the Euphrates, with the river between them, he sent Ḥasan his son on with an advance force, and then ordered 'Abdallāh al-Ṭā'ī, Mas'ūd b. 'Ilāj, Asad b. al-Marzubān and their troops to cross the Euphrates on their horses. They crossed in the late afternoon. The first rider of Ibn Hubayrah's men they met was speared, and the others took flight, as far as the bridge over the Sūrā. Here

---

[16]

346. A Persian military unit that had become mawlās of the Tamīm. See Crone, *Slaves on Horses*, 38, 237, n. 362.

Suwayd, Ibn Hubayrah's chief of security, opposed them, striking [17]
the leaders and their mounts until he had forced them to retreat to
their position at sundown. The Syrians pressed until they came up
against Mas'ūd b. 'Ilāj and his men, a force that they outnumbered.

Then Qaḥṭabah ordered al-Mukhāriq b. Ghiffār, 'Abdallāh b. Bassām and Salamah b. Muḥammad, who were attached to a contingent
of cavalry, to cross over and help Mas'ūd b. 'Ilāj. They crossed, and
Muḥammad b. Nubātah came against them. He surrounded Salamah and those with him in a village on the bank of the Euphrates.
Salamah and those with him dismounted, and the fighting grew hot.
Muḥammad b. Nubātah would attack Salamah and those with him,
and ten or twenty of Salamah's men would be killed. Then Salamah
and his men would attack Muḥammad b. Nubātah and kill one or
two hundred of his men. Salamah sent to Qaḥṭabah asking him for
reinforcements, and he sent all his officers to reinforce him. Then
Qaḥṭabah crossed over with his cavalry, ordering every horseman to
carry a footsoldier with him. This was on the eve of the first Thursday of Muḥarram (August 25, 749). Then Qaḥṭabah attacked Muḥammad b. Nubātah and those with him. They fought a violent battle, and Qaḥṭabah put the enemy to flight, forcing them to retreat
until they joined up with Ibn Hubayrah. He then fled as well, seeing
the rout of Ibn Nubātah. The Syrians abandoned their camp and all
that was in it in the way of wealth, weapons, furnishings, vessels
and other things. The rout continued until they cut the pontoon
bridge across the Ṣarāt Canal, and then, retreating all that night,
they came at morning to the mouth of the Nīl Canal. When Qaḥṭabah's men greeted the morning, they had already noted that he was
missing, but they kept on hoping to find him until the day was half
spent. Then they gave up hope and realized he had drowned. The officers agreed on al-Ḥasan, his son, and put him in command and
swore to follow him, whereupon he took charge. He ordered that
what was in Ibn Hubayrah's camp be reckoned. He put the booty in
charge of a Khurāsānī, called Abū al-Naḍr,[347] with two hundred
horsemen and ordered that it be taken to Kūfah in boats. Al-Ḥasan
moved on with the troops to camp at Karbalā', then moved again
and stopped at Sūra.[348] After that he halted at Dayr al-A'war, then [18]

---

347. The text is al-Naṣr; it should be read al-Naḍr, as in the Cairo edition.
348. That is, the settlement. See Yāqūt, Mu'jam, III, 184.

marched from there and settled at 'Abbāsiyyah. Hawtharah was informed of Ibn Hubayrah's flight, and he and such men as were with him joined Ibn Hubayrah at Wāsiṭ.

The cause of Qaḥṭabah's death, according to these authorities, was what Aḥlum b. Ibrāhīm b. Bassām the mawlā of the Banū Layth stated: When I saw Qaḥṭabah in the Euphrates, his horse had already carried him until he had nearly crossed over to the side where I was positioned with my brother Bassām b. Ibrāhīm who was in charge of Qaḥṭabah's vanguard. Then I thought of the sons of Naṣr b. Sayyār who had been slain, and of other things. I was apprehensive for my brother Bassām because of a report that had reached him about Qaḥṭabah, and I said, "May I never seek revenge again if you are spared this night." Bassām said, "Then go meet him." Qaḥṭabah's horse was about to emerge from the Euphrates, while I was standing on the bank. I struck him with my sword on the forehead. His horse reared and death came to him quickly, as he fell into the Euphrates with his weapons.[349]

A similar account was related by Ibn Ḥusayn al-Saʿdī after Aḥlum b. Ibrāhīm's death. Ibn Ḥusayn said of this, "Were it not that Aḥlum confirmed it as he was dying, I'd not have repeated anything about it."

This year Muḥammad b. Khālid al-Qasrī rebelled in Kūfah and put on black before al-Ḥasan b. Qaḥṭabah had entered the city. Ibn Hubayrah's governor left the city, and al-Ḥasan occupied it.[350]

Muḥammad b. Khālid al-Qasrī Revolts at Kūfah

Hishām reported the following from Abū Mikhnaf: Muḥammad b. Khālid rebelled in Kūfah on the eve of 'Ashūrā', while Ziyād b. Ṣāliḥ al-Ḥārithī was governing the city. 'Abd al-Raḥmān b. Bashīr al-'Ijlī was in charge of security for him. Muḥammad put on black and [19] marched to the fortress (qaṣr), and Ziyād b. Ṣāliḥ, 'Abd al-Raḥmān b. Bashīr al-'Ijlī and the Syrians they had with them moved out, aban-

---

349. Bassām had defected to Abū Muslim after first serving Naṣr in Khurāsān. He was to lead an uprising against the 'Abbāsids in 133 (749–750) at Tadmur. He had been in trouble with Abū Muslim for taking private revenge on members of the Bakr b. Wā'il. See Ṭabarī, II/3, 1996.

350. See *Akhbār al-Dawlah*, 371–73; *FHA*, 195ff; Azdī, 119ff; Yaʿqūbī, *Ta'rīkh*, II, 412–13.

doning the castle, which Muḥammad b. Khālid occupied. When he woke on Friday, the second morning after Qaḥṭabah's death, he learned that Ḥawtharah and those with him had camped at Madīnat Ibn Hubayrah,[351] and were getting ready to march against Muḥammad. Most of the common sort who were with Muḥammad split from him as soon as word reached them that Ḥawtharah was camped at Madīnat Ibn Hubayrah and was coming to fight him. The exceptions were some horsemen from the Yamanī cavalry drawn from those who had fled from Marwān, and Muḥammad's mawlās. Abū Salamah al-Khallāl, who had not yet declared himself, sent word to Muḥammad b. Khālid ordering him to go out of the castle and get to the lowlands of the Euphrates. He feared for Muḥammad due to the small number (of men) with him and the large number with Ḥawtharah—neither of the two groups had as yet learned that Qaḥṭabah had perished. Muḥammad b. Khālid declined to act until it was full day. Ibn Ḥawtharah prepared to march against Muḥammad when word reached him that few supported Muḥammad and that the common people had abandoned him. While Muḥammad was still at the fortress, one of his scouts came to him and said, "Horsemen are coming—Syrians." At this, he sent a detachment of his mawlās. They had positioned themselves at the door of the house of 'Umar b. Sa'd, when the Syrian standards came into view. They prepared to fight them, when the Syrians called out, "We are of Bajīlah![352] Malīḥ b. Khālid al-Bajalī is with us, and we've come to enter the service of the Amīr!" They then entered the fortress. Then came an even greater body of horsemen, with a man of the family of Bahdal. When Ḥawtharah saw what his followers were doing, he and those with him left for Wāsiṭ. That night Muḥammad b. Khālid wrote to Qaḥṭabah, not knowing he had perished, informing him that he had prevailed in Kūfah. He dispatched the message with a fast rider who then came before al-Ḥasan b. Qaḥṭabah. When he handed him Muḥammad b. Khālid's letter, al-Ḥasan read it to his people, and then set out for Kūfah. Muḥammad stayed in Kūfah Friday, Saturday, and Sunday, and al-Ḥasan b. Qaḥṭabah came to him early on Monday morning. They then went to Abū Salamah who   [20]

---

351. Not to be confused with Qaṣr b. Hubayrah, this government complex was situated adjacent to Kūfah. See n. 343 above.

352. Khālid b. 'Abdallāh al-Qasrī had been of the tribe of Bajīlah. Hence the tribesmen now deserted to his son.

was with the Banū Salamah and brought him out. Abū Salamah camped at Nukhaylah for two days, and then set out for Ḥammām Aʿyan,[353] sending Ḥasan b. Qaḥṭabah to Wāsiṭ to fight Ibn Hubayrah.

ʿAlī b. Muḥammad reported the following from ʿUmārah, the mawlā of Jibraʾīl b. Yaḥyā: The Khurāsānīs took the oath to al-Ḥasan after Qaḥṭabah, and went to Kūfah which was commanded at that time by ʿAbd al-Raḥmān b. Bashīr al-ʿIjlī. A man of the Banū Ḍabbah came to him and said, "Al-Ḥasan b. Qaḥṭabah will enter today or tomorrow." ʿAbd al-Raḥmān said, "You act as if you'd come to threaten me!" He then gave him three hundred lashes. Then ʿAbd al-Raḥmān fled, and Muḥammad b. Khālid al-Qasrī put on black. He came out with eleven men, called on the people to give their allegiance, and took control of Kūfah. Al-Ḥasan came in the next day. They had been asking on the way, "Where is Abū Salamah the wazīr of the family of Muḥammad staying?"[354] People guided them to him, and they came and stood at his door. He came out to them, and they presented him with one of Qaḥṭabah's horses, which he mounted and rode as far as the cemetery (jabbānah) of the Sabīʿ.[355]

The Khurāsānīs then swore allegiance to him. Abū Salamah Ḥafṣ b. Sulaymān the mawlā of al-Sabīʿ, who was called "wazīr of the family of Muḥammad," stayed where he was and appointed Muḥammad b. Khālid b. ʿAbdallāh al-Qasrī to govern Kūfah, and he was called the Amīr until Abū al-ʿAbbās appeared.

ʿAlī reported the following from Jabalah b. Farrūkh, Abū Ṣāliḥ al-Marwazī, ʿUmārah the mawlā of Jibrīl, Abū al-Sarī and others who knew about the beginnings of the ʿAbbāsid propaganda: Abū Salamah sent al-Ḥasan b. Qaḥṭabah against Ibn Hubayrah at Wāsiṭ.[356] The officers he attached to his command included Khāzim b. Khu-

---

353. Ḥammām Aʿyan was actually located in Ḥīrah, the old Christian town that stood three farsakhs (18 km) from Kūfah. The area of Ḥīrah had enjoyed a revival in late Umayyad times when it actually became the government center of Kūfah. It was only natural, then, that the ʿAbbāsid armies would prefer to situate themselves in an established military camp some distance from the unruly population of Kūfah. Ḥammām Aʿyan functioned as the first of several ʿAbbāsid administrative centers in Iraq. See Lassner, ʿAbbāsid Rule, 143–51, especially 143–45, also n. 29. (J.L.)

354. Abū Salamah's role in what followed is discussed in detail by Sharon, ʿAlīyat, 237ff. See also Lassner, ʿAbbāsid Rule, 59–64, 145–47. (J.L.)

355. See Yāqūt, Muʿjam, II, 16–17.

356. See Ibn Khayyāṭ, II 424ff; Azdī, 125ff.

zaymah, Muqātil b. Ḥakīm al-ʿAkkī, Khafāf b. Manṣūr, Saʿīd b. ʿAmr, Zīyād b. Mushkān, al-Faḍl b. Sulaymān, ʿAbd al-Karīm b. Muslim, ʿUthmān b. Nahīk, Zuhayr b. Muḥammad al-Azdī, al-Haytham b. Zīyād, Abū Khālid al-Marwazī and others; altogether sixteen officers, with al-Ḥasan b. Qaḥṭabah heading them. He sent Ḥumayd b. Qaḥṭabah to Madāʾin with officers, including ʿAbd al-Raḥmān b. Nuʿaym and Masʿūd b. ʿIlāj, each officer accompanied by his men. In addition, Abū Salamah sent al-Musayyab b. Zuhayr and Khālid b. Barmak to Dayr Qunnā,[357] and al-Muhallabī and Sharāḥīl with four hundred men to ʿAyn Tamr. Bassām b. Ibrāhīm b. Bassām was sent to Ahwāz where ʿAbd al-Wāḥid b. ʿUmar b. Hubayrah was.

When Bassām got there, ʿAbd al-Wāḥid left Ahwāz for Baṣrah. Bassām then sent a letter with Ḥafṣ b. al-Sabīʿ to Sufyān b. Muʿāwiyah (al-Muhallabī) appointing him to govern Baṣrah. Al-Ḥārith Abū Ghassān al-Ḥārithī, one of the Banū al-Dayyān who had some pretensions to being a soothsayer, said, "This appointment will not be carried out." Nonetheless Ḥafṣ forwarded the letter to Sufyān. Then Salm b. Qutaybah[358] fought Sufyān, and so his appointment came to nought.

Abū Salamah left where he was and camped at Ḥammām Aʿyan, some three *farsakh*s (18 km) from Kūfah, while Muḥammad b. Khālid resided in Kūfah.

The reason that Salm b. Qutaybah fought Sufyān b. Muʿāwiyah b. Yazīd b. al-Muhallab, according to what is mentioned, is that when Abū Salamah al-Khallāl assigned governors to the provinces, he sent Bassām b. Ibrāhīm the mawlā of the Banū Layth against ʿAbd al-Wāḥid b. ʿUmar b. Hubayrah who was at Ahwāz, and Bassām fought him until he chased him out. ʿAbd al-Wāḥid then joined Salm b. Qutaybah al-Bāhilī in Baṣrah. Salm was governing for Yazīd b. ʿUmar b. Hubayrah. Abū Salamah wrote to al-Ḥasan b. Qaḥṭabah to send whomever he thought best among his officers to fight Salm. He wrote to Sufyān b. Muʿāwiyah appointing him governor of Baṣrah and commanding him to proclaim there the claims of the Banū ʿAbbās in the city, to summon people to al-Qāʾim among them, and to

---

357. Dayr Qunnā, also known as the Monastery of Marmarī, was just east of the Tigris above Dayr al-ʿAqūl, the "Monastery of the River Loop," with a town which was the chief place of the Middle Nahrawān district. Yāqūt states that it had over a hundred places for monks and high walls like a castle. See LeStrange, *Lands*, 36–37.

358. That is, the local governor of the Umayyads.

drive out Salm b. Qutaybah.[359] Sufyān wrote to Salm, ordering him to vacate the Government Palace, and informed him of what Abū Salamah had in mind, on the basis of reports he had received. However, Salm refused to comply and prepared his defense. All the Yamanīs rallied to Sufyān, with their allies among the Rabī'ah and others. One of Ibn Hubayrah's officers went over to him—Ibn Hubayrah had sent this officer with two thousand men of the Kalb tribe to assist Salm. They concurred on a plan to march on Salm b. Qutaybah, and Salm prepared for the battle. Rallying to Salm were the Qays and divisions of the Muḍar over whom he had control, as well as those Umayyads and their mawlās who were at Baṣrah. The Banū Umayyah hastened to come to his aid.

Sufyān advanced on a Thursday in the month of Ṣafar 132 (25 September or 2, 9, or 16 October 749). Salm came to the Mirbad of Baṣrah[360] and took his stand there at the camel-market. He sent horsemen on the Mirbad Road and other roads into Baṣrah, to encounter those whom Sufyān sent against him. He also proclaimed, "Whoever brings a head shall have a thousand." Mu'āwiyah b. Sufyān b. Mu'āwiyah came with a special force of Rabī'ah, and the cavalry[361] of the tribe of Tamīm met him on the road which connects with (the settlement of) the Banū 'Āmir from the Mirbad Road—at the house which became the property of 'Umar b. Ḥabīb. One of the Tamīm speared Mu'āwiyah's horse, and it reared and threw him. At this, a man of the Banū Ḍabbah, called 'Iyāḍ, threw himself upon him and killed him, and he carried his head off to Salm b. Qutaybah, who gave him a thousand dirhams for it. Sufyān was shattered by the slaying of his son, and he and those with him retreated. He and the people of his house departed immediately and traveled to Qaṣr al-Abyaḍ,[362] and they occupied it. Then they moved from there to Kaskar.

After Salm got the upper hand at Baṣrah, Jābir b. Tawbah al-Kilābī

---

359. The term *al-Qā'im* is a title for a promised deliverer, a "messianic" title. See Ibn 'Abd Rabbihi, IV, 476, also above. The text has *"yaqiya* Salm," emended by the Cairo edition as *yanfiya.*

360. The Mirbad of Baṣrah was the famous caravan quarter at the western end of the city. See LeStrange, *Lands,* 45.

361. The text has *rajul,* emended by the Cairo edition as *khayl.*

362. The identification of this place is not given. It is not to be confused with locations of that name situated at Ctesiphon and in Fārs. This place was between Baṣrah and Wāsiṭ, the major city of the Kaskar district. For Kaskar, see LeStrange, *Lands,* 39.

and al-Walīd b. ʿUtbah al-Firāsī, descendants of ʿAbd al-Raḥmān b. Samurah, advanced toward him with four thousand men. Ibn Hubayrah had written to them to go to the aid of Salm while he was at Ahwāz. The next day Jābir and the men with him appeared at the dwellings of the Muhallab and the rest of the Azd. They attacked them, but the Azd who remained there fought them in a fierce battle until many of the defenders were slain. The Azd then fled, and Jābir and his followers took their women captive, destroyed the houses and plundered for three days. Salm stayed on at Baṣrah until he received word that Ibn Hubayrah was slain, whereupon he left the city. Then the descendants of al-Ḥārith b. ʿAbd al-Muṭṭalib who were in Baṣrah gathered behind Muḥammad b. Jaʿfar and selected him as leader. He governed for a few days, until Abū Mālik b. ʿAbdallāh b. Asīd al-Khuzāʿī came to Baṣrah on behalf of Abū Muslim and governed for five days. When Abū al-ʿAbbās became Caliph, he gave the city to Sufyān b. Muʿāwiyah to govern.

In this year the oath of allegiance was given to Abū al-ʿAbbās ʿAbdallāh b. Muḥammad b. ʿAlī b. ʿAbdallāh b. al-ʿAbbās b. ʿAbd al-Muṭṭalib b. Hāshim on the eve of Friday, the thirteenth of Rabīʿ II (November 26, 749). This is according to Aḥmad b. Thābit—someone—Isḥāq b. ʿIsā—Abū al-Maʿshar. Hishām b. Muḥammad said the same. As for al-Wāqidī, he says: Abū al-ʿAbbās had allegiance sworn to him as Caliph at Madīnah in Jumādā I 132 (December 6, 749–January 4, 750). Al-Wāqidī also says that Abū al-Maʿshar told him it was in the month of Rabīʿ I 132 (October 18–November 16, 749), and Abū Maʿshar is the trustworthy authority.

The Caliphate of Abū Al-ʿAbbās ʿAbdallāh b. Muḥammad b. ʿAlī b. ʿAbdallāh b. ʿAbbās

The Origins of His Caliphate

According to what has been mentioned as coming from God's Messenger, may God bless him, it all began when he informed al-ʿAbbās b. ʿAbd al-Muṭṭalib that he would pass the caliphate to his descendants. His descendants therefore never stopped expecting it, and passed on the tradition among themselves.

According to ʿAlī b. Muḥammad—Ismāʿīl b. al-Ḥasan—Rashīd b. Kurayb: Abū Hāshim (b. Muḥammad b. ʿAlī b. Abī Ṭālib) went to Syria and met Muḥammad b. ʿAlī b. ʿAbdallāh b. ʿAbbās and said, "Cousin, I have religious knowledge *(ʿilm)* which I shall leave to you by default. Do not divulge it to anyone; this authority which men long for will be in your family." He said, "I knew it already; by no means let anyone hear it from you!"

According to ʿAlī—Sulaymān b. Dāwud—Khālid b. ʿAjlān: When Ibn al-Ashʿath opposed al-Ḥajjāj b. Yūsuf and the latter wrote of it to ʿAbd al-Malik b. Marwān, ʿAbd al-Malik sent a message to Khālid, son of Yazīd b. Muʿāwiyah, informing him of developments. Yazīd replied, "If the rupture *(fatq)* is in Sijistān, then have no fear; we need only worry if it comes from Khurāsān."[363]

ʿAlī reported the following from al-Ḥasan b. Rashīd, Jabalah b. Farrūkh al-Tājī, Yaḥyā b. Ṭufayl Nuʿman b. Sarī, Abū Ḥafṣ al-Azdī and others: The Imām Muḥammad b. ʿAlī b. ʿAbdallāh b. ʿAbbās said, "There are three turning points for us: the death of the profligate Yazīd b. Muʿwiyah, the turn of the first century, and disruption in Ifrīqiyah. With that, propagandists will call men to our cause, then our helpers will advance from the east until the hooves of their horses strike the lands of the Maghrib and extract the treasures hidden there by tyrants." When Yazīd b. Abī Muslim was slain in Ifrīqiyah and the Berbers revolted, Muḥammad b. ʿAlī sent a man to Khurāsān, ordering him to call men to the Chosen One, not mentioning any other name.

We have already mentioned the story of Muḥammad b. ʿAlī and the propagandists whom he sent to Khurāsān.[364] Then Muḥammad [25] b. ʿAlī died, appointing his son Ibrāhīm as his legatee. Ibrāhīm sent Abū Salamah Ḥafṣ b. Sulaymān the mawlā of al-Sabīʿ to Khurāsān, with letters to the *naqībs* there. They received his letters and Abū Salamah remained with them. Then he returned to Ibrāhīm, who sent him back (to Khurāsān) with Abū Muslim, whose story we have mentioned earlier. A letter from Ibrāhīm b. Muḥammad to Abū Muslim then fell into the hands of Marwān b. Muḥammad. It was an answer to a letter from Abū Muslim, in which Ibrāhīm ordered him to kill everyone who spoke Arabic in Khurāsān. At this Marwān wrote to his governor in Damascus, ordering him to write to his colleague in the Balqāʾ to go to Ḥumaymah, seize Ibrāhīm b. Muḥammad, and send him to Marwān.[365]

---

363. This statement is typical of the many forebodings the Umayyads allegedly had of the revolt in Khurāsān and the coming of ʿAbbāsid rule. These traditions were to establish the legitimacy of ʿAbbāsid claims. The turn of the first Islamic century was to have ushered in the Messianic age. Various ʿAbbāsid traditions deal with these expectations and tie them to the transfer of authority from Abū Hāshim to Muḥammad b. ʿAlī. See Kūfī, *Futūḥ*, VIII, 153 and Ibn ʿAbd Rabbihi, IV, 476. A full study of these traditions is being prepared by J. Lassner. (J.L.)

364. See Ṭabarī, II/3, 1358 *sub anno* 100.

365. The internment of Ibrāhīm al-Imām is a complex problem. Later ʿAbbāsid tradition makes him out to be a revolutionary martyr. For a detailed discussion of his internment, death and succession, see Sharon, *ʿAlīyat*, 237ff, which includes full references to primary sources. (J.L.)

According to Abū Zayd 'Umar b. Shabbah—'Īsā b. 'Abdallāh b.
Muḥammad b. 'Umar b. 'Alī b. Abī Ṭālib—'Uthmān b. 'Urwah b.
Muḥammad b. Muḥammad b. 'Ammār b. Yāsir: I was with Abū
Ja'far at Ḥumaymah and his two sons Muḥammad and Ja'far. I was
bouncing them on my knee, when Abū Ja'far said, "What are you doing? Don't you see what's happening?" I looked, and there were the
messengers of Marwān looking for Ibrāhīm b. Muḥammad. I said,
"Let me go out to them." He said, "You would go out of my house,
and you're the descendant of 'Ammār b. Yāsir?"[366] They seized the
doors of the mosque when (the 'Abbāsids) were at dawn prayer, and
then said to the Syrians[367] who were with them, "Where's Ibrāhīm
b. Muḥammad?" They told them, "That's him there." And they
took him. When Marwān had ordered them to seize Ibrāhīm, he had
described the appearance of Abū al-'Abbās, as he found it in books
that such a one would kill the Umayyads. When they brought him
Ibrāhīm, Marwān said, "This is not the man I described to you!"
They said, "We did not see such a one as you described." He sent
them back to look for him, but the 'Abbāsids were warned and fled
from him to Iraq.[368]

According to 'Umar—'Abdallāh b. Kathīr b. al-Ḥasan al-
'Abdī—'Alī b. Mūsā—his father: Marwān b. Muḥammad sent a   [26]
messenger to Ḥumaymah to bring him Ibrāhīm b. Muḥammad, describing him to him, and the messenger came and found that the de-
scription fitted Abū al-'Abbās 'Abdallāh b. Muḥammad. When
Ibrāhīm b. Muḥammad appeared and was given safety, people told
the messenger, "You were ordered to bring Ibrāhīm, but this is 'Abdallāh!" When this was made clear to him he let Abū al-'Abbās go,
and he took Ibrāhīm and departed with him. Mūsā said, "We set out
with him, I and a crowd of the Banū 'Abbās and their mawlās. The
messenger went off with Ibrāhīm, who had with him a concubine
(umm walad) of whom he was very fond. We told Ibrāhīm, "Only
one man came for you, so come, let us kill him. Then we'll turn off

---

366. 'Ammār had been the staunch supporter of 'Alī b. Abī Ṭālib. His father, Yāsir,
had been tortured by the Meccan ancestors of the Umayyads in the time of the
Prophet. It was therefore not politic to be seen leaving the house of an 'Abbāsid to
confront them. See *EI*² s.v. 'Ammār b. Yāsir.

367. Following the Cairo edition.

368. This is another of the apocalyptical traditions spoken of earlier. See n. 363
above.

for Kūfah where the people are our Shī'ah." He replied, "That's for
you to do." We said, "Wait until we get to the road that takes us to
Iraq." So we went on until we reached the fork where one road goes
off to Iraq while the other goes on to the Jazīrah. Then we made
camp. Whenever Ibrāhīm stopped for the night, he would withdraw
to the place of his concubine. The time came for us to do what we
had agreed on, and we called out to him to come. He got up to come
out, but his concubine threw herself on him and cried, "This is no
time for you to leave; what's making you go?" He went aside with
her and explained to her, and she said, "I conjure you by God not to
kill this man and bring misfortune on your family! By God, if you
slay him Marwān will kill every member of the family of 'Abbās in
Ḥumaymah." She wouldn't let go of him until he'd sworn to her not
to do it. When he came out to where we were and informed us, we
said, "You know best."

'Abdallāh says that a son of 'Abd al-Ḥamīd b. Yaḥyā the secretary
of Marwān told his father: "I asked Marwān b. Muḥammad, 'Are
you suspicious of me?' 'No,' he replied. So I asked him, 'Is Ibrāhīm
related to you by marriage?' 'No,' he said. I told him, 'Well, in my
opinion this is what you must do—give him a wife and take a wife
from him. Then if he is victorious you will have tied a knot between
you that will not reduce you to beggary; and if you beat him, the
marriage won't dishonor you.' He told me, 'Woe to you! By God, if I
[27]   knew he was the one [foretold] I'd hurry to do it, but he's not the
man for that.'"

It is mentioned that when Ibrāhīm b. Muḥammad was seized to be
taken to Marwān, he foretold his death to the people of his house
who accompanied his departure. He ordered them to go to Kūfah
with his brother, Abū al-'Abbās 'Abdallāh b. Muḥammad, and to
hear and obey him. Then he bequeathed his authority to Abū al-
'Abbās, appointing him as his successor. At this, Abū al-'Abbās set
out with the people of his house for Kūfah. Among them were 'Abdallāh b. Muḥammad and Dāwud b. 'Īsā; Ṣāliḥ, Ismā'īl, 'Abdallāh
and 'Abd al-Ṣamad the sons of 'Alī; Yaḥyā b. Muḥammad and 'Īsā b.
Mūsā b. Muḥammad b. 'Alī; 'Abd al-Wahhāb and Muḥammad the
two sons of Ibrāhīm; Mūsā b. Dāwud and Yaḥyā b. Ja'far b. Tammām. They traveled until they arrived in Kūfah in Ṣafar (ca. September 15–October 17, 750), and Abū Salamah put them up in the
house of Walīd b. Sa'd, the mawlā of the Banū Hāshim, situated

among the Banū Awd. He concealed their business for some forty
nights from all the officers and the Shī'ah. According to what is
mentioned, Abū Salamah wanted to change the succession to the
family of Abū Ṭālib when word reached him of the death of Ibrāhīm
b. Muḥammad.

'Alī b. Muḥammad reported the following from Jabalah b. Farrūkh, Abū al-Sarī and others: The Imām came to Kūfah with some of
the people of his House, and Abū al-Jahm said to Abū Salamah,
"What is the Imām doing?" He replied, "He still has not come." But
Abū al-Jahm pressed him until Abū Salamah said, "You ask too
many questions. This is not the time for him to emerge." Finally
Abū Ḥumayd met a servant of Abū al-'Abbās, called Sābiq al-Khu-
wārizmī, and asked him where his masters were. He informed Abū
Ḥumayd that they were in Kūfah, and that Abū Salamah had told
them to conceal themselves. At this he went with Abū Ḥumayd to
Abū al-Jahm and informed him about the 'Abbāsids. Abū al-Jahm
then sent Abū Ḥumayd with Sābiq to learn where they were staying
in Kūfah, and he came back bringing with him Ibrāhīm b. Salamah, a
man with the 'Abbāsid family. He told Abū al-Jahm about their
lodging, that the Imām was staying among the Banū Awd, and that
when they arrived the Imām had sent to ask Abū Salamah for a hundred dīnārs, but he had not sent the money. Then Abū al-Jahm and   [28]
Abū Ḥumayd and Ibrāhīm went to Mūsā b. Ka'b and told him the
story, and they sent the Imām two hundred dīnārs. Abū al-Jahm
then went to Abū Salamah and questioned him about the Imām.
Abū Salamah told him, "This is no time for him to come out, for
Wāsiṭ has not been conquered."[369] Abū al-Jahm went back to Mūsā
b. Ka'b and informed him, and they decided to meet the Imām. Then
Mūsā b. Ka'b, Abū al-Jahm, 'Abd al-Ḥamīd b. Rib'ī and Salamah b.
Muḥammad, Ibrāhīm b. Salamah and 'Abdallāh al-Ṭā'ī,
Isḥāq b. Ibrāhīm, Sharāḥīl, 'Abdallāh b. Bassām, Abū Ḥumayd
Muḥammad b. Ibrāhīm, Sulaymān b. al-Aswad and Muḥammad b.
al-Ḥusayn all went to the Imām. Word of this got to Abū Salamah
and he made inquiries about them and was told, "They rode to
Kūfah on some errand they had."

The group came to Abū al-'Abbās, entered into his presence, and

---

369. That is, the Umayyad capital of Iraq held by Ibn Hubayrah, the governor of the
province.

said, "Which of you is ʿAbdallāh b. Muḥammad b. al-Ḥārithiyyah?" "This one," the ʿAbbāsids said. The officers then saluted him as the Prophet's successor. Mūsā b. Kaʿb and Abū al-Jahm left the last, remaining with the Imām. Then Abū Salamah sent to Abū al-Jahm, asking, "Where have you been?" He replied, "I rode to my Imām." At this, Abū Salamah rode to the ʿAbbāsids. Abū al-Jahm then sent word to Abū Ḥumayd, "Abū Salamah is on his way to you. By no means let him go in to the Imām unless he is alone." So when Abū Salamah arrived they forbade him to go in accompanied by anyone. Thus he entered alone and greeted Abū al-ʿAbbās as successor of the Prophet.

On Friday, Abū al-ʿAbbās went out on a piebald horse, and prayed with the people.[370] ʿAmmār the mawlā of Jibraʾīl and Abū ʿAbdallāh al-Sulamī reported that when Abū Salamah greeted Abū al-ʿAbbās as Caliph, Abū Ḥumayd said to him, "He's Caliph in spite of you, you mother-sucker!" And Abū al-ʿAbbās said, "Easy does it."

[29] It is mentioned that when Abū al-ʿAbbās ascended the minbar on the day they swore allegiance to him as Caliph, he stood at the top, while Dāwud b. ʿAlī ascended and stood below him. Abū al-ʿAbbās spoke, and said:

Praise be to God who has chosen Islam as the pillow of His glory, who has exalted it and made it great, who has chosen it for us, and aided it by means of us. He has made us the people of Islam, its cave and its fortress, and made us to uphold it, to protect it and support it. He has caused us to cleave to His word of piety, and deemed us worthy of that as the people of the Word. He has specified us as the kin of God's Messenger, God's benediction and peace be upon him and his family. He created us from the ancestors of the Prophet, causing us to grow from his tree, and be derived thereby from common origins, making him one of us, causing what distresses us to weigh heavy on him, and making him watchful over us, for with the faithful He is gentle, compassionate. God placed us in the exalted place with Islam and its folk, sending down to the people of Islam the written Word to be recited to them, for He has spoken—glorious is

---

370. See Ibn Khayyāṭ, II, 424; Azdī, 123ff; *FHA*, 200ff; Yaʿqūbī, *Taʾrīkh*, II, 413; Masʿūdī, *Murūj*, VI, 98ff.

He who speaks—in unambiguous verses sent down in the Qur-
ʾān, "God only desires to put far from you abomination, O people of the house, and to cleanse you with purification".[371] He
has said, "Say [O Muḥammad]: I ask not of you any wage for
this save affection for the kinfolk."[372] He has said, "And warn
your clan, your closest kin."[373] He has said, "Whatever spoils
God has given His Messenger from the people of the towns is for
God and for the Messenger, and the near kinsman, and orphans."[374] He has said, "Know that if you take anything as
booty, one fifth of it is for God and for the Messenger and for the
near kinsmen and for orphans".[375] So He, glorious be His
praise, has informed them of our merit and made our rights and
affection for us incumbent on them. He has bestowed upon us
our share of the booty and the spoils in kindness toward us and
in favor to us. God is the Lord of mighty favor.

The erring Sabaʾiyyah[376] have asserted that others than we
are more worthy of headship, authority, and the successorship
than we; may their faces be struck by an evil eye! By what and   [30]
for what, ye people? By us God guided the people when they
were gone astray, and caused them to see when they were ignorant, and delivered them after they had perished. By us He
caused right to prevail, and through us refuted falsehood, setting aright by us the corrupt, uplifting by us the vile, complet-
ing by us what was defective, and joining together the separa-
tion. Thus after their enmity men became a family of mutual
affection, kindness and solace in both their religion and their
worldly affairs, "brothers reclining on couches face to face"[377]
in their after-life. That is what God has opened up [for men] in
grace and favor to Muḥammad, God bless him and give him
peace. When God took him to Himself, his companions took on
this authority after him, and their affair was by mutual counsel.

---

371. Qur. 33:33.
372. Qur. 42:23.
373. Qur. 26:214.
374. Qur. 59:7.
375. Qur. 8:41.
376. The followers of ʿAbdallāh b. Sabaʾ, the extremist whom enemies of the Shīʿah
of ʿAlī accused of founding the ʿAlid doctrine in early Islam. See *EI*[2] s.v. ʿAbd Allāh b.
Sabaʾ.
377. Qur. 15:47.

They took possession of the inheritance of the nations and distributed it justly, put it in its proper place, gave it to those entitled to it, and left with their own bellies empty. Then up reared the Banū Ḥarb and the Banū Marwān.[378] They took it away and passed it among themselves, and did battle for it, appropriating it to themselves, tyrannizing, oppressing those entitled to it; and God forbore with them for long, until they had afflicted Him; and when they afflicted Him, He took revenge on them at our hands. He restored to us our rights, and our Community became united through us. He vouchsafed our victory and established our authority in order to grant benefit through us to those grown feeble on the earth, closing an (epoch) with us as He had begun it with us. Most truly I hope that tyranny will not come upon you even as good has come, nor corruption overtake you as soundness has done. For what support have we, as People of the House, except in God?

People of Kūfah, you are the halting-place of our love, the lodging of our affections. You it is who remained steadfast, you who were not deflected from our love by the injustice of the people of tyranny against you until you reached our epoch and God brought you our revolution. You of all mankind are most fortunate in us and most worthy of our generosity. We have increased your allowances to a hundred dirhams. Make ready, then; for I am the manifest Spiller *(Saffāḥ)*,[379] the desolating Avenger.

[31]   He had been exhausted by a fever, and his weakness now increased. So he sat in the minbar, and Dāwud b. 'Alī went up and stood below him on the steps of the minbar and said:

Praise be to God, with gratitude, gratitude, and yet more gratitude! Praise to Him who has caused our enemies to perish and brought to us our inheritance from Muḥammad our Prophet, God's blessing and peace be upon him! O ye people, now are the dark nights of this world put to flight, its covering lifted; now light breaks in the earth and the heavens, and the sun rises from

---

378. The two branches of the Umayyad dynasty.

379. This sobriquet, which does not appear to be a regnal title, can mean either a spiller of wealth or of blood; a generous or an implacable ruler. During his lifetime the first 'Abbāsid caliph seems always to have been known as Abū al-'Abbās.

the springs of day while the moon ascends from its appointed place. He who fashioned the bow takes it up, and the arrow returns to him who shot it. Right [to rule] has come back to where it originated, among the people of the house of your Prophet, people of compassion and mercy for you and sympathy toward you. O ye people, by God we did not rebel seeking this authority to grow rich in silver and in gold; nor to dig a canal or build a castle. What made us rebel was the shame of their taking away our rights, our anger for our cousins,[380] our grief for your affairs and the burden that oppressed us for your sakes. It was for your situation that we burned in anger on our beds, and the evil conduct of the Banū Umayyah toward you increased our pain: their coarseness with you, their contempt for you, their appropriation of your booty, your alms and your spoils. You are under the protection of His Messenger, may God bless him and his family and give them peace, and the protection of ʿAbbās, may God have mercy on him. We shall rule you according to what God has sent down and treat you in accordance with the Book of God, and act with the commoner and the elite among you according to the behavior of God's messenger. Woe, woe to the Banū Ḥarb b. Umayyah and the Banū Marwān! In their space and time they preferred the ephemeral to the eternal, the transient abode to the everlasting one. Crime them obsessed; God's creatures they oppressed; women forbidden to them they possessed, all honor grieving and by sin deceiving. They tyrannized God's servants by their deport with evil custom where they sought disport; themselves with vice's burdens decked and their idolatry unchecked; at management of every fault most lively, cheerful; withal to race on error's course not fearful; God's purpose in respiting sin not comprehending and trusting they had tricked Him by pretending![381] God's severity came on   [32] them like a night raid when they were sleeping, and at dawn

---

380. That is, the ʿAlids. The ʿAbbāsids professed to avenge the wrongs against their kinsmen, while at the same time denying them any prior right to rule.

381. According to the Qurʾān, God permits sinners to flourish, so as to increase their guilt. See 17:15–19; 57:20; 35:39. This section of rhymed prose, generally intended to denigrate Umayyad rule, is a rhetorical flight which can be only approximately translated.

they were only legends. They were torn all to tatters, and thus may an oppressive people perish!

God has let us prevail over Marwān, for by God he was deceived with delusions, an enemy of God given the rein until he should stumble because of the superiority of his harness; for this enemy of God supposed that we should never prevail over him. He called upon his factions, employed all his stratagems and threw in his squadrons. Yet he found before him, behind him, and to his right and left, God's stratagem, His affliction and His judgment, to put to death his falsehood and efface his error. It was He who appointed the changes of ill-fortune for him, and revived our honor and our glory, returning to us our rights and our heritage.

O ye people, God has indeed helped the Commander of the Faithful to a mighty victory, but he turned to the minbar only after the prayer, for he hated to mix aught else with the congregation's words [with God], and only the severity of his fever deterred him from finishing his remarks. So call upon God to restore the Commander of the Faithful's health; for God has given you an exchange for Marwān, the enemy of the Merciful, the vice-regent of Satan, followed by base folk who corrupted the world when once it was wholesome, who replaced the true religion and violated the honor of the Muslims' protected women. [God has replaced him] with a youthful man of maturity and deliberation, one who is guided by his forefathers, those just and best who made the earth wholesome once it was corrupted, by following the waymarks of guidance and the well-traced road of piety.

The people then raised their voices in prayers for Abū al-'Abbās, and Dāwud continued:

Men of Kūfah, surely we continued wronged and bereft of our rights, until God ordained for us our Shī'ah, the people of Khurāsān, and by them revivified our rights. By them He adduced our compelling argument, and made our revolution to prevail. God has let you behold what you were awaiting, and now you look upon him. He has made manifest among you a Caliph of the clan of Hāshim, brightening thereby your faces and making you to prevail over the army of Syria, and transferring the sover-

[33]

eignty and the glory of Islam to you. He has graced you with an Imām whose gift is equity, and granted him good government. Receive with gratitude what God has given you, cleave to our allegiance, and practice not deceit against yourselves, for surely this authority is your authority; surely every dynasty has its center-point, and you are our center-point.[382] Has any successor to God's Messenger ascended this your minbar save the Commander of the Faithful ʿAlī b. Abī Ṭālib and the Commander of the Faithful ʿAbdallāh b. Muḥammad?[383]

and he gestured with his hand toward Abū al-ʿAbbās

So know that the authority is with us, and shall not depart from us until we surrender it to Jesus the son of Mary[384]—God's benediction be on him—and praise be to God, Lord of the universe, for that with which He has tried us and entrusted us!

Then Abū al-ʿAbbās descended from the minbar, with Dāwud b. ʿAlī in front of him until they entered the palace. He had Abū Jaʿfar sit and receive the handclasp of allegiance *(bayʿah)* from the people in the mosque. He kept on receiving it until he had prayed both the afternoon and the sunset prayer with them and night had enfolded them. Then he entered (the palace).

It is mentioned that when Dāwud b. ʿAlī and his son Mūsā were in Iraq, or somewhere else, they had left wishing to reach Sharāt. Abū al-ʿAbbās met them at Dūmat al-Jandal while on his way to Kūfah. With him were his brother Abū al-Jaʿfar ʿAbdallāh b. Muḥammad, ʿAbdallāh b. ʿAlī, ʿĪsā b. Mūsā, and Yaḥyā b. Jaʿfar b. Tammām b. al-ʿAbbās and a party of their mawlās. Dāwud asked them, "Where are

---

382. This reference to Kūfah was hardly reflected by ʿAbbāsid practice. They immediately withdrew to Ḥīrah and eventually established their administrative center at a new capital, Baghdad. See n. 353 above.

383. The question has a twofold thrust: that all caliphs between ʿAlī and Abū al-ʿAbbās were in fact illegal usurpers, and that there is a special relationship between the Kūfans and the Prophet's family.

384. That is, at the Messianic age which will precede the end of the world. According to one ḥadīth, "There will be no Mahdī but Jesus." This is preserved only in Sunnī collections of ḥadīths, however. The ʿAlid Shīʿī sects emphasize the Mahdist ḥadīths which state that the Messianic rule of justice will be fulfilled by a Mahdī of the line of ʿAlī. This statement therefore rejects the claims of the ʿAlids and suggests that the ʿAbbāsids are ushering in a messianic age which will see the second coming of Jesus. For a detailed treatment of Mahdism see J.A. Williams, *Themes of Islamic Civilization*, Ch. V, "The Expected Deliverer."

you going, and what is your story?" Abū al-ʿAbbās told him their story, and said that they were heading for Kūfah to make their appearance there and openly proclaim their authority. Dāwud told him, "Abū al-ʿAbbās, you are coming to Kūfah when the shaykh of the Umayyads, Marwān b. Muḥammad, is at Ḥarrān to oversee Iraq along with the armies of Syria and the Jazīrah. And Yazīd b. ʿUmar b. Hubayrah, the shaykh of the Arabs, is already in Iraq with the cavalry[385] of the Arabs!" Abū al-ʿAbbās replied, "O uncle,[386] Abū al-Ghanāʾim says, 'He who loves life will be humbled.'" And he quoted the words of al-Aʿshā:

[34]

> 'Tis no kind of death if I die not powerless,
> and a shame if what destroys a life is not its own demon.

Then Dāwud turned to his son Mūsā and said, "By God, your cousin's right, so let us go back with him and either live graciously or die nobly." At this they all turned back together. ʿĪsā b. Mūsā used to say when he mentioned their exodus from Ḥumayah to Kūfah, "A party of fourteen men left their homes and families to stake our claim; mighty was their purpose, great were their spirits, and strong their hearts."

The Remaining Reports of Events of this Year

Completion of the account of the oath of allegiance that was given to Abū al-ʿAbbās ʿAbdallāh b. Muḥammad b. ʿAlī, and what came of his authority: As Abū Jaʿfar said, we have previously mentioned (information) concerning Abū al-ʿAbbās ʿAbdallāh b. Muḥammad b. ʿAlī on the authority of certain scholars. We have also mentioned something of his affair and that of Abū Salamah. A reason that the Caliphate of Abū al-ʿAbbās was confirmed is what I now mention. When word reached Abū Salamah that Marwān b. Muḥammad had killed Ibrāhīm, who had been called the Imām, he thought it proper to declare for the descendants of ʿAbbās. Thus he suppressed any declaration for others. When Abū al-ʿAbbās arrived in Kūfah, Abū Salamah had settled him and the people of his house who came with

---

385. The text is *ḥalbah*, "fast horses," Perhaps read *jillah*, "great men," as in *Akhbār al-Dawlah*, 410–11.

386. The text is *fa-qāla Abū al-Ghanāʾim*. Ibn Athīr supplies *fa-qāla yā ʿammī*.

him in the house of al-Walīd b. Saʿd among the Banū Awd. When
Abū Salamah was asked about the Imām, he would say, "Don't be
hasty." This situation continued while he was at his camp at Ḥammām Aʿyan, until Abū Ḥumayd went out to go to the Kunāsah[387]
and met a servant of Ibrāhīm called Sābiq al-Khwārizmī. He recognized him, for he used to come to them in Syria. Now he asked him,
"What is the Imām Ibrāhīm doing?" Sābiq then informed him that
Marwān had treacherously slain him and that Ibrāhīm had bequeathed his authority to his brother Abū al-ʿAbbās, appointing him
as his successor. Moreover, Abū al-ʿAbbās had come to Kūfah with
most of the people of his family. Abū Ḥumayd begged Sābiq to set
off with him to the ʿAbbāsids. Sābiq told him, "The appointment between us is tomorrow morning in this place;" he was reluctant to
show him where the ʿAbbāsids were without their permission. The
following day, Abū Ḥumayd went out to the place where he had
promised to meet Sābiq. He found him, and went off with him to
Abū al-ʿAbbās and the men of his family. When he entered where
they were, Abū Ḥumayd asked, "Which of them is the Caliph?"
Then Dāwud b. ʿAlī said, "Here is your Imām and Caliph," pointing
to Abū al-ʿAbbās. Abū Ḥumayd then greeted him with the title of
Caliph, and kissed his hands and his feet, saying, "We are at your
command." He also condoled with him on the death of the Imām
Ibrāhīm.

Ibrāhīm b. Salamah had entered the army of Abū Salamah in disguise. He went to Abū al-Jahm and asked him for protection. Then
he informed him that he was the messenger of Abū al-ʿAbbās and
the people of his house. He also told him who was in the group and
where they were. He added that Abū al-ʿAbbās had sent him to Abū
Salamah to ask him for a hundred dīnārs with which to pay the
cameldriver for the camels that brought them to Kūfah, but Abū
Salamah had not sent them the money. Abū Ḥumayd also went
back to Abū al-Jahm and informed them of their situation. Abū al-
Jahm and Abū Ḥumayd together with Ibrāhīm b. Salamah went on
foot until they entered where Mūsā b. Kaʿb was. Abū al-Jahm told
him the story, and what Ibrāhīm b. Salamah had related to him.
Mūsā then said, "Hasten to send him the dīnārs, and see that the

[35]

---

387. One of the major quarters of Kūfah on the western side of the town. See Yāqūt,
Muʿjam, s.v. Kunāsah, and LeStrange, *Lands*, 75.

man gets there." So Abū al-Jahm went off and handed the money over to Ibrāhīm b. Salamah. He put him on a mule and sent two men with him to see him into Kūfah. Then Abū al-Jahm told Abū Salamah, "It is rumored in the army that Marwān b. Muḥammad has slain the Imām. If he has been slain, then his brother Abū al-ʿAbbās is the successor and the Imām after him." Abū Salamah replied, "Abū al-Jahm, stop Abū Ḥumayd from entering Kūfah, for these people spread falsehood and corruption."

[36]

On the second night, Ibrāhīm b. Salamah came to Abū al-Jahm and Mūsā b. Kaʿb and delivered to them a letter from Abū al-ʿAbbās and the people of his family. He visited the officers and the Shīʿah that same night. They then gathered in the house of Mūsā b. Kaʿb. Among them were ʿAbd al-Ḥamīd b. Ribʿī, Salamah b. Muḥammad, ʿAbdallāh al-Ṭāʾī, Isḥāq b. Ibrāhīm, Sharāḥīl, ʿAbdallāh b. Bassām and other officers. They disagreed as to whether to go see Abū al-ʿAbbās and those of his family. Then they stole away the next morning into Kūfah, led by Mūsā b. Kaʿb, Abū al-Jahm and Abū Ḥumayd al-Ḥimyarī—that is, Muḥammad b. Ibrāhīm. They came at last to the house of al-Walīd b. Saʿd, and went in. Mūsā b. Kaʿb and Abū al-Jahm said, "Which of you is Abū al-ʿAbbās?" At this the people pointed him out. They then wished him peace and condoled with him on the death of the Imām Ibrāhīm. Afterward they went off to the camp leaving behind with him Abū Ḥumayd, Abū Muqātil, Sulaymān b. al-Aswad, Muḥammad b. al-Ḥusayn, Muḥammad b. al-Ḥārith, Nahār b. Ḥusayn, Yūsuf b. Muḥammad and Abū Hurayrah Muḥammad b. Farrūkh.

Abū Salamah then sent to Abū al-Jahm to come to him. The latter had let him know that he had gone into Kūfah. "Where were you?" Abū Salamah asked. "I was with my Imām," Abū al-Jahm replied. Abū al-Jahm went out and called Ḥājib b. Ṣaddān and sent him to Kūfah, saying, "Go in and salute Abū al-ʿAbbās as Caliph." He sent word to Abū Ḥumayd and his friends, "If Abū Salamah comes to you, let him in only by himself. If he enters and offers allegiance, then let him go his way; otherwise, cut off his head." They had not waited long before Abū Salamah came, went in by himself, and greeted Abū al-ʿAbbās with the title of Caliph. Abū al-ʿAbbās ordered him to go back to his camp, and he went off that night. The people waited for morning wearing their weapons and in formation, waiting for Abū al-ʿAbbās to emerge. They gave him horses, and he

[37]

and the members of his family who were with him rode until they entered the governor's palace of Kūfah on Friday, the twelfth night of Rabīʿ II (November 28, 729). He then entered the mosque from the govenor's palace and went up into the minbar, where he praised God and magnified Him, mentioning the mightiness of the Lord and the excellence of the Prophet. He then traced authority to the rule and the succession (to the Prophet) down to himself. He promised the people good times to come, and then was quiet.

Dāwud b. ʿAlī who was in the minbar three steps lower than Abū al-ʿAbbās then spoke. He praised God and glorified Him and spoke benedictions on the Prophet. Then he said, "Ye people, truly there has been no Caliph after God's Messenger save ʿAlī b. Abī Ṭālib and this Commander of the Faithful who now sits behind me." Abū al-ʿAbbās then came down and left. He made his camp at Ḥammām Aʿyan in the camp of Abū Salamah, staying with him in the same chamber, with a curtain between them. The chamberlain *(ḥājib)* of Abū al-ʿAbbās at this time was ʿAbdallāh b. Bassām. Abū al-ʿAbbās left his paternal uncle Dāwud b. ʿalī to govern Kūfah and its province and sent his uncle ʿAbdallāh b. ʿAlī to Abū ʿAwn b. Yazīd. He sent his nephew ʿĪsā b. Mūsā to al-Ḥasan b. Qaḥṭabah who was at this time at Wāsiṭ besieging Ibn Hubayrah. He also sent Yaḥyā b. Jaʿfar b. Tammām b. ʿAbbās to Ḥumayd b. Qaḥṭabah at Madāʾin, Abū al-Yaqdhān ʿUthmān b. ʿUrwah b. Muḥammad b. ʿAmmār b. Yāsir to Bassām b. Ibrāhīm b. Bassām at Ahwāz, and Salamah b. ʿAmr b. ʿUthmān to Mālik b. Ṭarīf.[388] Abū al-ʿAbbās stayed with the army for some months, and then moved and settled at (the new) Hāshimite City (Madīnah al-Hāshimiyyah) in the fortress at Kūfah.[389] He had disguised his intention to Abū Salamah before he moved, until Abū Salamah learned of it.

In this year, Marwān b. Muḥammad was put to flight at the Zāb.[390]   [38]

---

388. The ʿAbbāsid family thus began the transition from a secretive revolutionary leadership into a ruling family. See Lassner, *ʿAbbāsid Rule,* 7ff. (J.L.)

389. This appears to be a broken text. It is hard to believe that Abū al-ʿAbbās would have chosen to establish his government in the city itself. He had, in similar circumstances, abandoned the Kūfans and gone to Ḥammām Aʿyan. It is more likely that what was originally intended was a place in the general vicinity of Kūfah. The text apparatus suggests such a reading. See Lassner, *ʿAbbāsid Rule,* 152–53. (J.L.)

390. See Ibn Khayyāṭ, II, 427ff; Azdī, 126ff; *FHA,* 201ff; Yaʿqūbī, *Taʾrīkh,* II, 413ff; Masʿūdī, *Murūj,* VI, 85ff; *Tanbīh,* 327.

Marwan's Defeat at the Zāb and Why and How it Came

According to ʿAlī b. Muḥammad—Abū al-Sarī, Jabalah b. Farrūkh, al-Ḥasan b. Rashīd, Abū Ṣāliḥ al-Marwazī and others: Abū ʿAwn ʿAbd al-Malik b. Yazīd al-Azdī was sent by Qaḥṭabah to Shahrazūr from Nihāwand. He then slew ʿUthmān b. Sufyān and stayed in the neighborhood of Mosul. Marwān was informed that ʿUthmān had been killed, and he advanced from Ḥarrān. He stayed at a place along the way, and asked, "What's the name of this place?" "Balwā [Calamity]," they told him. "Bal ʿAlwā [Nay, Superiority]; a good omen," he replied. He came to Ra's al-ʿAyn,[391] then to Mosul. Camping at the Tigris, he dug a moat. Abū ʿAwn marched to him and camped at the Zāb, and Abū Salamah sent Abū ʿAwn, ʿUyaynah b. Mūsā, Minhāl b. Fattān and Isḥāq b. Ṭalḥah, each at the head of three thousand men. When Abū al-ʿAbbās was proclaimed Caliph, he reinforced Abū ʿAwn sending Salamah b. Muḥammad with two thousand men, ʿAbdallāh al-Ṭā'ī with two thousand, and Wadas b. Naḍlah with five hundred. Then he asked, "Who among the men of my house will march against Marwān?" ʿAbdallāh b. ʿAlī said, "I." And Abū al-ʿAbbās told him, "Go with God's blessing."[392] ʿAbdallāh b. ʿAlī came up with Abū ʿAwn, and Abū ʿAwn vacated his own pavilion, leaving it and all that was in it for ʿAbdallāh. The latter now appointed Ḥayyāsh b. Ḥabīb al-Ṭā'ī in charge of security and Nuṣayr b. al-Muḥtafiz in charge of his guard. Abū al-ʿAbbās put Mūsā b. Kaʿb in charge of the postal intelligence *(barīd)*[393] and sent him with thirty men to ʿAbdallāh b. ʿAlī. On the second night of Jumāda II 132 (January 16, 750), ʿAbdallāh b. ʿAlī asked where there was a ford of the Zāb, and one was pointed out to him. He gave the order to ʿUyaynah b. Mūsā, who crossed over with five thousand men and proceeded to Marwān's camp. Marwān gave battle until evening fell and fires were lit. They broke off fighting and ʿUyaynah returned to the camp of ʿAbdallāh b. ʿAlī, crossing the river at the

[39]

---

391. For Ra's al-ʿAyn, see LeStrange, *Lands*, 95–96.

392. ʿAbdallāh b. ʿAlī later based his claims to the caliphate on having taken the field against Marwān. See Ṭabarī, III/1, 92–93; Azdī, 163ff; Yaʿqūbī, *Ta'rīkh*, II, 438–39; Masʿūdī, *Murūj*, VI, 177.

393. The posting system existed primarily for getting information to the Caliph with maximum efficiency. The "postmaster" in each province operated as the eyes and ears of the Caliph, and controlled the system by which information was carried by post horses to the capital. See *EI*² s.v. Barīd.

ford. Upon rising in the morning, Marwān secured the pontoon bridge and sent his son ʿAbdallāh to dig a moat further downriver from the camp of ʿAbdallāh b. ʿAlī. At this, ʿAbdallāh sent al-Mukhāriq b. Ghifār with four thousand men. He advanced five miles from ʿAbdallāh b. ʿAlī before halting. ʿAbdallāh b. Marwān sent al-Walīd b. Muʿāwiyah against him. Al-Walīd engaged al-Mukhāriq, whose followers were put to flight or captured, and a good number of them were killed that day. Al-Walīd sent the prisoners to ʿAbdallāh, who sent them on to Marwān with the heads. Marwān ordered, "Send in one of the prisoners to me." They brought him al-Mukhāriq, who was a very thin man. Marwān said, "You're al-Mukhāriq." But he told him, "No, I am one of the slaves of the people of the army." "Then do you know al-Mukhāriq?" asked Marwān. "Yes," he said. "Then look at these heads—do you see him?" He looked at one of the heads and said, "He's the one." Then Marwān let him go. At the time, a man who was with Marwān stared at al-Mukhāriq and, not knowing him, said, "God curse Abū Muslim for bringing such as these to do battle with us!"

ʿAlī heard the following from a shaykh of the people of Khurāsān: Marwān said, "Do you know al-Mukhāriq when you see him? They say that his is among these heads that were sent to us." "I know him," al-Mukhāriq told him. Then Marwān said, "Show him those heads." And he looked and said, "I don't see his head among these. I can only suppose he escaped." Then they let him go. ʿAbdallāh b. ʿAlī learned of the rout of al-Mukhāriq, and Mūsā b. Kaʿb told him, "Go out to Marwān before news of the rout reaches the army and what happened to al-Mukhāriq becomes widely known." ʿAbdallāh b. ʿAlī called Muḥammad b. Ṣūl and put him in charge of the army. [40] Abū ʿAwn had command of the right wing, and in command of Marwān's left wing was al-Walīd b. Muʿāwiyah. With Marwān were three thousand of the Muḥammirah,[394] and he had with him the Dhakwāniyyah, the Ṣaḥṣaḥiyyah, and the Rāshidiyyah. When the two armies were face to face, Marwān told ʿAbd al-ʿAzīz b. ʿUmar b.

---

394. Literally, "Redwearers." Later this word is used for Iranian heretics with Mazdakite doctrines. However, the later Qays faction of Greater Syria used red as their distinctive color. See e.g., *EI*² s.v. Ḳays ʿAylān. The "Muḥammirah" appear here as one of several elite regiments that served the last Umayyad Caliph, For colors as political tags, see the article of Omar cited in n. 72. See also Crone, *Slaves on Horses*, 241, n. 93.

ʿAbd al-ʿAzīz, "If the sun declines today before they have fought us, then it is we who shall yield up rule to Jesus the son of Mary; if they fight us before it declines, then we are God's, and to Him we shall return!"[395]

Marwān sent to ʿAbdallāh b. ʿAlī asking for terms, and ʿAbdallāh said, "Ibn Zurayq[396] lied; God willing, before the sun declines our horses shall have trampled him." Marwān told the Syrians, "Hold off, and do not begin battle," while he kept looking at the sun. Then al-Walīd b. Muʿāwiyah b. Marwān (b. al-Ḥakam), who was married to Marwān's daughter, attacked. At this, Marwān became furious and cursed him. Ibn Muʿāwiyah fought the troops of the (ʿAbbāsid) right wing, and Abū ʿAwn fled toward ʿAbdallāh b. ʿAlī. Then Mūsā b. Kaʿb said to ʿAbdallāh, "Order the troops to dismount." At this the cry went out, "To the ground!" The troops dismounted and extended their lances while crouched. Then they engaged the enemy. The Syrians began to pause, as if they were quitting, and ʿAbdallāh went along on foot, saying, "Lord, how long shall we be slain for your sake?" He called out, "Men of Khurāsān! Revenge for Ibrāhīm! Yā Muḥammad! Yā Manṣūr!"[397] And the battle grew fiercer. Marwān shouted to the Quḍāʿah, "Dismount!" They replied, "Say it to the Banū Sulaym; let them dismount!" He sent word to the Saksakīs, "Attack." They replied, "Tell the Banū ʿĀmir; let them attack." He then sent word to the Sakūn, "Charge!" They said, "Tell the Ghaṭafān; let them charge." He told his chief of security, "Dismount!" The man replied, "No, by God, I'll never make myself a

[41] target!" Marwān told him, "Well, by God, I'll surely cause you harm!" He replied, "By God, I wish you were able!" The Syrians fled, and then Marwān fled too, cutting the pontoon bridge. More were drowned that day than were slain in battle. Among those drowned was Ibrāhīm b. al-Walīd b. ʿAbd al-Malik (the deposed Caliph). At ʿAbdallāh b. ʿAlī's command the pontoon bridge over the Zāb was retied, and they took out the drowned—some three hundred—among whom were Ibrāhīm b. al-Walīd b. ʿAbd al-Malik. ʿAbdallāh b. ʿAlī then recited the verse, "And we divided the sea for you,

---

395. See n. 384 above. The expression "We are God's" is found in several verses of the Qurʾān.

396. Ibn Zurayq is an insulting name for Marwān, perhaps reflecting the story that he was not the son of Muḥammad b. Marwān at all. See Ṭabarī, III, 51.

397. For the title Manṣūr mentioned in this battle cry, see n. 82 above.

and delivered you, and drowned Pharaoh's people while you were beholding."[398]

'Abdallāh b. 'Alī remained in his camp for seven days. A man descended from Sa'īd b. al-'Āṣ said these words, reviling Marwān:

Flight importunes Marwān, and I have told him,
    'now the oppressor is one oppressed, whose desire is to flee.

What are flight and abdication of kingship, once gone
    from you all forbearance? There is no religion or honor;

Lightwit in patience, a Pharaoh in persecution; and if
    you seek his generosity, he's a dog before whom is a mad dog.'

'Abdallāh b. 'Alī wrote to the Commander of the Faithful of the victory and Marwān's flight, and he took possession of Marwān's army and all it had carried with it. They found many weapons and much wealth, but they found no women except a slavegirl of 'Abdallāh b. Marwān. When 'Abdallāh b. 'Alī's letter reached Abū al-'Abbās, he prayed two prostrations, and then recited the verses, "When Saul set out with the host, he said, 'God will try you by a river; whosoever drinks thereof is not of me, and whosoever tastes it not, he is of me, save him who scoops it with his hand.' Yet they drank thereof, all save a few of them, and when he had crossed with those who believed with him, they said, 'We can do nothing this day against Goliath and his hosts.' Those who reckoned that they were to meet God however said, 'How often a little band has overcome a numerous company by God's leave! God is with the patient.' So, when they went out against Goliath and his hosts, they said, 'Our Lord, bestow on us patience, make firm our feet, and aid us against the people of the unbelievers!' And they routed him, by God's leave, and David slew Goliath, and God gave him the kingship, and wisdom, and taught him such as He willed."[399] Then Abū al-'Abbās ordered that each man who had been at the battle should receive five hundred (dirhams) and he raised their monthly salaries to eighty (dirhams).

Aḥmad b. Zuhayr reported the following from 'Alī b. Muḥammad

---

398. Qur. 2:47.
399. Qur. 2:249–51.

[42]

—ʿAbd al-Raḥmān b. Umayyah: When the men of Khurāsān met up with Marwān, he could manage nothing that was free of disorder and corruption. Aḥmad said that he received this account. On the day he was routed Marwān was standing firm, and the troops were engaged in combat, when he sent for money. It was brought, and he told the troops, "Stand fast and fight, and this money will be yours." Then some of the troops began to seize the money, and they sent word to him, "The troops are eager for the money, and we're not sure they won't run away with it." So he sent word to his son ʿAbdallāh, "Go with your men to the rear of your camp and kill anyone who takes that money, and stop them." ʿAbdallāh moved (to the rear) with his standard, and the troops said, "It's a retreat." and fled.

According to Aḥmad b. ʿAlī—Abū Jārūd al-Sulamī—a man from the Khurāsān army. We encountered Marwān at the Zāb, and the Syrians attacked us as if they were a mountain of iron; then we crouched and extended our lances and they turned from us like a cloud (of dust) and God gave us the backs of them. When they crossed (the river) the bridge was cut in front of those following them. A Syrian remained on it, so one of our men went out to him, and the Syrian slew him. Then another man went out, and he killed him, until finally he had killed three men. Then one of our men said, "Find me a sharp sword and a tough shield," so we got them for him. Then he went for him. The Syrian struck at him, but he fended him off with the shield and struck the Syrian's leg, cutting off his foot. He went on to kill him, and came back to us. We picked him up shouting, "*Allāhu Akhbar!*" The man was ʿUbaydallāh al-Kābulī.

The rout of Marwān at the Zāb, according to what is mentioned, took place on Saturday morning, the eleventh night of Jumādā II (January 25, 750).

In this year Ibrāhīm b. Muḥammad b. ʿAlī b. ʿAbdallāh b. ʿAbbās was killed.

The Death of the Imām Ibrāhīm the ʿAbbāsid

The biographers have differed on the matter of Ibrāhīm b. Muḥammad. Some of them say that he was not killed but that he died of plague in the prison of Marwān b. Muḥammad.[400]

---

400. See n. 365 above. However, death by plague is also regarded as a martyr's death, following a well-known ḥadīth.

Those Who Say He Died in Prison

According to Aḥmad b. Zuhayr—ʿAbd al-Wahhāb b. Ibrāhīm b. Khālid—Abū Hāshim Mukhallad b. Muḥammad b. Ṣāliḥ: Marwān b. Muḥammad came to Raqqah the time he set out against al-Ḍaḥḥāk. He had with him Saʿīd b. Hishām b. ʿAbd al-Malik and Saʿīd's two sons ʿUthmān and Marwān. All of them accompanied him in bonds. He sent them to his lieutenant at Ḥarrān, who put them in the prison there along with Ibrāhīm (b. Muḥammad) b. ʿAlī b. ʿAbdallāh b. ʿAbbās and ʿAbdallāh b. ʿUmar b. ʿAbd al-ʿAzīz, al-ʿAbbās b. al-Walīd, and Abū Muḥammad the Sufyānī, who was called the Farrier *(al-Bayṭār)*. Of them there perished in prison from an epidemic that broke out in Ḥarrān, ʿAbbās b. al-Walīd, Ibrāhīm b. Muḥammad and ʿAbdallāh b. ʿUmar b. ʿAbd al-ʿAzīz. One week before Marwān was routed at the Zāb by ʿAbdallāh b. ʿAlī, Saʿīd b. Hishām and those who were imprisoned with him escaped when they killed the man in charge of the prison. Abū Muḥammad al-Sufyānī stayed behind in confinement and did not leave with those who escaped. Others who did not view escape from the prison as lawful stayed with him. The people of Ḥarrān and some of the rabble *(ghawghā')* in the city killed Saʿīd b. Hishām, Sharāḥīl b. Maslamah b. ʿAbd al-Malik, ʿAbd al-Malik b. Bishr al-Taghlibī and the Patrikios of Armenia IV, whose name was Kūshān, by stoning them to death. Only fifteen days or so after they were killed, Marwān came to Ḥarrān fleeing from the Battle of the Zāb and set Abū Muḥammad and those confined with him in the prison free.

According to ʿUmar—ʿAbdallāh b. Kathīr al-ʿAbdī—ʿAlī b. Mūsā—his father: Marwān pushed down the walls of a room on Ibrāhīm b. Muḥammad and killed him.[401]

According to ʿUmar—Muḥammad b. Maʿrūf b. Suwayd—his father—al-Muhalhil b. Ṣafwān (ʿUmar: Later al-Mufaḍḍal b. Jaʿfar b. Sulaymān also told me that al-Muhalhil b. Ṣafwān told this story): I was with Ibrāhīm b. Muḥammad in the prison in which ʿAbdallāh b. ʿUmar b. ʿAbd al-ʿAzīz and Sharāḥīl b. Maslamah b. ʿAbd al-Malik were detained. They would visit each other, especially Ibrāhīm and

[43]

[44]

---

401. The same method of assassination was reportedly utilized by the Caliph al-Manṣūr against his uncle ʿAbdallāh b. ʿAlī. The latter tradition with full explication of the legal consequences of this kind of killing is discussed in Lassner, *ʿAbbāsid Rule*, 39–57, esp. 40–46. (J.L.)

Sharāḥīl. One day Sharāḥīl's messenger brought Ibrāhīm some milk and said, "Your brother says, 'I drank some of this milk and enjoyed it, and I'd like you to have some too.'" He accepted it and drank, and immediately thereafter became ill and collapsed. It was a day when he was supposed to go see Sharāḥīl, but he delayed, so Sharāḥīl sent word to him, "Let me be your ransom, you have delayed; what has detained you?" He sent word back, "When I drank the milk you sent me, it disagreed with me." Sharāḥīl came to him badly frightened, and said, "No, by God, no god there is but He; I drank no milk today and I sent none to you! Truly we are God's, and to Him we shall return. By God, you have been deceived!" By God, he survived only that night and no other. The following morning Ibrāhīm was dead.[402]

Ibrāhīm b. ʿAlī b. Salamah b. ʿĀmir b. Ḥurmah b. Hudhayl b. al-Rabīʿ b. ʿĀmir b. Subayḥ b. ʿAdī b. Qays, that is, Qays b. al-Ḥārith b. Fihr, lamented Ibrāhīm as follows:

> I reckoned myself strong, but my wits are scattered
>   by a grave at Ḥarrān in which is religion's defense.
>
> In it is the Imām and the best of all mankind,
>   among the slates and the stones and the clay;
>
> The Imām whose misfortune became widespread,
>   depriving every rich man or poor.
>
> May God not absolve Marwān for any wrongdoing,
>   but God pardon all who here say "Amen!"

This year Marwān b. Muḥammad b. Marwān b. ʿAbd al-Ḥakam was slain.

The Death of Marwān and His Battle with the Syrians

[45]   Aḥmad b. Zuhayr—ʿAbd al-Wahhāb b. Ibrāhīm b. Khālid—Abū Hāshim Mukhallad b. Muḥammad: When Marwān fled from the

---

402. Sudden or unexpected deaths from natural causes (e.g., appendicitis) were always prone to be later described as murder by poisoning. See Lassner, *ʿAbbāsid Rule,* 46ff.

Zāb I was in his army, and Marwān had one hundred twenty thousand men in his forces at the Zāb; sixty thousand were in his own army and about the same number were with his son ʿAbdallāh, with the Zāb between them. ʿAbdallāh b. ʿAlī engaged Marwān with the troops accompanying him, Abū ʿAwn and a group of officers among whom was Ḥumayd b. Qaḥṭabah. When Marwān's forces were put to flight, they went to Ḥarrān, where Abān b. Yazīd b. Muḥammad b. Marwān, his brother's son, was governor. Marwān stayed at Ḥarrān more than twenty days. When ʿAbdallāh b. ʿAlī drew near, he packed up his people and children and family and fled, leaving at Ḥarrān Abān b. Yazīd who was married to a daughter of Marwān called Umm ʿUthmān. ʿAbdallāh b. ʿAlī advanced and Abān went out to meet him dressed in black as a sign of his allegiance. Abān then took the oath to ʿAbdallāh and entered his service, while ʿAbdallāh gave him and all those in Ḥarrān and the Jazīrah guarantees of safety. Marwān continued past Qinnasrīn with ʿAbdallāh b. ʿAlī pursuing him. Then he moved on from Qinnasrīn to Ḥimṣ where the people met him in the markets ready to hear and obey. He stayed there for two or three days, and then set out. When people saw how few there were with him they became emboldened against him, saying, "He's a coward, running away." They pursued him after he had set out from them and caught up with him some miles away. When he saw the dust raised by their horses, he set two officers of his mawlās, one called Yazīd and the other Mukhallad, in two ravines (wādīs). When the pursuers came near him and passed the two ambush parties and his womenfolk had gone, he set his men in battle formation, and besought the pursuers in God's name. They refused to do anything but bandy words with him and do battle, so fighting broke out between them. Then the ambushers attacked them from the rear, and he put them to flight. His cavalry pursued them, killing them until they reached the vicinity of the city.

Marwān went on until he passed Damascus, which was governed by al-Walīd b. Muʿāwiyah b. Marwān, who was Marwān's son-in-law, married to a daughter of his called Umm al-Walīd. Marwān continued on his way, leaving al-Walīd b. Muʿāwiyah in charge of the city until ʿAbdallāh b. ʿAlī came against him. ʿAbdallāh besieged [46] Damascus some days, and the city was taken. He entered Damascus by force, opposing its people. Al-Walīd b. Muʿāwiyah fell among those who were slain. ʿAbdallāh b. ʿAlī tore down the walls of the city. Marwān passed by the Jordan, and Thaʿlabah b. Salāmah al-ʿĀmilī, who was his governor there, set off with him, leaving the district without a governor until ʿAbdallāh b. ʿAlī arrived and appointed one for it. Then Marwān came to Palestine, which was governed on his behalf by al-Rumāḥis b. ʿAbd al-ʿAzīz. Rumāḥis also left with him, and Marwān went on until he arrived at Miṣr.[403] Then he left there and stopped one stage away at a place called Būsir.[404] He was attacked by night and slain there by ʿĀmir b. Ismāʿīl and Shuʿbah, accompanied by some of the cavalry of Mosul. On the same night that he was attacked, ʿAbdallāh and ʿUbaydallāh, the two sons of Marwān, fled to the land of the Abyssinians. They met misfortune at the hands of the Abyssinians, who fought them and slew ʿUbaydallāh. ʿAbdallāh got away with a number of men who were with them, including Bakr b. Muʿāwiyah al-Bāhilī. Bakr stayed free until the caliphate of al-Mahdī, when Naṣr b. Muḥammad b. al-Ashʿath, the governor of Palestine, caught him and sent him to al-Mahdī.

According to ʿAlī b. Muḥammad—Bishr b. ʿĪsā, al-Nuʿmān Abū Sarī, Muḥriz b. Ibrāhīm, Abū Ṣāliḥ al-Marwazī and ʿAmmār the mawlā of Jibrīl: Marwān met ʿAbdallāh b. ʿAlī with one hundred and twenty thousand men, and ʿAbdallāh had only twenty thousand. The number who were with ʿAbdallāh that day is disputed, however, by other authorities.

Muslim b. al-Mughīrah reported the following from Muṣʿab b. al-Rabīʿ al-Khuthʿamī, father of Abū Mūsā b. Muṣʿab, who was a secretary of Marwān: When Marwān fled and ʿAbdallāh b. ʿAlī conquered Syria, I asked for a guarantee of safety, and he accorded it to me. One day I was sitting in his presence, and while he was reclining, someone mentioned Marwān and his flight. He asked, "Were you at the battle?" "Yes," I told him, "May God make things right with the [47] Amīr!" "Tell me about him," he said. So I said, "On that very day he told me, 'Count the enemy.' I told him, 'I'm only a man of the pen, not a man of war.' Then turning to the right and the left, he looked

---

403. Miṣr was both the name for Egypt and the general name for its capital, Fusṭāṭ. The context makes it clear that the city is intended here.

404. There were several locations of that name in Egypt. This was probably Būsir called Būsir al-Malaq on the west bank of the Nile at the entrance to the Fayyūm Oasis in Upper Egypt. Yāqūt calls it Būsir Qūrīdis. See *EI²* s.v. Būsir; Yāqūt, *Muʿjam*, I, 760.

and said, "They are twelve thousand." At this, 'Abdallāh sat up and said, "God smite him, what was with him? I do not reckon the military rolls carried more than twelve thousand men that day!"

Returning to 'Alī b. Muḥammad—his authorities: Marwān fled until he came to the city of Mosul which was governed by Hishām b. 'Amr al-Taghlibī and Bishr b. Khuzaymah al-Asadī, and they cut the pontoon bridge. The Syrians shouted to them, "It's Marwān!" But they replied, "You lie; the Commander of the Faithful doesn't run away!" He therefore went to a village. He crossed the Tigris and went to Ḥarrān and then to Damascus, where he left al-Walīd b. Mu'āwiyah in charge, saying, "Fight them, until the people of Syria are united." Then Marwān moved on to Palestine and stopped at the River of Abū Fuṭrus. Al-Ḥakam b. Dab'ān al-Judhāmī had seized power in Palestine, so Marwān sent word to 'Abdallāh b. Yazīd b. Rawḥ b. Zinbā' appointing him to power, but the treasury was in the hands of al-Ḥakam. Abū al-'Abbās wrote to 'Abdallāh b. 'Alī commanding him to pursue Marwān, so 'Abdallāh proceeded to Mosul. He was met by Hishām b. 'Amr al-Taghlibī and Bishr b. Khuzaymah who had displayed the color black with the people of Mosul, and they now opened up the city to him. He then marched to Ḥarrān, appointing Muḥammad b. Ṣūl as governor of Mosul. In Ḥarrān 'Abdallāh demolished the house in which Ibrāhīm b. Muḥammad had been confined. He then marched to Manbij, where the people had displayed black. He stopped in Manbij and appointed Abū Ḥumayd al-Marwazī as governor. The people of Qinnasrīn sent 'Abdallāh their oath of allegiance; one of those who came to him on their behalf was Abū Umayyah al-Taghlibī. 'Abd al-Ṣamad b. 'Alī arrived from Abū al-'Abbās to reinforce him with four thousand men. [48] 'Abdallāh stayed there a couple of days after the arrival of 'Abd al-Ṣamad, but then moved to Qinnasrīn. When he came there, the people had already displayed the color black. He stayed a couple of days, and then moved on to stop at Ḥimṣ. 'Abdallāh stayed there several days, while the inhabitants swore the oath of allegiance. Then he marched to Ba'albakk where he stayed a couple of days before moving on. He stopped next at 'Ayn al-Jarr,[405] remaining there two days

---

405. The Umayyad princely city built by al-Walīd II in the anti-Lebanon and known today as 'Anjar. See *EI*[2] s.v. 'Ayn al-Djarr.

before moving on. ʿAbdallāh then camped at Mizzah,[406] one of the villages of Damascus. Then Ṣāliḥ b. ʿAlī arrived with reinforcements and he camped at Marj ʿAdhrā'[407] with eight thousand men. With him were Bassām b. Ibrāhīm, Khafāf, Shuʿbah, and al-Haytham b. Bassām. Then ʿAbdallāh b. ʿAlī moved, and camped at the East Gate (Bāb Sharqī).[408] Ṣāliḥ b. ʿAlī settled at the Jābiyah Gate, Abū ʿAwn at Bāb Kaysān, Bassām at Bab al-Ṣaghīr and Ḥumayd b. Qaḥṭabah at Bāb Tūmā. ʿAbd al-Ṣamad, Yaḥyā b. Ṣafwān and al-ʿAbbās b. Yazīd were at Bāb al-Farādīs—al-Walīd b. Muʿāwiyah was still inside Damascus. The attackers laid siege to the people of Damascus and the Balqāʾ. Then the people of the city broke into factional rivalry; some of them killed others, and they slew al-Walīd. The ʿAbbāsids forced the gates on Wednesday, the twentieth of Ramadān (May 2, 750). The first to scale the wall of the city from the East Gate was ʿAbdallāh al-Ṭāʾī, and the first at Bāb al-Ṣaghīr was Bassām b. Ibrāhīm. They fought for three hours in the city. ʿAbdallāh b. ʿAlī stopped at Damascus for fifteen days, and then set out for Palestine and stopped at the Kuswah River.[409] From there he sent Yaḥyā b. Jaʿfar the Hāshimite to Madīnah, and then he moved to the Jordan. The people had already adopted black, and they came out to meet him. He camped at Baysān,[410] then moved to Marj al-Rūm and came to the River of Abū Fuṭrus.[411] Marwān had fled, and ʿAbdallāh stayed in Palestine. A letter from Abū al-ʿAbbās came to him, "Send Ṣāliḥ b. ʿAlī in pursuit of Marwān." And Ṣāliḥ b. ʿAlī marched from the

---

406. See LeStrange, *Palestine*, 237.

407. A meadow lying twelve *mīl* (24 km.) from Damascus. See LeStrange, *Palestine*, 503.

408. Bāb al-Farādīs was the northern gate of Damascus. The Kaysān Gate was southeast, and Bāb al-Saghīr on the south. Bāb Tūmā was on the northeast. See *EI²* s.v. Dimashk.

409. Meaning the Nahr al-Aʿwaj which flows from Mt. Hermon into the area known as al-Kuswah. The latter was situated some twelve *mīl* (24 km.) from Damascus. See LeStrange, *Palestine*, 488.

410. A town in the Jordan Valley known today as Bet Shan. See LeStrange, *Palestine*, 410ff.

411. Abū Fuṭrus was the ancient Antipatris on the Awjāʾ, near Ramlah. Ṭabarī barely mentions, later on, a massacre of some eighty members, more or less, of the Umayyad family here by ʿAbdallāh b. ʿAlī, though Ibn Athīr, Yaʿqūbī, Azdī, and *al-Aghānī* all give details. See Ibn Athīr, II, 333; Yaʿqūbī, *Taʾrīkh*, II, 355; and Wellhausen, *Arab Kingdom*, 551–52. Yaʿqūbī II, 356–57, also mentions how ʿAbdallāh b. ʿAlī opened the graves of the Umayyad caliphs and burned their bodies "sparing none." Others state that the tomb of ʿUmar II was spared.

River of Abū Fuṭrus in Dhū al-Qaʿdah 132 (June 11–July 10, 750). He
had with him Ibn Fattān, ʿĀmir b. Ismāʿīl al-Ḥārithī and Abū ʿAwn,   [49]
and he sent Abū ʿAwn to lead his vanguard along with ʿĀmir b.
Ismāʿīl. Ṣāliḥ marched on, stopping at Ramlah;[412] then he continued, and they camped at the seacoast. Ṣāliḥ b. ʿAlī gathered vessels
and provisioned them to go after Marwān who was at Faramā. Ṣāliḥ
marched along the coast road while the ships sailed alongside him
until he stopped at ʿArīsh.[413]

Word of this reached Marwān, so he had the fodder and foodstuffs
around him burned, and fled. Ṣāliḥ b. ʿAlī pressed on, and stopped at
the Nile, before moving on and camping in Upper Egypt (al-Saʿīd).
Word reached Ṣāliḥ that Marwān's cavalry along the banks of the
river were burning the fodder, so he sent some officers against them.
These captured ten men and brought them to Ṣāliḥ, who was at
Fusṭāṭ.[414] Marwān crossed the Nile, cut the pontoon bridge, and
burned the fields. Ṣāliḥ went in pursuit of him, and clashed with a
contingent of Marwān's cavalry at the Nile; they fought an engagement and Ṣāliḥ put them to flight. He then went on to a canal,
where some (more) of Marwān's cavalry chanced upon him. He
wounded some of them and drove the party away. Then he went on
to another canal, and his force crossed over. They then saw a cloud
of dust, and supposed it was Marwān, so Ṣāliḥ sent out a scouting
party under al-Faḍl b. Dīnār and Mālik b. Qādim. They found no one
to oppose, so they went back to Ṣāliḥ and he moved on. He then
stopped and camped at a place called Dhāt al-Sāḥil. Abū ʿAwn sent
ahead ʿĀmir b. Ismāʿīl al-Ḥārithī along with Shuʿbah b. Kathīr al-
Māzinī. Encountering some of Marwān's cavalry, they put them to
flight and took some men who were on foot as prisoners. Some of
these they slew, and some they let live. They asked about Marwān's
whereabouts, and the prisoners told them where he was, on condition that they be given guarantees of safety. They rode on, and found
Marwān staying at a church in Būsīr. They attacked his force at the

---

412. Situated between the hill country and the coast, Ramlah was the administrative center of Palestine. See LeStrange, *Palestine*, 303ff.

413. That is, he was marching along the Via Maris, the ancient route to Egypt.
Faramā' was between Egypt proper and ʿArīsh. The latter oasis was on the border between Sinai and Palestine. See Yāqūt, *Muʿjam*, III, 883.

414. See n. 403 above. Fusṭāṭ was the earliest Arab settlement in Egypt and the first
of a series of settlements that was to comprise the area of Greater Cairo. See *EI*[2] s.v.
al-Fusṭāṭ.

night's end, and his soldiers ran away. Marwān came out against them with a small party of men, and they surrounded him and killed him.

According to ʿAlī—Ismāʿīl b. al-Ḥasan—ʿĀmir b. Ismāʿīl: We [50] found Marwān at Būsīr. We were a small party, so they pressed us hard. We gathered together in a palm-stand, and if they had known how few we were, they would certainly have killed us. I said to the men with me, "If we wait until morning and they see how few we are in number, not one of us will get away." Then I recalled the words of Bukayr b. Māhān, "By God, you will slay Marwān; it's as though I hear you cry [in Persian], 'Give it to them, bullies! [dahīd yā juvānkashān].'"[415] Then I broke the sheath of my sword, and my companions broke theirs. And I cried out, "Dahīd yā juvānkashān!" It had the effect of molten fire poured on them, and they fled. Then a man attacked Marwān and struck him with his sword, killing him.

ʿĀmir b. Ismāʿīl rode back to Ṣāliḥ b. ʿAlī, who wrote to the Commander of the Faithful Abū al-ʿAbbās, "We pursued al-Jaʿdī, the enemy of God, until we caused him to seek refuge in the land of God's enemy, Pharaoh—he who made himself like unto God—and in that land I slew him."

ʿAlī reported the following from Abū Ṭālib al-Anṣārī: It was a man from Baṣrah they called al-Maghūd who stabbed Marwān; he didn't recognize him when he felled him. Then someone gave a great cry, "The Commander of the Faithful is down!" They raced over to him, and a man from Kūfah, who used to sell pomegranates, got there first and cut off his head. ʿĀmir b. Ismāʿīl sent Marwān's head to Abū ʿAwn, who sent it to Ṣāliḥ b. ʿAlī, and Ṣāliḥ b. ʿAlī sent the head with Yazīd b. Hāniʾ, his chief of security, to Abū al-ʿAbbās on Sunday, the third day before the end of Dhū al-Ḥijjah 132 (August 6, 750). Ṣāliḥ went back to Fusṭāṭ, then he left for Syria, turning over the booty to Abū ʿAwn, and the weapons, money and slaves to al-Faḍl b. Dīnār, and left Abū ʿAwn in command in Egypt.

According to ʿAlī—Abū al-Ḥasan al-Khurāsānī—a shaykh of the tribe of Bakr b. Wāʾil: I was at Dayr Qunnā with Bukayr b. Māhān, and we were talking together when a young man passed by with two [51] waterskins, went to the Tigris and got water. Then he returned, and

---

415. Following the Cairo edition.

Bukayr called him, saying, "What's your name, young man?"
"ʿĀmir," he said. "Son of whom?" asked Bukayr. "Of Ismāʿīl," he
replied. "Of Balḥārith?"[416] asked Bukayr. "I am of Balḥārith," he
said. "Then you'll be of the Banū Musliyyah," Bukayr said. "I am,"
he told him. "Then, by God," said Bukayr, "you will slay Marwān; it
is as though I hear you cry: *'Ya juvānkashān, dahīd!'*"

ʿAlī reported the following from al-Kinānī: I used to hear our
shaykhs at Kūfah say, "The Banū Musliyyah will be the death of
Marwān."[417] According to some, Marwān was sixty-two years old
on the day that he was slain. Others say he was sixty-nine, and still
others that he was fifty-eight. He was slain on Sunday three days before the end of Dhū al-Ḥijjah (August 6, 750), and his reign from the
time that allegiance was sworn to him until he was killed was five
years, ten months and sixteen days. His patronymic *(kunyā)* was
ʿAbū ʿAbd al-Malik. Hishām b. Muḥammad asserts that his mother
was a Kurdish concubine.

According to Aḥmad b. Zuhayr—ʿAlī b. Muḥammad—ʿAlī b.
Mujāhid and Abū Sinān al-Juhnī: It was said that the mother of
Marwān b. Muḥammad used to belong to Ibrāhīm b. al-Ashtar,[418]
and that Muḥammad b. Marwān b. al-Ḥakam acquired her the day
Ibn al-Ashtar was slain; he took her to be a refined woman, from Ibn
al-Ashtar's household. She bore Marwān in Muḥammad's bed.
When Abū al-ʿAbbās took power, ʿAbdallāh b. al-ʿAyyāsh al-Mantūf
came into his presence and said, "Praise be to God, who has exchanged for us the ass of the Jazīrah and the son of the slaughtered
man's bondmaid with a descendant of the paternal uncle of God's
Messenger and the son of ʿAbd al-Muṭṭalib!" This same year
ʿAbdallāh b. ʿAlī killed those of the Banū Umayyah who were slain
at the River of Abū Fuṭrus. They were seventy-two men.[419]

---

416. The Balḥārith were the Arab tribe of the Yaman which included the Christians
of the Najrān oasis. See *EI²* s.v. Ḥārith b. Kaʿb.

417. The Banū Musliyyah were the earliest supporters of the ʿAbbāsid revolution.
Most leaders of the Kūfah apparatus were counted among them. Abū al-ʿAbbās was
married to Rayṭah, one of the noble women of this clan. See *Akhbār al-Dawlah*,
192–93. (J.L.)

418. That is, the famous ʿAlid commander who also fought for the Zubayrids and
was killed in 72 (October 691). See *EI²* s.v. Ibrāhīm b. al-Ashtar.

419. See n. 411 above. The traditions concerning the annihilation of the Umayyad
house are problematic.

In this year Abū al-Ward threw off his allegiance to Abū al-ʿAbbās at Qinnasrīn, and adopted the color white along with others.[420]

[52]   *Abū al-Ward's Adopting White and What Happened*

The cause of this, according to Aḥmad b. Zuhayr—ʿAbd al-Wahhāb b. Ibrāhīm—Abū Hāshim Mukhallad b. Muḥammad b. Ṣāliḥ: Abū al-Ward, whose name was Majzaʾah b. Kawthar b. Zufar b. al-Ḥārith al-Kilābī, was a companion of Marwān and one of his cavalry officers. When Marwān was routed, Abū al-Ward was at Qinnasrīn, and ʿAbdallāh b. ʿAlī came there. Abū al-Ward gave him allegiance, and he and his troops placed themselves at ʿAbdallāh's disposal. The descendants of Maslamah b. ʿAbd al-Malik lived next to Abū al-Ward at Bālis and Nāʿūrah.[421] One of the "Thousanders,"[422] an officer of ʿAbdallāh b. ʿAlī, came to Bālis at the head of a hundred and fifty cavalry and manhandled the sons of Maslamah b. ʿAbd al-Malik and their womenfolk. Some people complained of this to Abū al-Ward, and he came out in an agricultural settlement there called Zarāʿat Banī Zufar—it was also called Khusāf—[423] with a number of people of his family to attack the officer, who was staying in Maslamah's fort. Abū al-Ward fought him until he had killed him and the men with him, and then he proclaimed the adoption of the color white and the deposing of ʿAbdallāh b. ʿAlī. He called on the people of Qinnasrīn to do the same, and all of them displayed the white. Abū al-ʿAbbās was staying at this time in Hīrah, and ʿAbdallāh b. ʿAlī was occupied in armed conflict with Ḥabīb b. Murrah al-Murrī, fighting him in the Balqāʾ, Bathaniyyah and Ḥawrān.[424] ʿAbdallāh b. ʿAlī had already encountered Ḥabīb with his

---

420. White became the color of the opposition to ʿAbbāsid rule. See the article on colors and politics by Omar cited in n. 72 above. See also Azdī, 146.

421. Bālis, the ancient Barbalissus, was situated on the Syrian side of the Euphrates west of Raqqah. Nāʿūrah was between Aleppo and Bālis. See Yāqūt, *Muʿjam*, I, 477ff, and IV, 832.

422. The text is al-*azārmardīn*," it should be read *hazārmard*, literally, "thousand-man." The epithet *hazārmard* occurs regularly for outstanding officers in this period, and is probably traceable to the old Sasanian practice of giving certain officers of great merit and bravery the pay and importance of a thousand ordinary soldiers. See Ibn ʿAbd al-Ḥakam, *Futūḥ Miṣr*, 61.

423. See Yāqūt, *Muʿjam*, II, 922, who lists a Zurāʿat Zufar near Bālis. He also lists a Khusāf in the same region (ibid, 441).

424. For these districts of Syria, see *EI*[2] s.v. al-Bathaniyya, Ḥawrān.

troops and engaged them in several clashes. Ḥabīb had been one of Marwān's cavalry officers, and his reason for adopting white had been fear for himself and for his people. The Qays and other groups allied to them among the inhabitants of these districts, Bathaniyyah and Ḥawrān, had sworn to follow him. However, when word reached ʿAbdallāh b. ʿAlī of their adopting white (in Qinnasrīn), he invited Ḥabīb b. Murrah to make peace, made peace with him, pardoned him and those with them, and set out for Qinnasrīn to engage Abū al-Ward. He passed by Damascus and appointed as his deputy there Abū Ghānim ʿAbd al-Ḥamīd b. Ribʿi al-Ṭāʾī, giving him command of four thousand men from his army. Also at Damascus at this time was the wife of ʿAbdallāh b. ʿAlī, Umm al-Banīn bt. Muḥammad b. ʿAbd al-Muṭṭalib al-Nawfaliyyah, the sister of ʿAmr b. Muḥammad, as well as concubine mothers of ʿAbdallāh's children, and some of his household. As ʿAbdallāh b. ʿAlī arrived at Ḥimṣ on his way, the people of Damascus rebelled against him when his back was turned, adopted white, and rose against him with ʿUthmān b. ʿAbd al-Aʿlā b. Surāqah[425] al-Azdī. They encountered Abū Ghānim and those with him and put him to flight, killing a great number of his followers. They carried off all that ʿAbdallāh b. ʿAlī had left behind in the way of household goods and chattels, but did not harm his family. Displaying white, the people of Damascus united in opposition to (the ʿAbbāsids). ʿAbdallāh b. ʿAlī however continued on his way. Some of the people of Qinnasrīn had joined with Abū al-Ward, and had corresponded with their associates at Ḥimṣ and Tadmur. Thousands had come to join them under Abū Muḥammad b. ʿAbdallāh b. Yazīd b. Muʿāwiyah b. Abī Sufyān.[426] The rebels made Abū Muḥammad their leader and called men to follow him, saying, "This is the Sufyānid who was foretold."[427] Their numbers were now about forty thousand.

[53]

---

425. The text is Surāqah; emended by the Cairo edition to Sarādiqah.

426. That is, the descendant of Yazīd I, the second Umayyad Caliph and the son of the founder of the dynasty.

427. There is frequent mention of a Sufyānid as an eschatological figure in the ḥadīth collections on *fitan*, "troubles." What his role will be depends on the orientation of the source, Umayyad, ʿAlid, or ʿAbbāsid. Al-Maqdisī, *al-Badʾ wa al-Taʾrīkh*, II, 186, reports, "The Banū ʿAbbās will be destroyed at the hands of a man from the house of this woman" (the Prophet's wife Umm Ḥabībah bt. Abī Sufyān). All of these ḥadīths are politically tendentious; some of them come from a Syria resentful of ʿAbbāsid domination.

When ʿAbdallāh b. ʿAlī was near them, he sent his brother ʿAbd al-
Ṣamad ahead with ten thousand of his cavalry. Abū Muḥammad had
camped with his following at a meadow called Marj al-Akhram. Abū
al-Ward was in charge of the camp, and was Abū Muḥammad's exec-
utive and battle-chief. He thus came cut to oppose them, and met
them on the field between the two armies. There was a confused engagement between the two forces, but the enemy stood fast. ʿAbd al-
Ṣamad and those with him were routed, and thousands of his men
were killed that day. When ʿAbd al-Ṣamad came back to him, ʿAb-
[54] dallāh advanced, along with Ḥumayd b. Qaḥṭabah and a group of officers who were with him. They engaged the enemy again at Marj al-
Akhram, and fought a fierce battle with them. A group of those who
were with ʿAbdallāh were put to flight, but they regrouped, while
ʿAbdallāh b. ʿAlī and Ḥumayd b. Qaḥṭabah stood firm and repulsed
the attackers. Abū al-Ward and about five hundred men of his family
and clan held fast and were all killed. Abū Muḥammad and the Kalb
who were with him fled until they got to Tadmur. ʿAbdallāh gave
the people of Qinnasrīn a guarantee of safety, and they displayed
black, swore allegiance to him, and became submissive to him. He
then set out to go back to the people of Damascus because they displayed white in rebellion against him and drove out Abū al-Ghānim.
As he neared Damascus, the people fled and scattered without any
battle between them, and ʿAbdallāh pardoned the city's inhabitants.
They swore allegiance to him, and he did not prosecute them for
what they had done.

Abū Muḥammad continued to absent himself as a fugitive, and he
reached the Ḥijāz. Word of his hiding place reached Ziyād b. ʿUbaydallāh al-Ḥārithī, Abū Jaʿfar al-Manṣūr's governor, and he sent cavalry for him. They engaged him in battle until he was killed and two
sons of his were captured. Ziyād sent his head and his two sons to
the Commander of the Faithful Abū Jaʿfar, who ordered that the
sons be set free, and he pardoned them.

ʿAlī b. Muḥammad reported the following from al-Nuʿmān Abū
al-Sarī, Jabalah b. Farrūkh, Sulaymān b. Dāwud and Abū Ṣāliḥ al-
Marwazī: Abū al-Ward threw off his allegiance at Qinnasrīn and
Abū al-ʿAbbās wrote to ʿAbdallāh b. ʿAlī at (Abū) Fuṭrus to engage
Abū al-Ward in battle. ʿAbdallāh sent ʿAbd al-Ṣamad to Qinnasrīn at
the head of seven thousand men, with Mukhāriq b. Shabīb in charge
of security. He then sent five thousand men after him under the

command of Dhu'ayb b. al-Ashʿath, and after that he began to send the main contingents. ʿAbd al-Ṣamad encountered Abū al-Ward at the head of a great force. The people fled from ʿAbd al-Ṣamad until [55] they came to Ḥimṣ, so ʿAbdallāh b. ʿAlī sent al-ʿAbbās b. Yazīd b. Ziyād, Marwān al-Jurjānī and Abū al-Mutawakkil al-Jurjānī, each with their own followers, to Ḥimṣ. ʿAbdallāh b. ʿAlī himself arrived, and camped four miles *(mīl)* from Ḥimṣ. ʿAbd al-Ṣamad b. ʿAlī was also at Ḥimṣ. ʿAbdallāh wrote to Ḥumayd b. Qaḥṭabah, and he came to him from the Jordan. The people of Qinnasrīn swore allegiance to the Sufyānid Abū Muḥammad Ziyād b. ʿAbdallāh b. Yazīd b. Muʿāwiyah, and Abū al-Ward b. . . . . .[428] They swore allegiance to him and he stayed forty days. ʿAbdallāh b. ʿAlī, together with ʿAbd al-Ṣamad and Ḥumayd b. Qaḥṭabah came against them, and the two forces engaged in the fiercest of battles. Abū Muḥammad drove them into a narrow pass, and the people began to scatter. Then Ḥumayd b. Qaḥṭabah said to ʿAbdallāh b. ʿAlī, "What are we waiting for? They are increasing in numbers, and our followers are decreasing! Let us go forth against them!" They fought each other on Tuesday, the last of Dhū al-Ḥijjah 133 (July 27, 751). Abū Muḥammad had Abū al-Ward on his right, and in command of his left was al-Aṣbagh b. Dhū'ālah. Abū al-Ward was wounded and carried back to his people, and then he died. A group of Abū al-Ward's followers fled into a bushy area, and it was set on fire over their heads. The people of Ḥimṣ had thrown off their allegiance and wanted to follow Abū Muḥammad, but when they learned of his flight they stayed where they were.

In this year, Ḥabīb b. Murrah al-Murrī threw off (black) and put on white along with those of the people of Syria who were with him.

Ḥabib b. Murrah Puts on White

ʿAlī reported the following from his authorities: Ḥabīb b. Murrah al-Murrī and the people of the Bathaniyyah and Ḥawrān put on white [56] while ʿAbdallāh b. ʿAlī was in the camp of Abū al-Ward, who was slain in this year.[429]

According to Aḥmad b. Zuhayr—ʿAbd al-Wahhāb b. Ibrā-

---

428. There is a lacuna in the text and in the Cairo edition.
429. See Azdī, 144ff *sub anno* 133.

him—Abū Hāshim Mukhallad b. Muḥammad: Ḥabīb b. Murrah's display of white and his struggle with ʿAbdallāh b. ʿAlī occurred before Abū al-Ward put on white, and Abū al-Ward only did this while ʿAbdallāh b. ʿAlī was occupied in fighting Ḥabīb b. Murrah in the Balqāʾ, or in the Bathaniyyah and Ḥawrān. ʿAbdallāh had already encountered Ḥabīb with his troops and engaged them in several clashes. Ḥabīb had been one of Marwān's cavalry officers, and the reason for his putting on white had been fear for his own safety and his people. The Qays and its allies among the inhabitants of those districts, i.e., Bathaniyyah and Ḥawrān, pledged allegiance to him. When word of the rebellion of the people of Qinnasrīn reached ʿAbdallāh b. ʿAlī, he invited Ḥabīb b. Murrah to make peace. ʿAbdallāh then made peace with him and pardoned him and his men and set out for Qinnasrīn to encounter Abū al-Ward.

In this year also the people of the Jazīrah put on white and threw off their allegiance to Abū al-ʿAbbās.

The Revolt of the Jazarīs

According to Aḥmad b. Zuhayr—ʿAbd al-Wahhāb b. Ibrāhīm—Abū Hāshim Mukhallad b. Muḥammad: The people of the Jazīrah displayed white and threw off their allegiance as soon as word came to them of the revolt of Abū al-Ward and the uprising of the people of Qinnasrīn. The rebels marched to Ḥarrān, where at this time Mūsā b. Kaʿb was stationed with three thousand men of the army. The defenders stuck fast to the city, and wearers of white flocked to it from every direction. They besieged Mūsā and those with him, but their command was not unified and they had no single chief to unite them.

[57] Following this, Isḥāq b. Muslim came from Armenia.[430] He had set out from there when word came to him of Marwān's defeat. The people of the Jazīrah made him their leader, and he besieged Mūsā b. Kaʿb upwards of two months. Abū al-ʿAbbās sent Abū Jaʿfar, his brother, with the troops he had with him besieging Ibn Hubayrah at Wāsit. He went on past Qarqīsiyyah, where the inhabitants had displayed white and locked the gates of the city. Then he came to Raq-

---

430. That is, Isḥāq b. Muslim al-ʿUqaylī, the "chief man of Qays," who was an Umayyad commander along the Armenian frontier. See Ṭabarī, II/3, 1871, 1940.

qah, which was in the same condition under Bakkār b. Muslim, brother of Isḥāq. Abū Jaʿfar continued on toward Ḥarrān, and Isḥāq b. Muslim then moved to Ruhāʾ.[431] This occurred in the year 133 (750–751). Mūsā b. Kaʿb and his followers came out of Ḥarrān and met Abū Jaʿfar, while Bakkār b. Muslim went to his brother, Isḥāq b. Muslim, who went to a group of the Rabīʿah at Dārā and Mārdīn. The leader of the Rabīʿah at this time was one of the Ḥarūriyyah (Khārijites) called Buraykah. Abū Jaʿfar went after him, and the two forces engaged in a violent battle in which Buraykah was killed. Bakkār then went back to his brother Isḥāq in Ruhāʾ. Isḥāq left him in charge of Ruhāʾ and went with most of their army to Sumaysāṭ,[432] where he entrenched himself with his troops. Abū Jaʿfar proceeded with his units until Bakkār confronted him at Ruhāʾ, and there were several battles between them.

Abū al-ʿAbbās wrote to ʿAbdallāh b. ʿAlī to march with his troops against Isḥāq at Sumaysāṭ, and he came from Syria to camp opposite Isḥāq at Sumaysāṭ. There were sixty thousand men, all of them from the Jazīrah. Between the two forces lay the Euphrates. Abū Jaʿfar now came from Ruhāʾ, whereupon Isḥāq wrote the ʿAbbāsid commanders requesting guarantees of safety (in return for surrender). They assented to this and wrote to Abū al-ʿAbbās, who ordered them to give him and all those with him pledges of safety. They therefore composed a document in which Isḥāq was given firm assurances. Isḥāq then came out to meet Abū Jaʿfar, and there was a complete reconciliation between them. He later became one of Abū Jaʿfar's chosen men. The people of the Jazīrah and of Syria were thus pacified, and Abū al-ʿAbbās appointed Abū Jaʿfar as governor of the Jazīrah, Armenia and Ādharbayjān. He continued in that capacity [58] until he became Caliph.

It is mentioned that Isḥāq b. Muslim al-ʿUqaylī stayed at Sumaysāṭ seven months while Abū Jaʿfar besieged him. He used to say, "There is an oath of allegiance on my neck, and I shall not put it aside until I know that the man to whom I gave it has died or been killed." At this, Abū Jaʿfar sent word to him that Marwān had been slain, and he replied, "Let me be sure of this." Then he sought peace,

---

431. For Ruhāʾ (Edessa), see LeStrange, *Lands*, 103–4.
432. For Sumaysāṭ, ancient Samosata, which lay on the north bank of the Euphrates, see LeStrange, *Lands*, 108.

saying, "I have learned that Marwān has been slain." So Abū Jaʿfar pardoned him, and he went with Abū Jaʿfar and held a place of great esteem with him. It has also been said that it was ʿAbdallāh b. ʿAlī who pardoned him.

Also in this year, Abū Jaʿfar set out for Abū Muslim in Khurāsān to seek his opinion about slaying Abū Salamah Ḥafṣ b. Sulaymān.

Abū Jaʿfar's Journey to Khurāsān

Earlier I mentioned the matter of Abū Salamah and what he had done to arouse the suspicions of Abū al-ʿAbbās and those of the Banū Hāshim who accompanied him when they arrived at Kūfah.

According to ʿAlī b. Muhammad—Jabalah b. Farrūkh—Yazīd b. Asīd—Abū Jaʿfar: When Abū al-ʿAbbās became Commander of the Faithful, we sat up one evening talking and mentioned what Abū Salamah had done. Then one man there said, "What do you know; maybe what Abū Salamah did was done by the advice of Abū Muslim!" Not one of us spoke, and then the Commander of the Faithful Abū al-ʿAbbās said, "Well, if that was by the advice of Abū Muslim, then we are up against trouble, unless God should rid us of him." Then we dispersed, and Abū al-ʿAbbās sent for me to ask, "What is your opinion of this?" I replied, "Whatever you think." He told me, "None of us is nearer to Abū Muslim than yourself, so go out to see him until you learn his thoughts. He will not disguise them from you. If you encounter him and discover that it was by his advice that Abū Salamah acted, we shall look to ourselves. If it was not, then our souls will be at peace."

[59]　　I left in some disquiet, and when I got to Rayy, the man in charge there had received a letter from Abū Muslim saying, "Word has reached me that ʿAbdallāh b. Muhammad is headed your way. When he arrives, send him on within the hour of his arrival." So, when I got there, the governor of Rayy came to me, informed me of Abū Muslim's letter, and ordered me to travel on. My disquiet increased; I left Rayy cautious and fearful and traveled on. As soon as I was at Naysābūr, the governor there came to me with a (second) letter from Abū Muslim, "If ʿAbdallāh b. Muhammad arrives there, send him on and do not let him tarry, for your area is one of rebels and there is no security for him there." I felt better then, and said, "I see he is concerned about me." So I went on, and when I was two *farsakh*s (12

km) from Marw, Abū Muslim came with the notables to meet me. As soon as he drew near, he (dismounted and) walked toward me to kiss my hand. I told him, "Mount," At this he got on his horse and we went into Marw. I stayed in a house there for three days, and he didn't ask me about anything. Then on the fourth day, he asked me, "What brought you here?" I told him, and he said, "That was Abū Salamah's doing! I shall take care of him for you." Then he called Marrār b. Anas al-Dabbī and told him, "Set out for Kūfah, and kill Abū Salamah as soon as you encounter him. Finish with this as the Imām thinks best." Marrār then arrived at Kūfah, when Abū Salamah was spending the evening with Abū al-ʿAbbās. He waited in his path, and when Abū Salamah came out, Marrār killed him. It was then said that it was the Khārijites who had killed him.

ʿAlī reported the following from a shaykh of the Banū Sulaym— Sālim:[433] I accompanied Abū Jaʿfar from Rayy to Khurāsān as his chamberlain. Abū Muslim would come to see him, dismount at the door of the house, sit down in the antechamber, and say, "Ask for leave for me to enter." Then Abū Jaʿfar grew angry at me, and told me, "Woe to you! When you see him, open the door for him and tell him to ride in on his mount!" I did so, and told Abū Muslim, "He says thus-and-so." "Yes," he said, "I know. Go and ask him for leave for me to enter."

It was also said that Abū al-ʿAbbās had a dislike for Abū Salamah [60] even before he left his camp at Nukhaylah. He then moved from his camp to Hāshimiyyah[434] and stayed at the government palace there. He was hostile to Abū Salamah; this was known about him. He wrote to Abū Muslim informing him what he thought, telling him about the duplicity that concerned him and what he feared in consequence. Abū Muslim wrote, "If the Commander of the Faithful has come across such information about Abū Salamah, then have him killed." But Dāwud b. ʿAlī told Abū al-ʿAbbās, "Do not do it, Commander of the Faithful. It will be used against you by Abū Muslim and the people of Khurāsān who now are with you—his position

---

433. The text is Sālim, probably an error. The chamberlain's name was Sallām b. Sulaym.

434. That is, the Hāshimiyyah that was at Madīnat b. Hubayrah, near Kūfah. There were several ʿAbbāsid administrative centers before the building of Madīnat al-Salām at Baghdad. Each was known as Hāshimiyyah. There is thus much confusion about them. For a full discussion, see Lassner ʿAbbāsid Rule, 151–62. (J.L.)

with them being what it is. Rather, write to Abū Muslim and let him send someone to kill Abū Salamah." So he wrote Abū Muslim to this effect, and Abū Muslim sent Marrār b. Anas al-Ḍabbī. He came to Abū al-ʿAbbās at the city of Hāshimiyyah and let him know the reason for his coming. Abū al-ʿAbbās then ordered a crier to proclaim, "The Commander of the Faithful is well pleased with Abū Salamah and has summoned him and given him robes of honor." Abū Salamah went to visit him one evening after that, and he did not quit him until the greater part of the night had passed. Then he went out to go home, walking alone, until he entered the arcade. Along with some confederates who accompanied him, Marar b. Anas confronted Abū Salamah and killed him. The city gates were locked, and they said, "The Khārijites have murdered Abū Salamah." He was carried out the next day. Yahyā b. Muhammad b. ʿAlī led prayers over him, and he was buried in Hāshimiyyah. On this, Sulaymān b. Al-Muhājir al-Bajalī said:

> Indeed the wazīr, the wazīr of the family of Muhammad
> has perished, and he who hates you became wazīr.

Abū Salamah was called "Wazīr of the Family of Muhammad," and
[61] Abū Muslim "Trustee (*amīn*) of the Family of Muhammad." Thus when Abū Salamah was slain, Abū al-ʿAbbās sent his brother Abū Jaʿfar at the head of thirty men to Abū Muslim; among them were al-Hajjāj b. Arṭāh and Ishāq b. al-Faḍl al-Hāshimī.

When Abū Jaʿfar came to Abū Muslim, ʿUbaydallāh b. al-Husayn al-Aʿraj kept pace with him. Alongside him rode Sulaymān b. Kathīr. Sulaymān then said to al-Aʿraj, "Friend, we have been hoping that your business would be done. If you wish, call on us, as regards your desire." ʿUbaydallāh then thought that he was an agent from Abū Muslim, and he became fearful. Word reached Abū Muslim of Sulaymān b. Kathīr's ride with him. ʿUbaydallāh went to Abū Muslim and mentioned what Sulaymān had said, thinking that if he did not do this, Abū Muslim would devise some mischief against ʿUbaydallāh and kill him. Abū Muslim sent for Sulaymān b. Kathīr and said to him, "Do you remember how the Imām told me, 'Whomever you suspect, kill him?'" "Yes," said Sulaymān. "Well," said Abū Muslim, "I suspect you." "I beseech you in God's name!" said Sulaymān. "Do not beseech me in God's name when you are plotting treachery to the Imām," said Abū Muslim. He then ordered his head cut off. Abū Ja'far saw no one else whom Abū Muslim had beheaded, but he went home from Abū Muslim and told Abū al-'Abbās, "You are no Caliph, and your rule is nothing, if you leave Abū Muslim alone and do not kill him." "How so?" said Abū al-'Abbās. "By God, he does just what he pleases," said Abū Ja'far. Abū al-'Abbās told him, "Be quiet, and keep this to yourself."[435]

The Battle for Wāsiṭ

In this year, Abu al-'Abbas sent his brother Abū Ja'far to Wāsiṭ to do battle with Yazīd b. 'Umar b. Hubayrah.[436] We have mentioned what happened when the troops of the Khurāsān army encountered Ibn Hubayrah (first) under Qaḥṭabah and then under Qaḥṭabah's son al-Ḥasan—how Ibn Hubayrah was routed and how his supporters among the Syrian troops had gotten to Wāsiṭ and fortified themselves in that city.

According to 'Alī b. Muḥammad—Abū 'Abdallāh al-Sulamī—   [62]
'Abdallāh b. Badr, Zuhayr b. Hunayd, Bishr b. 'Īsā and Abū al-Sarī: When Ibn Hubayrah was routed, people deserted him. He had put a group of men in charge of the baggage, and they ran away with it. At this, Ḥawtharah asked him, "Where will you go? These people's leader (Qaḥṭabah) has been killed. Go to Kūfah; you have many troops with you. Then fight them until you are slain or win the fight." Ibn Hubayrah replied, "No, we shall go to Wāsiṭ and see what happens." Ḥawtharah said, "You will only strengthen them yourself that way, and [in the end] you'll be slain." Yaḥyā b. Ḥuḍayn told him, "There is truly nothing dearer you could bring to Marwān than these troops. Follow the Euphrates until you come to him, and beware of Wāsiṭ; you'll walk into a siege there, with no future but death." He refused, however, since he was afraid of Marwān. He had

---

435. The murder of the veteran revolutionary was listed among the charges allegedly read against Abū Muslim shortly before the latter's execution. One could nevertheless argue that the 'Abbāsids would not have been sorry to see Ibn Kathīr eliminated since he seems to have represented an independent voice among the old guard operatives in Khurāsān. See *FHA*, 223. (J.L.)

436. See Ibn Khayyāṭ, II, 424ff; *FHA*, 208ff; Kūfī, *Futūḥ*, VIII, 202ff; Ya'qūbī, *Ta'rīkh*, II, 42; Dīnawarī, Ibn Ṭabāṭabā, 160.

written to Marwān about the situation, and Marwān had opposed
him. He therefore feared that Marwān would kill him if he came to
him. Hence he went to Wāsiṭ, entered the city and fortified it.

Abū Salamah sent al-Ḥasan b. Qaḥṭabah (off to Wāsiṭ), and al-
Ḥasan and his followers dug trenches and camped in the area between the Zāb and the Tigris. Al-Ḥasan pitched his pavilion opposite the Hipprodrome Gate (Bāb al-Miḍmār), and the first battle that
occurred between them was on a Wednesday. The Syrians said to
Ibn Hubayrah, "Give us permission to fight them." This he did.
They rode out and Ibn Hubayrah was with them. With his right
flank was his son Dāwud, along with Muḥammad b. Nubātah and
some men from Khurāsān.[437] Among them was Abū al-ʿŪd al-Khu-
rāsāni. The two armies met, with Khāzim b. Khuzaymah leading al-
Ḥasan's right flank. Now Ibn Hubayrah was just in front of the Hip-
[63]   podrome Gate, so Khāzim attacked him. He routed the Syrians, and
they sought refuge behind their trenches. The people ran for the gate
of the city, so many of them that the Hippodrome Gate was choked,
and the men manning ballistas hurled stones as al-Ḥasan stood by.
They began to move with the cavalry in the area between the river
and the trench. The Syrians turned back, and al-Ḥasan outflanked
them. At this, they shifted between him and the city and forced his
men into the Tigris, so that many of them were drowned. The defenders also came out against them in boats. Then the (ʿAbbāsid)
Khurāsānīs counterattacked. Ibn Nubātah threw away his weapons
that day and rushed blindly into the water. They followed him in a
boat, and he got in.

After this they abstained from fighting, remaining as they were for
seven days, but on Tuesday the defenders made a sortie and engaged
in battle. One of the Syrians attacked Abū Ḥafṣ Hazārmard[438] and
struck him. Referring to his tribe, the Syrian crowed, "I am the
Sulami lad!" Abū Ḥafṣ struck him back retorting, "And I am the
ʿAtaki lad!" and felled him. The Syrians fled in disgrace and entered
the city. They stayed there so long as God wished, fighting no more,
except to cast missiles from behind the barbican.

While he was besieged there, Ibn Hubayrah heard that Abū Umayyah al-Taghlibī had appeared in black garments. He thus sent Abū

---

437. These, of course, were Umayyad troops.
438. See n. 422 above.

'Uthmān to al-Taghlibī's quarters. He came upon Abū Umayyah in his tent and said, "The Amīr has sent me to you to search your tent. If there is a black livery in it, I am to hang it about your neck, put a halter on you, and go with you to him. If there are no black garments in your quarters, then these fifty thousand (dirhams) are a gift to you." Abū Umayyah declined to let him search his tent, so he took him to Ibn Hubayrah, who imprisoned him. Man b. Zā'idah and leading men of the Rabī'ah discussed this turn of events and then seized three men of the Banū Fazzārah. They detained them and insulted Ibn Hubayrah. Yaḥyā b. Ḥudayn then came to them and spoke with them, but they said, "We will not let them go until he lets our comrade go." Ibn Hubayrah refused, however, so Yaḥyā told him, "You are hurting no one but yourself. You are under siege; let [64] this man go his way." Ibn Hubayrah said, "No, not even as a favor." Ibn Ḥudayn returned to them and informed them (of his conversation). At this, Ma'n and 'Abd al-Raḥmān al-'Ijlī withdrew (their support from Ibn Hubayrah) and Ibn Ḥudayn told Ibn Hubayrah, "These are your cavalry. You have already alienated them. If you persist in this, they will be harder on you than those who are besieging you." At this, he called for Abū Umayyah, gave him a robe of honor and let him go. The disaffected were thus reconciled to Ibn Hubayrah, and they became obedient as before.

Abū Naṣr Mālik b. Haytham arrived from Sijistān, and al-Ḥasan b. Qaḥṭabah sent a delegation to inform Abū al-'Abbās of Abū Naṣr's arrival, putting Ghaylān b. 'Abdallāh al-Khuzā'ī at the head of it. Ghaylān was grieved with al-Ḥasan because he had sent him to reinforce Rawḥ b. Ḥātim, and when he came before Abū al-'Abbās, he said, "I bear witness that you are the Commander of the Faithful, that you are God's firm bond, that you are the Imām of the pious." Abū al-'Abbās replied, "What do you want, Ghaylān?" He then said, "I beg your pardon." Abū al-'Abbās said, "May God pardon you." Dāwud b. 'Alī added, "May God prosper you, Abū Fuḍālah." Then Ghaylān said, "Commander of the Faithful, favor us with a man from the people of your house [to lead us]!" Abū al-'Abbās said, "Why, is there not already a man from the people of my house in command of you, al-Ḥasan b. Qaḥṭabah?" Ghaylān repeated "Commander of the Faithful, favor us with a man from the people of your house!" Abū al-'Abbās replied as he had done at first. Then Ghaylān said, "Commander of the Faithful, favor us with a man from the people of your house, that we may look on his face and our eyes be consoled by him" Abū al-ʿAbbās said, "Alright, Ghaylān." He then sent Abū Jaʿfar. He appointed Ghaylān as chief of security for him, and Abū Jaʿfar went to Wāsiṭ. Abū Naṣr then said to Ghaylān, "What I wished was not what you did." Ghaylān replied, "It was better this way [*beh būd*]." He stayed some days as chief of security, then he said to Abū Jaʿfar, "I am not forceful enough for the security, but I can point out someone who is tougher than I." "Who is he?" Abū Jaʿfar asked. "Jahwar b. Marrār," he told him. "I am not able to release you," Abū Jaʿfar said, "because it was the Commander of the Faithful who appointed you." "Write to him and inform him," Ghaylān told him. So Abū Jaʿfar wrote to Abū al-ʿAbbās, who replied, "Do as Ghaylān advises." He then made Jahwar his chief of security. Abū Jaʿfar said to al-Ḥasan, "Tell me a man I can appoint to command my guard." Al-Ḥasan said, "My own choice would be ʿUthmān b. Nahīk." At this, he put ʿUthmān in command of the guard.

According to Bishr b. ʿĪsā: When Abū Jaʿfar got to Wāsiṭ, al-Ḥasan turned over his quarters to him, and Abū Jʿfar engaged the enemy in combat. One day Abū Naṣr fought with the Syrians, and they fled to their defensive trenches. Maʿn b. Zāʾidah and Abū Yaḥyā al-Judhāmī had concealed themselves in ambush. When the Khurāsānīs passed through, they came out against them and fought them until nightfall. Abū Naṣr dismounted to engage them, and they fought each other at the trenches. Fires were lit for them while Ibn Hubayrah was at the tower at the Vinegar-sellers' Gate (Bāb al-Khallālīn). They fought each other for as long as God wished that night; then Ibn Hubayrah gave word to Maʿn to turn back, whereupon he returned. They remained this way for some days. Then the Syrians came out again, with Muḥammad b. Nubātah, Maʿn b. Zāʾidah, Ziyād b. Ṣāliḥ and certain cavaliers of Syria. The Khurāsānīs fought them, and drove them toward the Tigris. They began to fall into the river, and Abū Naṣr called in Persian, "Men of Khurāsān, be waterless for these men of treachery, make them rise!"[439] The Khurāsānīs returned. Abū Naṣr's son had been felled, and Rawḥ b. Ḥātim had protected him. His father passed by him and said in Persian, "They've killed you, my son, and so to hell with all the world, now that you're

---

439. Persian: *mardumān-i khāʾineh beyābān hastīd ve bar khīzīd.*

gone." Then they charged the Syrians and chased them back into
Wāsit. The Syrians began to tell each other, "No, by God, there's no
good fortune for us after this. We went out against them—we the
cavalry of the Syrian army—and they drove us back into the city."
Killed that evening among the Khurāsānī army were Bakkār al-   [66]
Anṣarī and another man, both of them cavalrymen. During the siege
of Ibn Hubayrah, Abū Naṣr used to fill boats with wood and set
them ablaze to consume all that passed by, while Ibn Hubayrah had
prepared fireboats with iron hooks to drag these boats away. So
things remained for eleven months, and when this grew too tedious
for them the defenders asked for peace. However, they did not ask
for peace until the news of Marwān's slaying reached them. It was
brought by Ismāʿīl b. ʿAbdallāh al-Qasrī who asked them, "Why are
you killing yourselves? Marwān has been slain!"

It has been said that Abū al-ʿAbbās sent Abū Jaʿfar to fight Ibn
Hubayrah as soon as he arrived from Khurāsān, coming back from
Abū Muslim. Abū Jaʿfar traveled to reach al-Ḥasan b. Qaḥṭabah who
was besieging Ibn Hubayrah at Wāsit. Al-Ḥasan turned over his
quarters to Abū Jaʿfar, and Abū Jaʿfar settled there. When the siege
grew tedious to Ibn Hubayrah and his followers, they became disaffected. The Yamanīs said, "We see no Marwān, and what he did to
us, he did." The Nizārīs said, "We won't fight until the Yamanīs
fight alongside us." The only people who did fight for him were the
ragamuffins (ṣaʿālīk) and young toughs (fityān). Then Ibn Hubayrah
thought of appealing to Muḥammad b. ʿAbdallāh b. Ḥasan b. Ḥasan,[440] and wrote to him, but he delayed his answer. Abū al-ʿAbbās
corresponded with Ibn Hubayrah's Yamanī followers and raised
their hopes. Then the Ḥārithīs Ziyād b. Ṣāliḥ and Ziyād b. ʿUbaydallāh went over to Abū al-ʿAbbās. They promised Ibn Hubayrah
that they would bring about good relations between him and Abū al-
ʿAbbās, but they did not do it. Emissaries went back and forth between Abū Jaʿfar and Ibn Hubayrah until the latter sent him a (version of) a guarantee of safety. Ibn Hubayrah had consulted the
experts for forty days until he was satisfied with it. He then sent it   [67]
to Abū Jaʿfar, who transmitted it to Abū al-ʿAbbās, and he ordered

---

440. The strategy was to get a person of the Banū Hāshim to intercede. In this case
the ʿAlid known as al-Nafs al-Zakiyyah was chosen.

Abū Ja'far to implement it.[441] It was Abū Ja'far's opinion that everything in it must be faithfully carried out, but Abū al-'Abbās was not accustomed to making a final decision without Abū Muslim. Abū al-Jahm was the "eye" that Abū Muslim kept on Abū al-'Abbās, and Abū Jahm thus wrote to him with all the news about him. So Abū Muslim wrote Abū al-'Abbās, "Truly an easy road is spoiled if a boulder is thrown into it: by God, no road with Ibn Hubayrah in it is in good order."

When the document was completed, Ibn Hubayrah came out to Abū Ja'far at the head of thirteen hundred warriors.[442] He wanted to enter Abū Ja'far's enclosure while on his horse; however, the chamberlain Sallām b. Sulaym stood before him and said, "Welcome to you, Abū Khalīd! Dismount in good order!" The enclosure was encircled by upwards of ten thousand men of Khurāsān, so Ibn Hubayrah dismounted. Sallām called for a cushion for Ibn Hubayrah to sit upon, and he sent for the officers to come in. Then Sallām said, "Go in, Abū Khālid." The latter asked, "I and who else with me?" Sallām replied, "I sought permission for you alone." He went in, and a cushion was placed for him, and he spoke with him a while. Then he rose to leave and Abū Ja'far followed him with his gaze until he disappeared from view. Ibn Hubayrah continued to visit Abū Ja'far, absenting himself one day and waiting on him the next, at the head of five hundred riders and three hundred foot soldiers. Yazīd b. Ḥātim then said to Abū Ja'far, "Truly, Amīr, Ibn Hubayrah comes here and the whole camp is humble before him; nothing is lacking in his sovereignty. If he is to make a progress with all this cavalry and infantry, what will 'Abd al-Jabbār and Jahwar say?" Then Abū Ja'far told Sallām, "Tell Ibn Hubayrah to leave this crowd behind him and come to us with a retinue [of about thirty]."[443] Sallām told Ibn Hubayrah this and his face changed. He then came with a retinue of about thirty, and Sallām said to him, "It seems you come so proudly!" He replied, "If you order us to, we shall come on foot."

[68]

---

441. The text of the document was reportedly framed by Ibn al-Muqaffa'. The agreements forced upon Abū Ja'far by the document were so carefully worded that they made him very uneasy.

442. The text has *bukhāriyyah*, which seems most unlikely. Following a suggestion in the textual apparatus, the reading *muhāribah* has been adopted.

443. The words in brackets are missing in the text, and are supplied by the Cairo edition.

Sallām told him, "We do not wish to treat you lightly; the Amīr ordered what he did so as to pay full attention to you." After that, Ibn Hubayrah would come with three companions.

The Death of Ibn Hubayrah

Abū Zayd reported the following from Muḥammad b. Kathīr: Ibn Hubayrah spoke to Abū Jaʿfar one day and said, "Look here," or "O man." Then he came back and said, "O Amīr, it has been my fashion to address people as I just spoke to you, and my tongue slipped, forcing me to say something I did not intend." Abū al-ʿAbbās used to press Abū Jaʿfar, ordering him to kill Ibn Hubayrah. But Abū Jaʿfar would refer it back to him, until finally Abū al-ʿAbbās wrote him, "By God, you shall certainly kill him, or I will certainly send someone to drag him out of your enclosure." At this, he undertook to have Ibn Hubayrah killed and made up his mind to do it. He sent Khāzim b. Khuzaymah and al-Haytham b. Shuʿbah b. Zuhayr and ordered them to seal the treasuries. He then sent for the leading men of the Qays and Muḍar who were with Ibn Hubayrah. Coming to him were Muḥammad b. Nubātah, Hawtharah b. Suhayl, Ṭāriq b. Qudāmah, Ziyād b. Suwayd, Abū Bakr b. Kaʿb al-ʿUqaylī, Abān and Bishr the two sons of ʿAbd al-Malik b. Bishr, with twenty-two men of the Qays, as well as Jaʿfar b. Ḥanẓalah and Hazzān b. Saʿd. Sallām b. Sulaym went out and said, "Where are Hawtharah and Muḥammad b. Nubātah?" They both stood up and went in. ʿUthmān b. Nahīk, al-Faḍl b. Sulaymān and Mūsā b. ʿAqīl had been sitting with one hundred men in an enclosure outside Abū Jaʿfar's enclosure. Both men had their swords taken away and their hands pinioned behind their backs. Then Bishr and Abān the sons of ʿAbd al-Malik b. Bishr entered, and the same was done with them. Then Abū Bakr b. Kaʿb and Ṭāriq b. Qudāmah entered. At this, Jaʿfar b. Ḥanẓalah rose up and said, "We are the chiefs of the army; why have these men been given precedence over us?" Sallām said, "What tribe [69] are you from?" "From Bahrāʾ," he said. And Sallām said, "You would do well to get out of here." Then Hazzān stood and spoke, and he was held back. Rawḥ b. Ḥātim then said, "Abū Yaʿqūb, the men's swords have been taken away!" Mūsā b. ʿAqīl now came out against them, and they told him, "You gave us an oath before God, and now you break it. We hope that God may catch up with you."

Ibn Nubātah began to make rude noises in his beard, and Ḥawtharah told him, "That will be of no use to you." He replied, "It seems to me I told you this would happen." Then they were slain, and their signet rings were taken from them.

Khāzim, al-Haytham b. Shuʿbah and al-Aghlab b. Sālim went off with about a hundred men and sent word to Ibn Hubayrah, "We intend to transport the money." Ibn Hubayrah told his chamberlain, "Go, Abū ʿUthmān, and show them where it is." They posted some men in each room, and began to look throughout the house. With Ibn Hubayrah were his son Dāwud, his secretary ʿAmr b. Ayyūb, his chamberlain, and a number of his mawlās. Also with him was a very young son whom he held in his arms. He began to feel misgiving at their looks, and said, "I swear by God that there is evil in the faces of these men." They came towards him, and his chamberlain stood up to them, and said, "Get out of here!" Al-Haytham b. Shuʿbah struck the chamberlain in the shoulder tendon, and felled him. His son Dāwud put up a struggle and was killed, and his mawlās were slain. Ibn Hubayrah put aside the child in his arms and said, "You have no need for this little boy." Then he prostrated himself in prayer, and was slain while prostrating himself. The slayers went with the heads to Abū Jaʿfar, whereupon he proclaimed amnesty for all the important poeple except al-Ḥakam b. ʿAbd al-Malik b. Bishr, Khālid b. Salamah al-Makhzūmī and ʿUmar b. Dharr. However, Ziyād b. ʿUbaydallāh sought pardon for Ibn Dharr, and Abū al-ʿAbbās accorded it. Al-Ḥakam fled. Abū Jaʿfar gave a guarantee of safety to Khālid, but Abū al-ʿAbbās had Khālid killed and did not honor Abū

[70] Jaʿfar's guarantee. Abū ʿAllāqah and Hishām b. Hāshim b. Ṣafwah b. Mazyad, both of the Banū Fazzār, fled, but Ḥujr b. Saʿīd al-Ṭāʾī caught up with them and killed them both at the Zāb. Abū al-ʿAṭāʾ al-Sindī recited in lament:[444]

> Surely an eye that did not find that day at Wāsiṭ
>   for you its tears overflowing was incapable of tears,
>
> At evening when the wailing women rose, and torn
>   were neck-openings at their hands, and cheeks were gashed.

---

444. A Kūfan poet known for his pro-Umayyad activity. The elegy on the death of Ibn Hubayrah is one of his most famous poems. See *EI²* s.v. Abū ʿAṭa al-Sindī.

And if your courtyard is empty at evening now, yet often
    there used to stay in it envoys after envoys.

You are not far away from one who frequents your grave,
    though surely one who lies beneath the dust is far.

Munqidh b. ʿAbd al-Raḥmān al-Hilālī recited in a lament:

The burning in my breast forbade all consolation
    and grief prevented my heart's firm resolve on patience,

When once I heard a blow that struck
    all white my hair at its place of parting.

Vanished those noble defenders, when appeared
    snares of treachery, and promises were broken.

That noose entrapped in its toil a man
    like the full moon, by stars surrounded.

A crier proclaimed the report of their death, and I said,
    "Why did you not come with the cry of Doomsday?

May God reckon with you, you who assert to us
    that the vicissitudes of time have encompassed him."

Who is there for the minbars, after their perishing,
    or who could supply their excellent qualities of character?

Whenever I remember them, my heart complains
    of pain for the bright-faced cavaliers

Slain at the Tigris; nothing could cover them
    but billows of raging waves of the sea.

Now let our womenfolk weep for their riders,
    best of defenders, through nights of terror.

According to Abū Zayd—Abū Bakr al-Bāhilī—a shaykh of the   [71]
Khurāsānīs: (The Caliph) Hishām b. ʿAbd al-Malik asked Yazīd b.

ʿUmar b. Hubayrah for his daughter as wife for Hishām's son Muʿāwiyah, but Yazīd refused. After this some words passed between Yazīd b. ʿUmar and al-Walīd b. al-Qaʿqāʿ, and Hishām sent Yazīd to al-Walīd b. Qaʿqāʿ, who beat him and had him incarcerated. Then Ibn Ṭaysalah recited:

> Little good is there for men who have no intelligence.
>   who will justly treat the man detained at Aleppo,
>
> A man never struck by time's mischances
>   but he made light of it, with heart at ease?

It is said that when Abū al-ʿAbbās sent Abū al-Jaʿfar to Wāsit to fight Ibn Hubayrah, he wrote to al-Ḥasan b. Qaḥṭabah, "The army is your army, and the officers are your officers. Still, I should like for my brother to be present, so listen to him and obey him and help him as best you can." He wrote something similar to Abū Naṣr Mālik b. Haytham. Then al-Ḥasan was the one who managed the army, by al-Manṣūr (Abū Jaʿfar)'s orders.

Other Events

This same year Abū Muslim sent Muḥammad b. al-Ashʿath to rule Fārs, commanding him to seize the governors of Abū Salamah there and cut off their heads. This he did.

In the same year Abū al-ʿAbbās sent his paternal uncle ʿĪsā b. ʿAlī to Fārs, which Muḥammad b. al-Ashʿath was controlling, and Muḥammad b. al-Ashʿath worried what to do. Someone told him, "This is not a man you can treat like others." He however replied, "On the contrary, Abū Muslim ordered me not to let anyone he had not sent come here claiming to be a governor without cutting off his head." He shrank from that, fearing what the consequences might be, but he obliged ʿĪsā by the most binding oath not to go up into a minbar, [72] nor to gird on a sword except on jihād. ʿĪsā never held a governorship after that, nor put on a sword except in a campaign. After this, Abū al-ʿAbbās sent Ismāʿīl b. ʿAlī as governor over Fārs.

In this year, Abū al-ʿAbbās sent his brother Abū Jaʿfar to the Jazīrah, Adharbayjān and Armenia as governor, and his brother Yaḥyā as governor for Mosul.[445]

He also removed his paternal uncle Dāwud b. ʿAlī as governor of Kūfah and its territory and gave him Madīnah, Mecca, the Yaman and Yamāmah to govern. In his place over Kūfah and its territory he appointed ʿĪsā b. Mūsā.

In this year, while he was in the Jazīrah Marwān had dismissed al-Walīd b. ʿUrwah as governor of Madīnah, and he appointed in his place al-Walīd's brother Yūsuf b. ʿUrwah. Al-Wāqidī mentions that he came to Madīnah on the fourth of Rabīʿ I (October 10, 750).

This year ʿĪsā b. Mūsā appointed Ibn Abī Laylā as judge for Kūfah.

The governor for Baṣrah this year was Sufyān b. Muʿāwiyah al-Muhallabī. Al-Ḥajjāj b. Arṭāh was in charge of the judiciary there. The governor of Fārs was Muḥammad b. al-Ashʿath, and that of Sind was Manṣūr b. Jumhūr.[446] ʿAbdallāh b. Muḥammad governed the Jazīrah, Armenia, and Ādharbayjān, while Yaḥyā b. Muḥammad governed Mosul. ʿAbdallāh b. ʿAlī governed the Syrian provinces, Abū ʿAwn ʿAbd al-Malik b. Yazīd governed Egypt, Abū Muslim ruled Khurāsān and Jibāl, and the Landtax Bureau was headed by Khālid b. Barmak. The leader of the Pilgrimage this year was Dāwud b. ʿAlī b. ʿAbdallāh b. al-ʿAbbās.

---

445. Azdī states that this occurred the following year, 133 (749–750), and gives eye-witness reports of the pitiless massacre of the inhabitants carried out by Yaḥyā to punish them for repudiating the previous governor, a mawlā of the Ḥijāz tribe of Khathʿam. See Azdī, 145–53; Ibn Athīr, IV, 339–40. Ṭabarī does not mention this act of the new dynasty, in which the people were persuaded to come out of hiding by proclamation of a general amnesty and then slain, it is said to the number of about thirty thousand men, women and children. Azdī also alludes to ʿAbbāsid massacres in Syria.

446. Ṭabarī does not discuss it, but this perennial rebel against the Qaysīs had at last joined the ʿAbbāsid revolt and had been rewarded with the governorate of Sind. See Omar, 161.

THE
EVENTS OF THE YEAR

133

(AUGUST 9,750–29 JULY, 751)

The Events of this Year

Among the events, Abū al-ʿAbbās sent his paternal uncle Sulaymān b. ʿAlī as governor for Baṣrah and its dependencies, as well as the Tigris districts, Baḥrayn, ʿUmān and Mihrijānqadhaq.[447] His paternal uncle Ismāʿīl b. ʿAlī was made governor of the districts of Ahwāz.

This year Dāwud b. ʿAlī slew all members of the family of Umayyah arrested at Mecca and Madīnah.

In this year also, Dāwud b. ʿAlī died at Madīnah during Rabīʿ I (ca. October 18–November 16, 750). His governorship, according to Muḥammad b. ʿUmar, lasted three months. He had chosen his son Mūsā to succeed him when his death drew near, but when the word of his death reached Abū al-ʿAbbās, the Caliph sent his maternal uncle Ziyād b. ʿUbaydallāh b. ʿAbdallāh b. ʿAbd al-Madān al-Ḥārithī as governor for Madīnah, Mecca, Ṭāʾif and Yamāmah, and he sent Muḥammad b. Yazīd b. ʿAbdallāh b. ʿAbd al-Madān as governor for the Yaman. This man arrived in the Yaman in Jumādā I (December

---

447. Mihrijānqadhaq was a fertile district in the extreme west of Jibāl. The major town was Saymarah. See Yāqūt, *Muʿjam* s.v. Mihrijānqadhaq, and LeStrange, *Lands*, 184, 202.

16, 750–January 14, 751). Ziyād stayed at Madīnah, while Muḥammad went on to the Yaman. Then Ziyād sent Ibrāhīm b. Ḥassān al-
Sulamī, who was Abū Ḥammād al-Abraṣ, against al-Muthannā b.
Yazīd b. ʿUmar b. Hubayrah, who was in Yamāmah. Abū Ḥammād
killed him and slew his followers.

This year Abū al-ʿAbbās wrote to Abū ʿAwn, continuing his appointment as governor of Egypt. He did the same with ʿAbdallāh and
Ṣāliḥ, the sons of ʿAlī, who ruled over the military districts in Syria.

He also sent Muḥammad b. al-Ashʿath to Ifrīqiyah, and the latter   [74]
engaged in fierce combat with (the Berber Khārijites) until he conquered the province.

This year Sharīk b. Shaykh al-Mahrī rebelled against Abū Muslim
in Khurāsān at Bukhārā and reviled him, saying, "It was not for this
that we followed the family of Muḥammad, to shed blood and act
unjustly."[448] More than thirty thousand men followed his banner,
so that Abū Muslim sent Ziyād b. Ṣāliḥ, who fought him and slew
him.

Also, Abū Muslim sent Abū Dāwud Khālid b. Ibrāhīm from the
Oxus to Khuttal, and he entered the country. Ḥanash b. al-Subul,[449]
the king there, did not oppose him, but the leading men among the
dihqāns of Khuttal came to him and put themselves in the fortress
with him, while some of them resisted along the roads and in the
mountain passes and forts. When Abū Dāwud pressed Ḥanash, he
went out from his fortress by night accompanied by his dihqāns and
his Shākiriyyah to the land of Farghānah, and from there to the land
of the Turks, until he came to the King of China. Abū Dāwud took
those he captured among the enemy and crossed back to Balkh,
where he sent the captives to Abū Muslim.

In this year ʿAbd al-Raḥmān b. Yazīd b. al-Muhallab was slain by
Sulaymān, called al-Aswad, who killed him with a safe-conduct he
had written for him.

In this year Ṣāliḥ b. ʿAlī sent Saʿīd b. ʿAbdallāh to lead the summer
expedition behind the frontiers (of the Byzantines). Yaḥyā b.

---

448. This man had been an early ʿAbbāsid partisan. Narshakhī states that his rebellion was in favor of the ʿAlids, though Ṭabarī, writing under the ʿAbbāsids, draws a
veil over his affiliations. Sharīk is quoted as saying that the plagues of the house of
ʿAbbās should not afflict him, and that the children of the Prophet must be the Prophet's successors. See Narshakhī (trans.), 62.
449. Ibn Athīr gives his name as Ḥubaysh b. al-Shibl (IV, 342).

[75] Muḥammad was removed from the governorship of Mosul, and Ismāʿīl b. ʿAlī was appointed in his place. Ziyād b. ʿUbaydallāh al-Ḥārithī led the Pilgrimage this year, as I was told by Aḥmad b. Thābit—Isḥāq b. ʿĪsā—Abū Maʿshar. Al-Wāqidī and others say the same.

ʿĪsā b. Mūsā governed Kūfah and its surrounding territory, while Ibn Abī Laylā was in charge of the judiciary there. Sulaymān b. ʿAlī governed Baṣrah, its dependencies, the Tigris districts, Baḥrayn, ʿUmān, ʿIrd[450] and Mihrijānqadhaq. In charge of the judiciary was ʿAbbād b. Manṣūr. Ismāʿīl b. ʿAlī governed Ahwaz, and Muḥammad b. al-Ashʿath governed Fārs. The governor of Sind was Manṣūr b. Jumhūr, and Abū Muslim governed Khurāsān and Jibāl. ʿAbdallāh b. ʿAlī governed Qinnasrīn, Ḥimṣ, the districts of Damascus and the Jordan. Ṣāliḥ b. ʿAlī governed Palestine.

ʿAbd al-Malik b. Yazīd, Abū ʿAwn, governed Egypt; ʿAbdallāh b. Muḥammad al-Manṣūr governed the Jazīrah. Ismāʿīl b. ʿAlī governed Mosul, Ṣāliḥ b. Ṣubayḥ governed Armenia, and Mujāshiʿ b. Yazīd was governor of Adharbayjān.

Khālid b. Barmak headed the Landtax Bureau.

---

450. An ʿirḍ is an Arabian wādī with villages and palms. *The* ʿIrḍ was a district contiguous to ʿUmān, part of Yamāmah in East Arabia. See Yāqūt, *Muʿjam* s.v. ʿIrḍ.

THE
EVENTS OF THE YEAR

134

(JULY 30, 751–JULY 17, 752)

The Rebellion of Bassām b. Ibrāhīm

In this year Bassām b. Ibrāhīm b. Bassām rebelled and threw off his allegiance.[451] According to what has been mentioned, he was a leading cavalryman of Khurāsān. He left the army of Abū al-ʿAbbās the Commander of the Faithful with a group of sympathizers who sought to keep their departure secret.[452] The Caliph made close inquiries to their purpose and where they were heading, until it was found that they were at Madāʾin. Abū al-ʿAbbās then sent Khāzim b.   [76] Khuzaymah after them. When he found Bassām, they came out to fight him. Bassām and his followers were put to flight, and most of them were slain. His camp was destroyed, and Khāzim and his followers went on to pursue them in the district of Jūkhā[453] until he came to Māh. Khāzim slew all of them he encountered, whether they fled or stood to fight. Then Khāzim turned back and passed by Dhāt al-Maṭāmīr, or a village resembling it, where were some of the Banū al-Ḥārith b. Kaʿb, of the Banū ʿAbd al-Madān—they were the

---

451. See Azdī, 140, *sub anno* 133, who says that Bassām revolted in Tadmur, among the Kalb, and called for an ʿAlid caliphate.

452. The text is *mustabshirīn*, corrected by the Cairo edition to *mustasirrīn*.

453. A district along what was then the dried-up eastern bed of the Tigris, stretching northwest to Kaskar. See LeStrange, *Lands*, 42.

less prestigious maternal kindred of Abū al-ʿAbbās. He passed by them while they were holding a gathering. They were thirty-five men, eighteen being from their own clan and others, and seventeen from their mawlās. Khāzim did not salute them, and as he passed they reviled him.[454] He held a grudge against them already because of what he had heard that they had done regarding al-Mughīrah b. al-Fazʿ, one of Bassām b. Ibrāhīm's followers who had taken refuge with them. Khāzim wheeled around and went back, and he asked them about al-Mughīrah's stay among them. They replied, "A man passed through here. We did not know him. He stayed in our village one night and left." Then Khāzim said, "You are the maternal relatives of the Commander of the Faithful and his enemy comes to you and finds shelter in your village! Why didn't you get together and seize him?" They gave him a rough answer, whereupon he ordered that all of them be beheaded. Their houses were demolished, and their property plundered. Then he went back to Abū al-ʿAbbās.

Word of what Khāzim had done came to the Yamanī tribesmen, who dwelt on the magnitude of it in full accord. Then Ziyād b. ʿUbaydallāh al-Ḥārithī went to see Abū al-ʿAbbās with ʿAbdallāh b. al-Rabīʿ al-Ḥārithī, ʿUthmān b. Nahīk and ʿAbd al-Jabbār b. ʿAbd al-Raḥmān, who at that time was chief of security for Abū al-ʿAbbās. [77] They said, "Commander of the Faithful, a servant of yours[455] has dared to do something which the nearest and dearest of your father's sons would not venture to do against you. That is, he has made light of your justice and has slain your maternal relatives. They had left their home and come to you to glory in you, seeking your benevolence—then, when they had come to your abode and sought protection in your vicinity, Khāzim pounced on them and cut off their heads, destroyed their homes, carried off their possessions and ruined their estates, without their having done anything against him!" At this, Abū al-ʿAbbās proposed killing Khāzim, and word of it came to Mūsā b. Kaʿb and Abū al-Jahm b. ʿAṭīyyah. They went to Abū al-ʿAbbās and said, "Word has reached us, Commander of the Faithful, of what these people have said to you against Khāzim, how they have advised you to kill him, and what you have proposed to do

---

454. Khāzim was a Northern Tamīmī, and they were from the once Christian Yamanī tribe of Najrān and its vicinity, which may have predisposed them to hostility. Khāzim offered offense by not saying "peace" as he rode by.

455. The text is *khāzim*; read *khādim* with the Cairo edition.

about this. We invoke God's protection upon you against that. He has a record of obedience and long service. May he be forgiven for what he has done. Your Shī'ah among the people of Khurāsān have preferred you to their closest sons and fathers and brothers, and they killed all those who opposed you. You are the one whom their wrongdoing has strengthened most. If you are absolutely determined on his death, then do not undertake that yourself. Rather, put him among those who are sent where, if he is slain, you will have attained what you desire, and if he is victorious, then his victory will be yours." They advised him to send Khāzim against those of the (Ibāḍī) Khārijites who were in 'Umān, i.e., against al-Julandā and his followers, and against the (Ṣufrī) Khārijites who were on the island of Ibn Kāwān with Shaybān b. 'Abd al-'Azīz al-Yashkurī. Thus Abū al-'Abbās commanded that he be sent with seven hundred men and wrote to Sulaymān b. 'Alī at Baṣrah to transport them in vessels to the island of Ibn Kāwān and 'Umān. Khāzim then set out.

In this year, Khāzim b. Khuzaymah set out for 'Umān, and attacked the Khārijites situated there. He conquered it and the neighboring lands and slew Shaybān the Khārijite. [78]

The Account of What Occurred in 'Umān

It is mentioned that Khāzim b. Khuzaymah set out at the head of seven hundred men whom Abū al-'Abbās had given him. He also chose men of his house as well as cousins of his and his mawlās and men of Marwarrūdh whom he knew and could depend upon. They went to Baṣrah, where Sulaymān b. 'Alī supplied them with ships, and where a number of the Banū Tamīm at Baṣrah joined him. They sailed until they landed at the island of Ibn Kāwān, and Khāzim sent Naḍalah b. Nu'aym al-Nahshalī with five hundred of his men against Shaybān. They met and fought a violent battle. Shaybān and his followers then took to boats and crossed over to 'Umān. They were Ṣufrīs, and when they came to 'Umān, al-Julandā and his followers, who were Ibāḍīs, stood ready to do combat with them. They fought a pitched battle, and Shaybān and those accompanying him were killed. Then Khāzim set sail with his following until they reached the coast of 'Umān, and there went into the desert. Al-Julandā and his followers encountered them, and they fought a sharp engagement. Many of Khāzim's followers were killed that day. At the time they were on a stretch along the sea. Among those slain was a brother of Khāzim by the same mother, called Ismā'īl, along with ninety men of the Marwarrūdh contingent. They clashed again on the following day and fought a sharp battle. Commanding Khāzim's right wing was a man from Marwarrūdh called Ḥumayd al-Wartakānī, on his left was a man of Marwarrūdh called Muslim al-Arghadī, and Naḍalah b. Nu'aym al-Nahshalī was in command of the vanguard. On this day, nine hundred of the Khārijites were killed, and some ninety of them were burned. Seven days later, Khāzim's chief men agreed on an expedient suggested to him by a man of al-Ṣughd who happened to be in that country. He advised him to command his followers to fix tow on the ends of their spears and soak this in naptha and set fire to it, and then go with these and set fire to the dwellings of al-Julandā's followers, which were made of wood and withes. They did this and set fire to the houses. While the Khārijites were busy saving them and their children and families who were in them, Khāzim and his men pressed the attack and laid on with their swords, meeting little resistance from them. Al-Julandā was one of those who were slain, and the number came to ten thousand. Khāzim sent their heads to Baṣrah where they remained some days before being sent to Abū al-'Abbās. Khāzim stayed (in 'Umān) some months until a letter from Abū al-'Abbās arrived bidding him to come back, and they returned.

This year Abū Dāwud Khālid b. Ibrāhīm raided the people of Kashsh[456] and killed its ruler, al-Ikhrīd. He was a loyal vassal who had come before this to Abū Dāwud at Balkh. Then he met him at Kandak,[457] near Kashsh. When he slew them Abū Dāwud took from al-Ikhrīd and his followers some ornamented and gilded Chinese vessels, the likes of which had not been seen. He also took Chinese saddles and furnishings, all of brocade and other stuffs, and many rare things of China. He transported all of this to Abū Muslim, who was at Samarqand. Abū Dāwud slew the dihqān of Kashsh along with a number of other dihqāns, but he spared Ṭārān, the brother of al-Ikhrīd, and made him ruler of Kashsh. He took Ibn al-Najāh and returned him to his own country, and Abū Muslim de-

---

456. Also known as Kash, later as Shahr-i Sabz. It was a town situated in the province of Ṣughd. See LeStrange, *Lands*, 441–43, 465, 470, 472; *EI²* s.v. Kash.

457. See LeStrange, *Lands*, 472.

parted for Marw after slaying some of the people of Sughd and Bukhārā. He ordered a wall to be built around Samarqand. He appointed Ziyād b. Ṣāliḥ over Sughd and Bukhārā, and then Abū Dāwud went back to Balkh.

In this year Abū al-ʿAbbās sent Mūsā b. Kaʿb to India to fight Manṣūr b. Jumhūr.[458] He assigned him monies for three thousand men,
Arabs and mawlās of Baṣrah, and a thousand men specifically chosen from the Banū Tamīm. He then set out, and al-Musayyab b.
Zuhayr replaced him as chief of security for Abū al-ʿAbbās, subject
to his arrival from Sind. Mūsā met Manṣūr b. Jumhūr at the head of
twelve thousand men and put him and his followers to flight. Manṣūr kept going, and died of thirst in the sands.

It has been said that a member of Manṣūr's clan killed him. Manṣūr's lieutenant learned of his defeat at Manṣūrah[459] and set off
with Manṣūr's family and treasures. Leaving with them a number of
trusted men, he entered the land of the Khazars.[460]

This year Muḥammad b. Yazīd b. ʿAbdallāh died while he was
governor of the Yaman, so Abū al-ʿAbbās wrote to ʿAlī b. al-Rabīʿ b.
ʿUbaydallāh al-Ḥārithī, the functionary of Ziyād b. ʿUbaydallāh for
Mecca, appointing him as governor of the Yaman. ʿAlī then went
there.

This same year Abū al-ʿAbbās moved from Ḥīrah to Anbār.[461]
This, according to al-Wāqidī and other authorities, was in Dhū al-
Ḥijjah (June 19–July 13, 752).

In this year Ṣāliḥ b. Ṣubayḥ was removed from Armenia, and
Yazīd b. Asīd[462] was appointed in his place. In this year Mujāshiʿ b.
Yazīd was removed from Adharbayjān, and Muḥammad b. Ṣul was
appointed for that province.

In this year the beacon system and milestones were set up from

[81]

---

458. Al-Balādhurī states that Abū Muslim appointed another governor for Sind,
whom the old Kalbite warrior then slew. At this, Abū Muslim sent Mūsā b. Kaʿb.
Ṭabarī says the Caliph sent Mūsā and does not say why. See al-Balādhurī, *Futuḥ* III, p.
343.

459. The capital of Sind. See LeStrange, *Lands*, 331.

460. The kingdom of Turks and Huns in the south Russian steppes which later converted to Judaism. See *EI*² s.v. Khazar. It is a very long way from Sind to the land of
the Khazars.

461. For the ʿAbbāsid capital at Anbār known as Hāshimiyyah, see Lassner,
ʿAbbāsid Rule, 153–57.

462. The text is Usayd. The Cairo edition gives Asīd, a rare name, but here probable. See n. 150 above.

Kūfah to Mecca. The leader of the Pilgrimage was 'Īsā b. Mūsā, who was governor of Kūfah and its territories.

In charge of the judiciary at Kūfah was Ibn Abī Laylā, and Ziyād b. 'Ubaydallāh was governor of Mecca, Madīnah, Ṭā'if and Yamāmah. 'Alī b. al-Rabī' al-Ḥārithī governed the Yaman. Sulaymān b. 'Alī b. 'Alī was governor of Baṣrah and the Tigris districts, Baḥrayn, 'Umān, 'Irḍ and Mihrijānqadhaq. 'Abbād b. Manṣūr was in charge of its judiciary. Mūsā b. Ka'b was governor of Sind; Abū Muslim was governor of Khurāsān and Jibāl; Ṣāliḥ b. 'Alī governed Palestine; Abū 'Awn governed Egypt; Ismā'īl b. 'Alī governed Mosul; Yazīd b. Asīd governed Armenia; and Muḥammad b. Ṣūl governed Ādharbayjān. The Landtax Bureau was headed by Khālid b. Barmak. 'Abdallāh b. Muḥammad (Abū Ja'far) governed the Jazīrah, and 'Abdallāh b. 'Alī governed Qinnasrīn, Ḥimṣ, the districts of Damascus and the Jordan.

THE
EVENTS OF THE YEAR

135

(JULY 18, 752–JULY 7, 753)

The Rebellion of Ziyād b. Ṣāliḥ in Transoxania

Among the events of this year was the rebellion of Ziyād b. Ṣāliḥ, beyond the river of Balkh (the Oxus).[463] Abū Muslim set out from   [82]
Marw, prepared to encounter him, while Abū Dāwud Khālid b.
Ibrāhīm sent Naṣr b. Rāshid to Tirmidh[464] and ordered him to establish himself at the town, to prevent Ziyād b. Ṣāliḥ from sending
men and gaining possession of the fortress and the boats there. This
Naṣr did. He stayed there for some days, and then some of the people
of the Rāwandiyyah[465] from Ṭālaqān,[466] led by a man with the pat-

---

463. For this revolt see Daniel, *Khurāsān Under ʿAbbāsid Rule,* 111–12.

464. The major town of the Ṣaghāniyān district north of the Oxus at its junction
with the Zamil river. It was a great entrepot for trade coming from the north to
Khurāsān. See LeStrange, *Lands,* 240.

465. Named after the village of Rāwand near Naysābūr (Nishāpūr) the Rāwandiyyah were apparently identical with the Hāshimiyyah Shīʿah, who believed that
Abū Hāshim b. Muḥammad b. ʿAlī had passed the Imāmate to the ʿAbbāsids. The
Rāwandiyyah included many Iranian converts. See Baghdadī, *Farq,* trans. by Halkin,
74–75; also Lassner, *ʿAbbāsid Rule,* 109ff.

466. A great city between Balkh and Marwarrūdh. See LeStrange, *Lands,* 423–24
(Ṭāliqān). Ṭālaqān was the scene of the first great victory won by Abū Muslim. See
Yāqūt, *Muʿjam,* II, 129–30 s.v. Junduwayh.

ronymic of Abū Ishāq,[467] rebelled against him and slew him. When Abū Dāwud learned this, he sent 'Īsā b. Mahān in pursuit of Naṣr's murderers, and 'Īsā tracked them down and killed them.

Abū Muslim marched quickly, until he arrived at Āmul.[468] With him was Sibā' b. al-Nu'mān. This was the man who had brought the appointment of Ziyād b. Ṣāliḥ on behalf of Abū al-'Abbās[469] and ordered him, if he found an opportunity, to fall upon Abū Muslim and slay him. Abū Muslim was informed of that, so he gave Sibā' b. Nu'mān over to al-Ḥasan b. Junayd, his governor at Āmul, and ordered al-Ḥasan to confine him there. Then Abū Muslim crossed over to Bukhārā, and when he halted there, Abū Shākir and Abū Sa'd al-Sharawī came to him with officers who had deserted Ziyād. Abū Muslim questioned them about Ziyād's affair and who had corrupted him. They told him, "It was Sibā' b. al-Nu'mān." At this he wrote to his governor at Āmul to give Sibā' a hundred lashes and then behead him. This he did.

When Ziyād's officers betrayed him and went over to Abū Muslim, he fled to the dihqān of Bārkath,[470] but the dihqān pounced on him, cut off his head and brought it to Abū Muslim.

---

467. Ṭabarī is reticent here. This man is Abū Isḥāq Khālid b. 'Uthmān, 'Abbāsid *dā'ī* and mawlā of Khuzā'ah, who had once been chief of Abū Muslim's guard. The slaying is linked with rebellion against Abū Muslim among the 'Abbāsid Shī'ah, possibly fomented by the Caliph and his brother.

468. That is, the Āmul on the Oxus about 120 miles northeast of Marw. See Le-Strange, *Lands*, 404.

469. Here Ṭabarī lets out the secret. Abū Muslim had appointed Ziyād b. Ṣāliḥ, a mawlā of Khuzā'ah and 'Abbāsid *dā'ī*, governor of Ṣughd. The Caliph however had sent him a deed of appointment of his own behalf, with instructions to kill Abū Muslim. A key to this covert struggle between the Caliph and the governor of Khurāsān was the control of appointments of governors in the eastern provinces, as we have seen in Fārs and Sind. Balādhurī indicates that the Caliph had appointed Ziyād governor of Khurāsān; no doubt in the event that he could rid him of Abū Muslim. See Omar, *'Abbāsid Caliphate*, 159–60, quoting *Ansāb al-Ashrāf*, Paris manuscript, fol. 800b. Abū Muslim apparently intended to appoint the governors of the eastern provinces and wage jihād in Central Asia (and India?) at his own discretion, as the Umayyad viceroys of Iraq and the East had once done. The 'Abbāsids however planned a more centralized regime. The man the Caliph chose as his messenger to Ziyād b. Ṣāliḥ, Sibā' b. Nu'man al-Azdī, had been a follower of Juday' al-Kirmānī, and then had been appointed by Abū Muslim as his governor for Samarqand (Ṭabarī, II, 2001). Abū al-'Abbās had now acquired his services. When Abū Muslim took his revenge on Ziyād, and later on 'Īsā b. Māhān, however, the Caliph feigned innocence and congratulated Abū Muslim on dealing with them. See Omar, *'Abbāsid Caliphate*, 161, quoting Balādhurī in the unpublished portion of the *Ansāb.*

470. Bārkath was the major town of the Būzmajān district one day's journey north-

Abū Dāwud delayed in presenting himself before Abū Muslim, due to the affair of the Rāwandiyyah who had rebelled. At this, Abū Muslim wrote him as follows, "Let your dread be eased and your heart be at peace, for God has slain Ziyād; so come." Abū Dāwud then went to Kashsh and sent ʿĪsā b. Mahān to Bassām.[471] He sent al-Najāḥ to the Ispahbadh at Shāwaghar,[472] and Ibn al-Najāḥ besieged the fortress there. As for the people of Shāwaghar, they asked for peace, and it was granted. As for Bassām, ʿĪsā b. Mahān could get nowhere with him. Then Abū Muslim uncovered sixteen letters from ʿĪsā b. Mahān to Kāmil b. Muẓaffar, the friend of Abū Muslim, in which he blamed Abū Dāwud, accusing him of tribalism (ʿaṣabiyyah), and of preferring Arabs and his own tribe to all people of the ʿAbbāsid movement. ʿĪsā also accused him of having thirty-six tents in his camp for those to whom he had guaranteed protection. These letters Abū Muslim sent to Abū Dāwud, and wrote to him, "These are the letters of a barbarian (ʿilj) whom you rendered even as yourself; do with him as you will." At this, Abū Dāwud wrote ʿĪsā b. Mahān to come back to him from Bassām. When he arrived, he arrested him and handed him over to ʿUmar al-Naghm, at whose hands he remained in confinement. Then after two or three days he sent for ʿĪsā and reminded him of all that he had done for him and how he had preferred him even above his own sons, and he acknowledged all of that. Abū Dāwud then said, "Then the reward for all that I did for you was that you slandered me and desired my death?" This ʿĪsā denied, whereupon Abū Dāwud produced his letters, and he confessed that they were his. Abū Dāwud inflicted two legal punishments on him at that time, one of them on account of al-Ḥasan b. Ḥamdān.[473] Abū Dāwud then said, "As for me, I have left you in

[83]

---

east of Samarqand. See LeStrange, *Lands*, 466. The dihqāns of Central Asia were, for the most part, loyal to Abū Muslim out of fear or self-interest, or both.

471. Bassām b. Ibrāhīm was still at large, after leading a pro-ʿAlid revolt against the ʿAbbāsids in 133 (749–750), though where he was is not clear.

472. "Isbahbadh" was a title used by a number of Persian and even Turkish princes. See *EI*² s.v. Ispahbadh. Shāwaghar was a city in the land of the Turks, probably the one later called Yasi. See LeStrange, *Lands*, 435. We are not told why Ibn al-Najāḥ was sent there, but as the ʿAbbāsids expanded to the east and the Chinese to the west, the Turkish principalities were being asked to take sides.

473. Ṭabarī mentions this man only here and gives no reason for ʿĪsā's culpability. Narshakhī however mentions one Ḥamzah al-Hamdānī, a supporter of Sharīk b. Shaykh at Bukhārā, who was ambushed with his men. See Narshakhī, Frye translation, 63.

your sins, but the army has the final word. Depart in your chains."
When he was sent out from the tents, Ḥarb b. Ziyād and Ḥafṣ b.
Dīnār, the mawlā of Yaḥyā b. Ḥuḍayn, fell upon him striking him
with clubs and battleaxes, and he fell to the ground. Some men of
[84] Ṭālaqān[474] and others ran to him, put him in a sack, and struck him
with clubs until he died. Abū Muslim then returned to Marw.

Other Events

Sulaymān b. ʿAlī led the Pilgrimage for this year, and he was governor for Baṣrah and its dependencies. ʿAbbād b. Manṣūr was in
charge of the judiciary. The governor of Mecca was al-ʿAbbās b.
ʿAbdallāh b. Maʿbad b. ʿAbbās, and the governor of Madīnah was
Ziyād b. ʿUbaydallāh al-Ḥārithī. The governor of Kūfah and its territory was ʿĪsā b. Mūsā, and Ibn Abī Laylā was in charge of the judiciary. Abū Jaʿfar al-Manṣūr was governor of the Jazīrah, and Abū
ʿAwn was governor of Egypt. ʿAbdallāh b. ʿAlī governed Ḥimṣ, Qinnasrīn, Baʿalbakk, the Ghūṭah, Ḥawrān, the Jawlān, and the Jordan.
Ṣāliḥ b. ʿAlī was governor of the Balqāʾ and Palestine, and Ismāʿīl b.
ʿAlī governed Mosul. Muḥammad b. Ṣūl was governor for Ādharbayjān, and Khālid b. Barmak headed the Landtax Bureau.

---

474. Ibn Māhān may have slain relatives of theirs in fighting the Rāwandiyyah of
Ṭalaqān. Wrapping him in a sack and beating him to death in concert would have
avoided any specific guilt for killing him for which revenge could be exacted from an
individual.

THE
EVENTS OF THE YEAR

136

(JULY 7, 753–JUNE 26, 754)

In this year Abū Muslim came to Iraq from Khurāsān to visit Abū al-ʿAbbās the Commander of the Faithful.

What Happened When Abū Muslim Came to the Caliph

According to ʿAlī b. Muḥammad—al-Haytham b. ʿAdī, also al-Walīd b. Hishām—his father: Abū Muslim stayed on in Khurāsān until finally he wrote to Abū al-ʿAbbās requesting permission to present himself. The Caliph assented to this, and Abū Muslim came to Abū al-ʿAbbās at Anbār with an enormous contingent of the Khurāsān army, as well as others who followed him. Abū al-ʿAbbās ordered the important people to go and meet him, and they did. Then he went to where Abū al-ʿAbbās was, and went in to meet him. Abū al-ʿAbbās made much of him and showed him favor. Then he requested Abū al-ʿAbbās's permission to go on the Pilgrimage, and he told him, "If only Abū Jaʿfar were not making the Pilgrimage this year, I would have made you my appointee for the Pilgrimage season." He lodged Abū Muslim close by, and each day the latter would present himself and offer his respects. There was however a coolness between Abū Jaʿfar and Abū Muslim, because Abū al-ʿAbbās had sent Abū Jaʿfar to Abū Muslim when he was at Naysābūr, after matters regarding Abū Muslim's rule in Khurāsān were described to him, to exact his alle-

[85]

giance to Abū al-ʿAbbās and to Abū Jaʿfar as his heir. Abū Muslim and the army of Khurāsān had given the oath of allegiance to him, and Abū Jaʿfar stayed there for some days until he was finished with the matter of the oath. He then left, but Abū Muslim had slighted Abū Jaʿfar upon his arrival, and when he came back to Abū al-ʿAbbās he told him how he had been slighted.

According to ʿAlī—al-Walīd—his father: When Abū Muslim came to Abū al-ʿAbbās, Abū Jaʿfar told the Caliph, "Commander of the Faithful, tell me and I will kill Abū Muslim, for by God, his head is full of treachery." However, Abū al-ʿAbbās said "My brother, you know the tests he has come through and what has happened because of him." Abū Jaʿfar replied, "Commander of the Faithful, that was only because of our revolution. By God, if you had sent a cat, it would have taken his place and done what he has done for this revolution." Then Abū al-ʿAbbās said, "How could we slay him?" Abū Jaʿfar replied, "When he has come in to see you and you are engaging him in conversation, while he is in front of you, I could come in and take him unawares and strike him a blow from behind that would take his life." Abū al-ʿAbbās said, "And what of his followers who hold him above their religion and all the world?" He replied, "All [86] will result as you would desire. If they know he is already slain they will split up and be tractable." Abū al-ʿAbbās told him, "I beseech you not to carry this out." Abū Jaʿfar replied, "By God, I fear that if you do not breakfast on him today, he will dine on you tomorrow." The Caliph replied, "Then it is up to you. You know best [how to handle it]."

Abū Jaʿfar left his presence determined to carry it out, but Abū al-ʿAbbās had regrets and sent word to him, "Do not do that thing."

It is said that when Abū al-ʿAbbās had given Abū Jaʿfar permission to kill Abū Muslim, the latter came in to see the Caliph. Abū al-ʿAbbās sent a eunuch of his, saying, "Go see what Abū Jaʿfar is doing." He came to Abū Jaʿfar and found him sitting on his heels propped up by his sword. He asked the eunuch, "Is the Commander of the Faithful sitting in audience?" He replied, "He is just ready to sit." Then the eunuch went back to Abū al-ʿAbbās and told him what he had seen. At this, Abū al-ʿAbbās sent him back to Abū Jaʿfar, saying, "Tell him, 'Do not carry out the matter you have determined upon.'" At this Abū Jaʿfar desisted.

It was in this year that Abū Ja'far al-Manṣūr led the Pilgrimage, and Abū Muslim went on the Pilgrimage with him.

Their Journey and a Description of
Their Return to Abū al-'Abbās

As for Abū Muslim, according to what is mentioned, when he wished to present himself before Abū al-'Abbās, he also wrote asking for permission to go on the pilgrimage. This was granted. Abū al-'Abbās told him to come with five hundred soldiers, and Abū Muslim wrote, "I have irritated important people and am not sure that my life would be safe." Abū al-'Abbās then wrote him, "Come with a thousand. After all, you will be within the sovereignty of your own family and your own revolution. The road to Mecca will not bear any army." He set off at the head of eight thousand, and thinned them out between Naysābūr and Rayy. He brought with him great wealth and treasures, and left these at Rayy. He also gathered together the money of Jibāl,[475] and then left Rayy with a thousand men and came on. When he was ready to enter (the capital), the officers and various important people went to meet him. He then sought Abū al-'Abbās's permission to make the pilgrimage, and he granted it to him, saying, "If only Abū Ja'far were not making the pilgrimage I should appoint you to lead it this season." [87]

As for Abū Ja'far, he was the governor of the Jazīrah. According to al-Wāqidī, besides the Jazīrah, Abū Ja'far had Armenia and Ādharbayjān. He chose Muqātil b. Ḥakīm al-'Akki as his deputy, and he came to Abū al-'Abbās and asked his permission to make the pilgrimage.

According to 'Alī b. Muḥammad—al-Walīd b. Hishām—his father: Abū Ja'far went to Mecca as a pilgrim and Abū Muslim made the pilgrimage with him in the year 136 (753–754). When the season of the pilgrimage was at an end, Abū Ja'far and Abū Muslim started back. When they were between Bustān and Dhāt 'Irq,[476] a letter

---

475. The text is al-Jabal. The province of Jibāl must be intended, and the textual apparatus supports such a reading.

476. See Yāqūt, *Mu'jam*, III, 651 for Dhāt 'Irq. The reference to Bustān is to Bustān b. 'Āmir, also known as Bustān b. Ma'mar. See Yāqūt, I, 611. The letter arrived when Abū Ja'far and Abū Muslim were still in the pilgrimage territory.

came for Abū Jaʿfar that Abū al-ʿAbbās had died. Abū Jaʿfar who had preceded Abū Muslim by one stage, wrote to him, "Something has happened. Come quickly, quickly." The messenger arrived and informed Abū Muslim, who came on and joined Abū Jaʿfar, and together they came on to Kūfah.

In this year Abū al-ʿAbbās ʿAbdallāh b. Muḥammad b. ʿAlī had had the oath taken to his brother, Abū Jaʿfar, to have the caliphate after him. He made him the heir-apparent of the Muslims, with ʿĪsā b. Mūsā b. Muḥammad b. ʿAlī as his successor. The Caliph recorded the deed of these appointments in a document, placed it in a container, sealed it with his own seal and the seals of his family, and entrusted it to ʿĪsā b. Mūsā.[477]

This year Abū al-ʿAbbās the Commander of the Faithful died at Anbār on Sunday, the thirteenth of Dhū al-Ḥijjah 136 (June 10, 754). His death is said to have been due to smallpox.

[88]   According to Hishām b. Muḥammad: He died on the twelfth night of Dhū al-Ḥijjah (June 9, 754). There is a difference as to his age when he died; some have said he was thirty-three. Hishām b. Muḥammad says he was thirty-six years old, while others say he was twenty-eight.

His reign, from the time that Marwān b. Muḥammad was slain, lasted four years. From the time that he was acclaimed Caliph until he died, he ruled four years and eight months; some say nine. According to al-Wāqidī, he ruled four years and eight months, of which he spent eight months and four days fighting Marwān. He then reigned four years after the death of Marwān.

According to what is mentioned, he had curly hair, and was tall and white-skinned, with a hooked nose and a handsome face and beard. His mother was Rayṭah bt. ʿUbaydallāh b. ʿAbdallāh b. ʿAbd al-Madān b. al-Dayyān al-Ḥārithī. His wazīr was Abū al-Jahm b. ʿAṭiyyah.

His paternal uncle ʿĪsā b. ʿAlī prayed over him and buried him in his palace in the old city of Anbār. According to what is mentioned in the sources, he left behind nine full-sleeved gowns, four long gowns, five pairs of trousers, four cloaks, and three silk gowns.

---

477. The significance of Abū Jaʿfar's appointment is discussed in Lassner, ʿAbbāsid Rule, 19–38.

BIBLIOGRAPHY

Akhbār al-dawlah al-ʿAbbāsiyyah wa fīhi akhbār al-ʿAbbās. Edited by ʿA. ʿA. Dūrī and ʿA.J. al-Muṭṭalibī. Beirut, 1971.

al-Azdī, Yazīd b. Muḥammad. *Taʾrīkh al-Mawṣil.* Edited by ʿAlī Ḥabībah. Cairo, 1967.

al-Azraqī, Abū al-Ḥasan Muḥammad. *Akhbār Makkah.* Edited by F. Wüstenfeld in *Chroniken der Stadt Mekka.* Leipzig, 1858.

al-Baghdadī, ʿAbd al-Qāhir b. Ṭāhir. *al-Farq bayn al-firaq.* Edited by M. Badr. Cairo, 1910; translated and annotated as *Moslem Schisms and Sects.* 2 vols. K. Seelye, vol. 1, Columbia University Oriental Series Vol XV, 1920, and A. Halkin, vol. 2, Tel-Aviv, 1935.

al-Balādhurī, Aḥmad b. Yaḥyā. *Futūḥ al-buldān.* Edited by M. J. de Goeje. Leiden, 1966; translated by P. K. Hitti and F. C. Murgotten as *Origins of the Islamic State,* New York, 1916 and 1924.

K./ansāb al-ashrāf, Vol. I. Edited by M. Hamidullah, Cairo, 1959; IV. Edited by M. Schloessinger and M. J. Kister, Jerusalem, 1971; IV. Edited by M. Schloessinger, Jerusalem, 1938; Vol. V. Edited by S. Goitein, Jerusalem, 1939; Vol. XI. Edited by W. Ahlwardt, Greifswald, 1883, as *Anonyme arabische Chronik.*

Bibliotheca Geographicorum Arabicorum

Crone, P. *Slaves on Horses.* Cambridge, 1980.

Daniel, E. *The Political and Social History of Khurasan Under Abbasid Rule.* Minneapolis and Chicago, 1979.

Encyclopaedia of Islam, 1st and 2nd edition, Leiden.

al-Dīnawarī, Aḥmad b. Dāwud. *K./al-akhbār al-ṭiwāl.* Edited by V. Guirgass. Leiden, 1888.

Fragmenta Historicorum Arabicorum. Edited by M. J. De Goeje. 2 vols. Leiden, 1869.

Hinz, W. *Islamische Masse und Gewichte.* Leiden, 1955.

Ibn Abd al-Ḥakam, ʿAbd al-Raḥman. *Futūḥ Miṣr.* Edited by C. C. Torrey, New Haven, 1922.

Ibn 'Abd Rabbihi, Aḥmad b. Muḥammad, *al-'Iqd al-Farīd.* Edited by A. Amīn, I. al-Zayn and I. al-Abyarī. 6 vols. Cairo, 1940–1965.

Ibn 'Asākir, 'Alī b. al-Ḥasan. *Ta'rīkh Madīnat Dimashq.* Edited by B. and A. 'Ubayd. 7 vols. Damascus, 1911–32; S. al-Munajjid. vols. 1–2. Damascus, 1965, vol. 10 in 1965.

Ibn al-Athīr, 'Izz al-Dīn. *Al-Kāmil fī al-Ta'rīkh.* Edited by C. Tornberg. 12 vols. Leiden, 1851–76.

Ibn Khayyāṭ, Khalīfah al-'Uṣfurī, *Ta'rīkh.* Edited by A. al-'Umarī. 2 vols. Najaf, 1967.

Ibn Manẓūr, Muḥammad b. Mukarram, *Lisān al-'Arab.* Edited Cairo, 1966, and Beirut, 1953–57.

Ibn Qutaybah, 'Abdallāh b. Muslim *K. al-Ma'ārif.* Edited by F. Wüstenfeld. Göttingen, 1850.

'Uyūn al-Akhbār. Edited by A. Z. al-'Adawī. Cairo, 1925–30.

Ibn Ṭabāṭabā, Muḥammad b. 'Alī. *Al-Kitāb al-fakhrī.* Edited by H. Derenbourg. Paris, 1895; Beirut, 1966.

al-Iṣfahānī, 'Alī b. al-Ḥusayn. *K. al-aghānī.* Beirut, 1955.

al-Jāḥiẓ, 'Amr b. Baḥr. *Al-Bayān wa al-Tabyīn.* Edited by A. M. Hārūn. Cairo, 1948–50.

Kennedy, H. *The Early Abbasid Caliphate.* New York and London, 1981.

Lassner, J. *The Shaping of 'Abbāsid Rule.* Princeton, 1980.

LeStrange, G. *Lands of the Eastern Caliphate.* Cambridge, 1930.

———. *Palestine Under the Moslems.* London, 1890.

Lewis, B. "Regnal Titles of the First 'Abbāsid Caliphs," in *Dr. Zakir Husain Presentation Volume.* New Delhi, 1968; and in *Studies in Classical and Ottoman Islam.* London, 1976.

al-Maqdisī, Muṭahhar b. Ṭāhir. *Al-Bad' wa al-Ta'rīkh.* Paris, 1899–1918.

al-Mas'ūdī, 'Alī b. al-Ḥusayn. *Murūj al-Dhahab.* Edited and translated by C. Barbier de Meynard and Pavet de Courteille. 5 vols. Paris, 1861–77; edited by Y. A. Daghir. 4 vols. Beirut, 1965.

———. *Kitāb al-Tanbīh wa al-Ishrāf.* Edited by M. J. de Goeje. Leiden, 1894. *BGA,* 8.

Narshakhī, Muḥammad b. Ja'far. *Ta'rīkh-i Bukhārā.* Translation by R. N. Frye as *History of Bukhara.* Cambridge, Massachusetts, 1954.

Omar, F. *The 'Abbāsid Caliphate* 132/750—170/786. Baghdad, 1969.

———. "al-Alwān wa dalālatuhā al-siyāsiyyah fī al-'aṣr al-'Abbāsī al-awwal." in *Bulletin, Faculty of the Arts.* Baghdad University. 14 (1971): 827–36.

Shaban, M. A., *The 'Abbāsid Revolution.* Cambridge, 1970.

al-Ṭabarī, Muḥammad b. Jarīr. *Ta'rīkh al-Rusul wa al-Mulūk.* Edited by M. Abū al-Faḍl Ibrāhīm. Cairo, 1960–69.

al-Tha'ālibī, Abū Manṣūr 'Abd al-Malik. *Laṭā'if al-Ma'ārif.* Edited by P. de

Jong. Leiden, 1867, and by I. al-Abyarī and H. K. al-Ṣayrafī. Cairo, 1960; translated by C. E. Bosworth. Edinburgh, 1968.

Van Vloten, G. *De Opkomst der Abbasiden in Chorasan.* Leiden, 1890; English translation in Philadelphia, 1977.

Watt, W. M. *The Formative Period of Islamic Thought.* Edinburgh, 1873.

Wellhausen, J. *The Arab Kingdom and its Fall.* Calcutta, 1927.

al-Yaʿqūbī, Aḥmad b. Abī Yaʿqub. *Taʾrīkh (Historiae).* Edited by M. Th. Houtsma. 2 vols. Leiden, 1883.

Yāqūt, Abū ʿAbdallāh al-Ḥamawī. *Muʿjam al-Buldān.* Edited by F. Wüstenfeld. 6 vols. Leipzig, 1866–73.

Index

The index contains all proper names of persons, places, tribal and other groups, as well as topographical data, occurring in the introduction, the text, and the footnotes. However, as far as the footnotes are concerned, only those names that belong to the medieval or earlier periods are listed.

The definite article, the abbreviation b. (for ibn, son) and bt. (for bint, daughter), and everything in parentheses are disregarded for the purposes of alphabetization. Where a name occurs in both the text and the footnotes on the same page, both page and footnote are given, separated by a comma. If it occurs only in the footnote, there is no comma.